Public Drinking and Popular Culture
in Eighteenth-Century Paris

THOMAS BRENNAN

Public Drinking
and Popular Culture
in Eighteenth-Century
Paris

PRINCETON UNIVERSITY PRESS

PRINCETON, NEW JERSEY

Copyright © 1988 by Princeton University Press

Published by Princeton University Press, 41 William Street,
Princeton, New Jersey 08540
In the United Kingdom: Princeton University Press,
Guildford, Surrey

All Rights Reserved

Library of Congress Cataloging in Publication Data will
be found on the last printed page of this book

ISBN 0-691-05519-X

Publication of this book has been aided by a grant from the
Paul Mellon Fund of Princeton University Press

This book has been composed in Linotron Caslon type

Clothbound editions of Princeton University Press books are
printed on acid-free paper, and binding materials are chosen for
strength and durability. Paperbacks, although satisfactory
for personal collections, are not usually
suitable for library rebinding

Printed in the United States of America by Princeton
University Press, Princeton, New Jersey

To my parents

Contents

Illustrations

Tables

Acknowledgments

I would like to drink a toast to all those whose assistance I here acknowledge. I wish to thank the National Endowment for the Humanities and the Naval Academy Research Council for several grants to assist my research. The University of California Press and *Eighteenth-Century Studies* have kindly allowed me to use, in different form, the following articles: "Social Drinking in the Old Regime," in Robin Room and Susanna Barrows, eds., *The Social History of Alcohol* (Berkeley, forthcoming); and "Beyond the Barriers: Popular Culture and Parisian *Guinguettes*," *Eighteenth-Century Studies* 18, 2 (1984-85):153-169.

Guy Lytle fostered my first steps as a professional historian. I owe an enormous debt to Orest Ranum and Robert Forster for their guidance throughout this project, first as mentors and then as colleagues. Hans Medick taught me a great deal about popular culture, for which I am deeply grateful. *Les familles* Gouhier, Mollier, and Hamon welcomed me and nourished my love of France, especially their corner of it. Daniel Roche and Marcel Lachiver kindly offered me advice about the archives and my work. Steven Kaplan generously shared his prodigious knowledge of Paris and its records and just as generously gave an earlier draft of this study the benefit of his searching criticism. I have depended heavily on the support and criticism of colleagues in the Works-in-Progress Seminar of the U.S. Naval Academy's History Department, particularly its organizer Richard Abels, and in the Baltimore-Washington Old-Regime Study Group and its organizers, Timothy Tackett and Jack Censer. Rae Jean Goodman gave unstintingly of her time and expertise with recalcitrant computers. Marti Betz patiently prepared my maps. The encouragement and suggestions of Susanna Barrows, Natalie Zemon Davis, Robert Darnton, and Ezra Suleiman have sustained me through the years. Fritz Stern has helped me in countless ways, not the least of which was a careful reading of this work. I thank him and the whole Stern family. My parents have given me a love of history and their unfailing confidence, for which I offer this book in gratitude. Special thanks goes to my son Philip for his patience. Finally Katherine, my wife, has given freely of her own historical skills, her editor's pen, and her optimism. I have relied on her completely, and she has always been there.

Public Drinking and Popular Culture
in Eighteenth-Century Paris

Introduction

"Disreputable cabarets, otherwise called taverns. You will not go there delicate reader, I will go for you. You will only see the place in description and that will spare you some disagreeable sensations. This is the receptacle of the dregs of the populace."[1] Thus the essayist Louis-Sébastien Mercier, in his *Tableau de Paris* written shortly before the Revolution, introduced his eighteenth-century audience to Parisian taverns. His description is doubly appropriate today. In the first place, the taverns of old-regime Paris now lie beyond the reach of the modern reader; we too will go only vicariously. The culture and behavior of the common people who used taverns and gave them significance are equally inaccessible, and left largely unrecorded. Historians have relied necessarily on a few contemporary descriptions to discover popular culture, and that of Mercier has been particularly influential.[2] Secondly, his is not a sympathetic portrait, either of the populace or of their comportment. Mercier, like those of his contemporaries in the government or elite society who wrote about popular culture, dismissed taverns and those who went there as unsavory, violent, and even dangerous. A study of public drinking, then, must deal with several related questions: What was popular culture,

[1] Louis-Sébastien Mercier, *Tableau de Paris* (Amsterdam, 1782-1788), 7:233.

[2] See Norman Hampson, *Will and Circumstances* (Norman, Okla., 1983), pp. 65-83, for further discussion of Mercier's ideas. Jeffry Kaplow, *The Names of Kings: The Parisian Laboring Poor in the Eighteenth Century* (New York, 1972), relies heavily on Mercier, although elsewhere, in Louis-Sébastien Mercier, *Le Tableau de Paris*, ed. Jeffry Kaplow (Paris, 1982), p. 19, Kaplow notes Mercier's "visceral distrust of the *peuple*." Daniel Roche, *Le Peuple de Paris* (Paris, 1979), p. 46, expresses even more caution about Mercier's information on popular culture.

3

how do we find and understand it, and what role can elite evidence play in such an investigation?

Historians studying popular culture or the urban lower classes, particularly in Paris, have drawn heavily on accounts like Mercier's, as well as on government reports, literary evidence, and police codes. As a result, information on the lives of the common people has always come from an external and socially superior perspective. In this way the opinions of elite observers have shaped historical accounts for generations by providing the most accessible and coherent evidence. These literate intermediaries belonged to a heterogeneous elite of "the three robes": the clergy, the nobility, and the liberal professions. They could be doctors, writers, courtiers, or bureaucrats—in short, anyone who shared an elite culture of literacy and learning. Popular culture belonged to the rest of society: the popular or laboring classes, which included the lower classes in the city, as well as the master artisans and shopkeepers, who might be considered members of a lower middle class.[3] Historians continue to debate the distinction between elite and popular culture, and some argue that, because popular culture neither excluded nor was abandoned by the elites, at least until fairly recently, it is misleading to identify it only with the populace.[4]

[3] I have used Daniel Roche's category of "the three robes" as cited in Roger Chartier, "Culture as Appropriation: Popular Cultural Uses in Early Modern France," in Steven L. Kaplan, ed., *Understanding Popular Culture* (Berlin, N.Y., 1984), p. 237. For the popular classes I am considering a broader group than either Kaplow's "laboring poor" or Roche's *peuple*. I also refer to this broader group as the "laboring classes."

[4] Among those who have taken the position that there was little distinction are Robert Isherwood, in "Entertainment in the Parisian Fairs in the Eighteenth Century," *Journal of Modern History* 53 (1981):24-48; and in *Farce and Fantasy: Popular Entertainment in Eighteenth-Century Paris* (New York, 1986); Peter Burke, *Popular Culture in Early Modern Europe* (New York, 1978), pp. 24-28, 270-281. More recently, Burke, "Popular Culture Between History and Ethnology," *Ethnologia Europaea* 14 (1984):5-8, has recognized the need for some distinction between high and low culture and for a concept of cultural hegemony to explain their relationship.

But by the eighteenth century the elites were rapidly developing a sense of distance from the common people. Mercier expressed this distance in his distaste for the cabarets he described and clearly expected his "delicate readers" to avoid such places altogether. In fact the elites had abandoned taverns early in the eighteenth century and appear to have isolated themselves increasingly from other aspects of popular culture. Their descriptions of public drinking and popular culture grew correspondingly more hostile with their alienation from what they described.

With the weight of elite evidence so firmly opposed to the popular consumption of alcohol, it is hardly surprising to find that historians have condemned taverns—and the public drinking, leisure, and sociability associated with them—to the margins of old-regime society, if indeed they have bothered to mention them at all.[5] Taverns have become a cliché in descriptions of the old regime, a symbol of misery and debauchery, and continue to play that role for many modern historians. Despite all that has been written about the wine produced in France, discussions of its consumption have tended to focus on the rise of alcoholism in cities and later in the countryside. These accounts miss the cultural significance of alcohol and, more generally, the importance of public consumption and comportment in popular culture. This study, however, attempts to discover the positive uses of public drinking through

5 I discuss this traditional depiction in greater detail elsewhere, but several prominent examples include Francisque Michel and Edouard Fournier, *Histoire des hôtelleries, cabarets, hôtels, garnies, restaurants et cafés* (Paris, 1859); Albert de La Fizilière, *Vins à la mode et cabarets au XVIIIe siècle* (Paris, 1886); François Fosca, *Histoire des cafés de Paris* (Paris, 1934); and more recently Fernand Braudel, *Capitalism and Material Life*, trans. Miriam Kochan (New York, 1973); Philippe Ariès, *Centuries of Childhood: A Social History of the Family*, trans. Robert Baldick (New York, 1962); Kaplow, *The Names of Kings*; Robert Mandrou, *Introduction à la France moderne (1500-1640): essai de psychologie historique* (Paris, 1961; rpt. 1974); Jacques Saint-Germain, *La Vie quotidienne en France à la fin du grand siècle* (Paris, 1965). In contrast to these, Roche, *Le Peuple de Paris*, pp. 256-271, offers a remarkably good discussion of taverns.

evidence that has come more directly from the people in taverns. The juxtaposition of this evidence with more traditional descriptions offers an example of the opacity of popular culture to elite observers and modern researchers and provides a key with which to understand what made that culture unique.

Most attempts to find an autonomous "popular voice" have been frustrated by the lack of direct evidence for the common people's *mentalité*. Some historians have suggested that a limited number of cultural artifacts (for example, the *bibliothèque bleue* of chapbooks or the plays in the *poissard* genre) may reflect popular beliefs more directly, but there is considerable skepticism about their claim at this point.[6] We simply know too little about the authors and the audience of such works to accept them as evidence of popular beliefs. Our insight into popular culture, as a consequence, is necessarily dominated by intermediaries who produced the records of popular attitudes and behavior. Is there then such a thing as popular culture, beyond the defining discourse of elite criticism? Robert Darnton has argued that it exists and may be found when we encounter some aspect of the culture that we cannot understand. When we fail to "get" a story, joke, or proverb, then he is confident that its very opacity will bring us soonest to some aspect of popular culture.[7] In the same vein it is possible that popular culture emerges from those moments when the elites failed to "get" what they were hearing from the populace. The dissonances that arose between elite and popular discourse, even when pop-

[6] See for example Robert Mandrou, *De la culture populaire aux XVIIe et XVIIIe siècles: la bibliothèque bleue de Troyes* (Paris, 1964); or Geneviève Bollème, *Les Almanachs populaires aux XVIIe et XVIIIe siècles* (Paris, 1969). Trenchant criticism has come from Carlo Ginzburg, *The Cheese and the Worms: The Cosmos of a Sixteenth-Century Miller*, trans. John and Anne Tedeschi (Harmondsworth, 1982), and Robert Muchembled, *Culture populaire et culture des élites* (Paris, 1978). Frequently used words are not italicized in the text after their initial appearance.

[7] Robert Darnton, *The Great Cat Massacre and Other Episodes in French Cultural History* (New York, 1983), pp. 4-6, 77-78.

ular discourse was carefully staged, reveal alternative values and behavior.[8] For this reason, historians attempting to overcome the limitations of elite sources have been subjecting them to more critical analysis. Such an approach not only avoids too naive an acceptance of their information but also may penetrate the layers of distortion in elite evidence to reach a more objective description of popular practice. Taverns are a particularly good example of such dissonance since they provoked some of the harshest elite criticism of popular culture. As taverns and drink came to symbolize what was wrong with the populace and with its comportment and values, they offer us a remarkable vantage point for exploring both the nature of elite perceptions of the populace and the dissonance between elite portrayals and popular comportment.

The effort to reconstruct the institution of the public drinking place and its role in popular culture need not rely solely on testimony such as Mercier's. The people of Paris left their own testimony in various judicial, notarial, and fiscal archives. Judicial records in particular form the basis of this study's reevaluation of popular behavior. The records of petty contentions, banal disputes, and brawls occurring in and around taverns abound with details about the actions and attitudes of individual participants, as they were recounted to the police. Such documents offer a very different depiction of men in taverns: far from being "receptacles of the dregs of the populace," public drinking places drew people from all ranks of society to shops that served alcohol and gave them a place to consume it in the company of friends. They left their work and homes to find in public drinking places a neutral terrain in which to engage in the public reproduction of their social relations. Public drinking in taverns reenacted a fundamental communion among men, a symbolic consumption and sharing with which they created their solidarities and reaffirmed their values.

[8] Ginzburg, *The Cheese and the Worms*, p. xix.

7

Little more than a table and chairs with a roof overhead, the tavern managed to perform several crucial functions in urban society. A tavern sold different kinds of alcohol, of course, according to the elaborate distinctions of guild monopoly. More importantly, a tavern sold space and the freedom to use it within broad constraints. Its room was particularly cherished by the laboring classes, who supplemented their own inadequate domestic space by living publicly in the community of their fellows. As a predominantly male enclave, a tavern offered men leisure and recreation away from wives and work. A place to meet and to wait, to revel and relax, the tavern brought men together in endless permutations of their networks of friends, colleagues, rivals, and allies. Taverns also encouraged men to consume, preferably together and in ways that enhanced their solidarities. As public space, open to nearly everyone in a neighborhood, the tavern acted as a forum for local politics and contests of honor and status. Public drinking there embraced many of the more public and sociable, though less formal, aspects of popular culture.

Mercier observed taverns quite differently. Like other elite commentators discussing the populace and its behavior, he decried the lower classes' use of alcohol, especially their public drinking, as a major contribution to, and expression of, their degraded nature: "The brutalized father is deaf to the voices [of his crying children], and sells off the furniture piece by piece to reimmerse himself in drunkenness."[9] Mercier was certainly not alone in his jaundiced views. Contemporary jurists agreed that "the innumerable multitude of cabarets . . . yields drunkenness, thefts, debauchery, idleness, a passion for gambling, quarrels, bad households and the ruin of poor families."[10] Medical authorities, churchmen, and "moral observers" joined

[9] Mercier, *Le Tableau de Paris*, ed. Jeffry Kaplow, p. 283.
[10] Des Essarts, *Dictionnaire universel de police* (Paris, 1786-1789), 1:472. He claims that he is quoting from an unnamed "modern publicist."

in these denunciations.[11] Thus as taverns played an integral role in the lives of the laboring classes, so they also enjoyed a prominent position in the elite's critique of popular culture. The public drinking place epitomized the undisciplined, spendthrift behavior of the populace; it gave focus to elite hostility toward the laboring classes' unrepentant reliance on sociability and public consumption. Yet the very fact of this hostility helps both to establish the autonomy of a popular perspective and to delineate an important element in the struggle between elite and popular cultures. As a recurring metaphor for what made popular culture different, degenerate, and unacceptable in the eyes of the elites, taverns provide an avenue to investigating the dialectic between elite and popular culture. From that dialectic emerge the very things that make popular culture distinct.

Although evidence from elite observers on public drinking cannot be taken at face value, it does reveal their attitudes and the nature of their social and political relations with the rest of society. Such testimony makes clear that the Drink Question had already emerged in the eighteenth century as a powerful metaphor for talking about the lower classes. The middle class in the late nineteenth century experienced a sudden surge of alarm over the extent and consequences of lower-class alcohol consumption, known as the Drink Question, during which time the issue seemed particularly urgent.[12] The invention of

[11] See Georges Durand, *Vin, vigne et vignerons en Lyonnais et Beaujolais* (Paris, 1979), pp. 44-45; and Roche, *Le Peuple de Paris*, pp. 38-47, on the moral observers.

[12] See Susanna Barrows, "After the Commune: Alcoholism, Temperance and Literature in the Early Third Republic," in John M. Merriman, ed., *Consciousness and Class Experience in 19th-Century Europe* (New York, 1979), pp. 205-218; Susanna Barrows, *Distorting Mirrors* (New Haven, 1981), pp. 61-72; P. E. Prestwich, "French Workers and the Temperance Movement," *International Review of Social History* 28 (1980):36-52; Louis Devance, "Stratégies de l'antialcoolisme en France au début du xxe siècle," in *Les Boissons: production et consommation aux XIXe et XXe siècles*; Michael Marrus, "Social Drinking in the Belle Epoque," *Journal of Social History* 7 (1974):115-141. For the literature on this question in other countries, and for an excellent introduction to the Drink

the term *alcoholism* in the middle of the nineteenth century allowed the middle classes to condemn the insurgency and hostility of the lower classes with "scientific" objectiveness. But even before then the elites were using drink and its abuses to explain the impoverished condition of the lower classes in terms of their own failure and indiscipline.[13] Although the volume of elite denunciation reached a pitch only in the nineteenth century, a firm pattern of elite responses to popular drinking had clearly been established in the previous two centuries. Because public drinking was so integral to popular culture in the old regime, the Drink Question implicated the very things that made popular culture different and dangerous in elite eyes.

The Drink Question is not the only issue raised by public drinking, however. There is the related problem of elite perceptions and control of popular leisure.[14] Taverns figured prominently in popular leisure, and thus in the growing desire to control its uses and forms. Indeed the condemnation of taverns as a pernicious threat to the productivity and work ethic of the laboring classes played a larger role in elite commentaries than even worries about drunkenness. Closely linked to taverns and leisure was the problem of lower-class gambling. Here too the elites identified an activity that interfered with its program

---

Question, see especially James S. Roberts, *Drink, Temperance and the Working Class in Nineteenth-Century Germany* (Boston, 1984), pp. 2-10. See also W. J. Rorabaugh, *The Alcoholic Republic, An American Tradition* (Oxford, 1979), pp. 187-209, passim; Peter Clark, *The English Alehouse: A Social History, 1200-1830* (London, 1983).

[13] See Louis Réné Villermé, *Tableau de l'état physique et moral des ouvriers employés dans les manufactures de coton, de laine et de soie* (Paris, 1840), and its treatment by William H. Sewell, Jr., *Work and Revolution in France: The Language of Labor from the Old Regime to 1848* (Cambridge, 1980), pp. 231-232.

[14] Muchembled, *Culture populaire*, pp. 381-390; Gareth Stedman Jones, *Languages of Class: Studies in English Working Class History, 1832-1982* (Cambridge, 1983), pp. 76-89; Michael Marrus, *The Emergence of Leisure* (New York, 1974), pp. 1-10; Eileen Yeo and Stephen Yeo, "Ways of Seeing: Control and Leisure versus Class Struggle," in Eileen Yeo and Stephen Yeo, eds., *Popular Culture and Class Conflict, 1590-1914: Explorations in the History of Labor and Leisure* (Brighton, 1981), pp. 128-154.

to reform the morals and productivity of the populace. Less immediately linked to perceptions of public drinking, but still fundamental to the discussion, was the fear of violent, even criminal behavior, which focused most often on taverns as the chief cause. Thus the perception of public drinking places helped to define a dangerous class, or rather began the process of blurring the distinctions between laboring classes and dangerous classes. The attack on drink itself simply formed part of a larger rejection of popular culture and its manifestations in public drinking places.

The role of public drinking in popular culture is perhaps not entirely clear. Popular culture generally refers to the behavior and beliefs of the common people, the popular or laboring classes. Their religion and "superstitions," their rituals and celebrations, and their youth groups and confraternities played a large role in popular culture and have been investigated in recent studies. Less is known about ordinary life, lived daily and only punctuated by religion or festivals. But what can we learn about beliefs and ideas from unthinking routine? Public drinking raises the problem of interpreting popular behavior as a sign of meaning. Indeed, with little or no consideration of many of the mainstays of the genre, such as chapbooks, witchcraft, or popular religion, some may question whether I am writing about popular culture at all.[15] There is no coherent cosmology, no clear mentalité articulated in the records of public drinking. But popular culture refers also to social conduct, understood broadly enough to mean not only the elaborate rituals of carnival or religion, but the trivial and routine gestures and behavior of daily life as well. A system of meaning surely informs social conduct in its whole range of expressions, making sense of the insult and the toast, of sociability in its various

[15] According to Chartier, "Culture as Appropriation," p. 229, the popular culture of old-regime France "has been identified in two sources: a set of texts such as the *Bibliothèque bleue* and a set of beliefs and rituals considered a constituent part of a popular religion."

guises, as well as of the charivari.[16] People's values and priorities inform their behavior, especially their public comportment in front of their peers. The study of public drinking focuses on patterns of consumption and expenditure, of sociability and reciprocity, of fellowship and confrontation. It uses this behavior as a key to understanding popular beliefs and values. Thus it reflects the tendency to expand the definition of culture to overlap with society, preferring to use culture to refer to the way people live in, and make sense of, their environment.[17] Because the public drinking place stood at the juncture between public and private, between work and recreation, it provides an opportunity to pursue this conception of popular culture.

Taverns allow us to witness much of the social and public behavior of the Parisian people. Such behavior conveys meaning, much as a text would, though less explicitly. The laboring classes used public drinking to express their fundamental values and beliefs, and to give a structure to their social relations. In particular, tavern comportment rested on the pervasive need for sociability, both as a form of solidarity that shaped communities and allegiances and as an ethical imperative that inspired certain kinds of behavior. An historian of popular culture has placed this need for a "thick sociability" at the basis of the "quest for security" in the early modern period.[18] The idea of sociability, particularly in its first sense of configurations of

---

[16] Natalie Zemon Davis, *Society and Culture in Early Modern France* (Stanford, 1975), p. xvi.

[17] " 'Culture' is coming to be less and less distinguishable from 'society' as 'society' is seen more and more as a cultural construct," according to Burke, "Popular Culture Between History and Ethnology," p. 5. As Günther Lottes, "Popular Culture and the Early Modern State in 16th Century Germany," in Kaplan, ed., *Understanding Popular Culture*, p. 148, puts it, "the culturally oriented new social history sees culture as an entire way of life." For an excellent discussion of recent books on popular culture, see William Beik, "Searching for Popular Culture in Early Modern France," *Journal of Modern History* 49 (1977):266-281.

[18] Muchembled, *Culture populaire*, pp. 45-55.

solidarity, has also contributed greatly to the study of political organization and action, especially when unions or communities were emerging politically. Nineteenth-century taverns have been identified in a number of such studies as centers of protopolitical solidarity, schools of sociability that encouraged political self-awareness and cooperation.[19] Eighteenth-century taverns appear to have operated in much the same way. Certainly some taverns offered themselves in the service of the shadowy and illegal journeymen's associations, or as salons for third-rate *philosophes* and writers. But the tavern also served to define a more general solidarity, a structural identity common to a community or a class, through the reiterated patterns of routine encounters going on in taverns around the city and over time. This study attempts to identify the communities that revealed themselves in tavern sociability, aggregating the social networks of drinking groups in order to find common themes in the behavior of thousands of individuals.

The social relations evidenced through aggregate patterns of drinking companions shed some light on the major social questions of the eighteenth century. Prerevolutionary Paris presents many of the same kinds of problems in interpreting political action as do those nineteenth-century situations so well studied already. In particular historians would like to know more about the identity and sources of solidarity among the sans-culottes, that frustrating social hybrid whose composition seems so ill defined yet whose existence was so crucial.[20] This study suggests

[19] Maurice Agulhon, *Republic in the Village*, trans. Janet Lloyd (Cambridge, 1982); Ted Margadant, *French Peasants in Revolt* (Princeton, 1979); Michael P. Hanagan, *The Logic of Solidarity* (Urbana, Ill., 1980).

[20] For the ongoing discussion of this question, see R. B. Rose, *The Making of the Sans-Culottes: Democratic Ideas and Institutions in Paris, 1789-1792* (Manchester, England, 1983); Morris Slavin, *The French Revolution in Miniature* (Princeton, 1984); Richard Mowery Andrews, "Social Structures, Political Elites and Ideology in Revolutionary Paris, 1792-1794: A Critical Evaluation of Albert Soboul's *Les Sans-culottes en l'an II*," *Journal of Social History* 19 (1985):71-112.

that the revolutionary coalition of professional, artisan, and laborer that managed to cooperate despite social differences can be found manifested throughout the preceding century in networks of tavern fellowship, when they learned, if not the grounds for common interest, at least the habits of familiarity. Sociability also implied certain values, particular attitudes toward public life, social obligations, and male comportment.[21] These attitudes motivated the associations of men in taverns, long before the need for solidarity became politically urgent. This second aspect of sociability, its motivations and ethical implications, is obviously related to the first, yet tends to be less carefully analyzed. Most studies of sociability assume that this kind of sentiment is the reason for men congregating but focus more on the forms of association. Understood in this sense, sociability might be seen as little more than a general urge to associate, a kind of pervasive extroversion. Something like this has been claimed by scholars for various societies, particularly Mediterranean societies such as those in the south of France.[22] This study, however, attempts to show that the values inherent in sociability entail specific attitudes toward consumption, generosity, honor, and leisure. These attitudes bear more than a passing resemblance to the culture of reciprocity encountered in "primitive" societies.[23] Sociability means not only that men sought each others' companionship, but that their conviviality imposed certain obligations of consumption and expenditure, obligations that brought them into conflict with other imperatives in their society. Such consumption not only acted to fortify

---

[21] "Both participation in beer parties and the giving of parties are tokens of essential sociability, and sociability indicates to Iteso a willingness on the part of other actors to participate in social and economic exchanges"; see Ivan Karp, "Beer Drinking and Social Experience in an African Society," in Ivan Karp and Charles S. Beard, eds., *Explorations in African Systems of Thought* (Bloomington, Ind., 1980), p. 89.

[22] Maurice Agulhon, *Pénitents et francs-maçons de l'ancienne Provence* (Paris, 1968), pp. 15-16; Ariès, *Centuries of Childhood*, p. 405.

[23] Marshall Sahlins, *Stone Age Economics* (New York, 1972), pp. 188-220.

the fellowship of drinking groups and, ultimately, of social networks, but also competed with the requirements of the domestic economy and with an emerging definition of "rational" behavior.

Sociability in taverns should not be taken to refer solely to friendship and cordial relationships. A number of historians stress the importance of conflict in social relations, pointing out the degree to which competition and distrust pervaded communities.[24] I take the idea of sociability to encompass social relations of this kind as well and see the rivalries in a community as equally as instructive as, and often congruent with, the friendships. One of the reasons for the tavern's centrality in popular culture was its suitability as a place for public contests and rivalries. Inevitably, with so much of the evidence for popular culture coming from records of judicial contests, the contentious aspects of social relations figure prominently.

This study relies primarily on the voices of the inarticulate, unlearned people themselves, in the records of the judicial process. Like much of the literary artifacts used by historians of chapbooks and theater, the testimony in legal records purports to be the words of the populace, transcribed by a literate secretary. Unlike fiction, however, the veracity of legal testimony could be a matter of life and death. There is little question, of course, that transcriptions systematically condensed, and perhaps at times even distorted, testimony. In theory, however, a plaintiff or witness had the transcription read back before signing or making his mark. If the transcription changed his evidence, at least we may hope that the deponent kept it from doing violence to his testimony. Then too the testimony of the poor, destitute, and desperate might be fabricated, particularly by the accused on the spot in the *commissaire's* office. The bulk of the testimony in this study, however, comes not

[24] Ronald Weissman, *Ritual Brotherhood in Renaissance Florence* (New York, 1982); Yves Castan, *Honnêteté et relations sociales en Languedoc, 1715-1780* (Paris, 1974).

from the miserable thief apprehended in some crime, but from "ordinary" people complaining about petty disputes. The testimony in these kinds of cases probably suffers less from distortion than testimony in the intimidating circumstances of an arrest.[25] Plaintiffs too employed strategies of embellishment, no doubt, seeking to tarnish their assailant while asserting their innocence, but could afford to acknowledge most of the basic facts without jeopardy. It is always instructive to find a countersuit, with the defendant's version of an incident. The context of a confrontation—where it occurred, who was present, at what hour—is of equal importance as the specifics of the fight, and the information is less likely to be distorted. In this regard, I have attempted in this study to examine behavior and attitudes that attended the events of a dispute only peripherally.

Judicial records offer a unique view of popular culture. Despite the obvious problems with a source devoted to aberrant behavior, it is possible both to "look past" this behavior, to see daily life as it unfolded around an incident, and to discern attitudes and norms from the reaction to violence and crime.[26] The best records for this purpose come from the lowest level of the judicial system, those dealing with the most banal, commonplace affairs. Such records lie in the registers of the guard and nightwatch or the papers of the forty-eight police commissaires supervising Paris. The guard and nightwatch patrolled the city at all hours and brought the problems they encountered back to the office of the nearest commissaire. An even larger number of incidents came to the commissaire's attention in the form of complaints from individual citizens. Many of the disputes recorded in his papers never even reached the courts for a hearing

[25] Arlette Farge, *Délinquance et criminalité: le vol d'aliments à Paris au XVIIIe siècle* (Paris, 1974), pp. 145-149.

[26] David Garrioch, *Neighborhoods and Community in Paris, 1740-1790* (Cambridge, 1986), appeared too late for me to use his book in this study, but he also demonstrates the wealth of information on daily life in these archives as well as using them to address many of the topics in this study.

and were solved by the commissaire in his office. Others were dropped or settled by the parties themselves. A few, usually those dealing with theft, then made their way to a police or criminal court. The records of these courts form the basis of several interesting studies, and contribute to this study as well, but they suffer from certain limitations.[27] Much of the aggression and contention in daily life is left out of these records. More seriously, they scarcely exist before the middle of the eighteenth century. The commissaires' papers, on the other hand, embarrass the researcher with riches, both in their evidence about daily life and in their volume. As a consequence, it has been necessary to sample their records, at ten-year intervals, to cover a time span long enough to detect changing patterns.

The evidence for this study draws on records from various judicial archives chosen from years that ended with "I" between the years 1691 and 1771 (see Appendix). The choice of time spanned and the individual years sampled is not as arbitrary as might first appear. The volume of commissaires' papers dwindle away rapidly before the 1690s and explode in the 1770s. The period chosen begins roughly with the introduction of the café and the *guinquette* and ends before the Revolution. The endpoint reflects a deliberate decision to focus on a society undergoing no radical political changes, to look for public comportment in a less political era, and to leave to someone else the problem of the tavern's role in the Revolution. I suspect its role was little different than before the Revolution, still giving people a place to meet and talk about the things that mattered to them, but am disinclined to let the Revolution dominate the discussion of the old-regime institution, as it so often does. The

[27] Porphyre Petrovich, "Recherches sur la criminalité à Paris dans la seconde moitié du xviiie siècle," in André Abbiateci et al., eds., *Crimes et criminalité en France sous l'ancien régime, XVIIe et XVIIIe siècles* (Paris, 1971), pp. 190-268. Arlette Farge and André Zysberg, "Les Théâtres de la violence à Paris au xviiie siècle." *Annales, économies, sociétés, civilizations* 34 (1979):984-1015.

years ending with "1" are as good as any, and they avoid—barely—some of the events that shook Paris (Law's collapse, the kidnapped children affair, the carnage at the Dauphin's marriage), although it is difficult to see how these events could seriously disrupt the daily drinking habits of the Parisian populace. This study focuses rather on the larger structure of these habits, and on the gradual changes that affected long-term behavior.

The study begins with the documents at the point of their greatest ambiguity, in the fights and contentions that gave birth to these judicial records. Although the reliance on judicial records poses problems of interpretation, it reveals at the same time the things that men thought were worth fighting for. Contentions also identify an important facet of the tavern's clientele; these were men who belonged in large measure to the laboring classes, who insisted on their self-respect and the respect of others and fought to defend it. Their fights in taverns also attest to the importance of the public drinking place as an arena in which to provoke and settle disputes. Men fought in public here, seeking the support and approbation of peers and neighbors.

A discussion of the arena itself, the decor and arrangment of the tavern's space, follows in Chapter Two. The logistics of supplying alcohol and the manner of its sale both played an important part in the tavern's occupation, but the space presented to the customers was of equal importance. The diversity of drink and decor increased dramatically in the eighteenth century with the emergence of new public drinking institutions. This leads to an analysis in Chapter Three of patterns of use; the social, economic, and geographical distinctions among taverns; and the nature of recreation in taverns. The growing diversity among public drinking places paralleled an increasing stratification of urban society and popular recreation. Some of the new public drinking institutions also developed a different relation to their clientele, with a more commercial, and less "local" atmosphere.

The investigation of drink in Chapter Four addresses the symbolic role of drink in popular sociability. Drink functioned as a medium of social exchange, in a role very different from that described by elite discourse. This is followed in Chapter Five by a consideration of sociability in a larger context: the patterns of associating, the strategies of focusing sociability, and the emergence of new forms of sociability. The analysis also attempts to understand the values expressed through sociability. The study concludes with an explicit comparison of elite and popular perceptions of the tavern, seeking to find the reasons for the disparities and to understand the implications of these different perceptions. The evidence suggests that elite and popular perceptions were separated less by disagreement over the reality of what went on in taverns than by radically opposing assessments of the implications of tavern culture. What was for the police a center of disorder, dissolution, and debauchery was for the populace a space in which to create a public theater for its culture.

One. Honor and Public Violence

Violence and crime have characterized the taverns and tavern patrons of eighteenth-century Paris in descriptions of the institution from the old regime to the present. "If a brawl erupts from the effects of adulterated wine fists fly together; the guard comes running, for without it these *canaille* who had been dancing would kill each other to the sound of a violin. The populace, accustomed to this guard, needs it to be controlled and relies on the guard to end the frequent fights that break out in cabarets."[1] Thus Mercier, in one of his few descriptions of tavern comportment, captured the essence of this vision of a brutal lower class unleashing its aggressions in taverns; elsewhere he portrayed tavern patrons as beggars and thieves roistering on their ill-gotten gains. In addition to the violence endemic to taverns, they harbored dangerous, even criminal customers. His depictions contributed to an image of the tavern that has informed attitudes up to the present. "Tavernkeepers were more than ever [in the eighteenth century] the hosts of thieves and assassins," a pair of historians writing in the nineteenth century assures us, "all the wicked deeds were done in their dens." In particular, "very few cabarets in Paris were not a witness to a theft or a murder" by the notorious band of Cartouche and his men (in the 1720s).[2] "Most cabarets were veritable nests of cut-throats," states an historian of taverns earlier this century, and quite recently Philippe Ariès agreed that "the tavern was a place of ill-repute, reserved for criminals, prostitutes. . . ."[3] Whether viewed as merely disreputable or down-

---

[1] Mercier, *Tableau de Paris*, 7:239.
[2] Michel and Fournier, *Histoire des hôtelleries*, 2:342.
[3] George de Wissant, *Le Paris d'autrefois: cafés et cabarets* (Paris, 1928), p. 24. Ariès, *Centuries of Childhood*, p. 391.

right criminal, taverns were clearly not a place that Mercier's delicate readers might wish to visit.

Mercier's contemporary, Restif de la Bretonne, treated the reader to a more detailed version of the same thing in his brief essay on cabarets in *Les Nuits de Paris*. He had entered a cabaret on the rue Arbre-Sec where he heard laughing and singing. After taking a seat in the large and noisy "room of drinkers," he noted the "errand boys, shoe-cleaners, Auvergnats," and others with their wives and children, all seated in the room. "All these people are ugly, gross and hateful from every point of view, but this was because of their misery." With such a promising start he went on to describe a scene that could have come straight out of the boulevard theater. "By their second quart of wine, their heads began to ferment," Restif asserts and he recounts the ensuing quarrels. Practically everyone ends up arguing—wives with husbands, mothers with children, family with family—and the action culminates in a fight. The script was no different than dozens of others written by Vadé or Cailleau or other authors in the poissard genre, though Restif disguised his account as journalism.[4] He employed the same lampooning poissard speech, "J't'assènerai mon poing su'la mine!," and the same patronizing tone, as he discreetly paid for the other customers' drinks on his way out.[5]

The police of Paris expected no better from tavern crowds than did Mercier or Restif. They took every opportunity to condemn taverns for the illegal activities, particularly gambling and illicit assemblies, that they harbored, for the unsavory and dangerous customers they attracted, and for the violence that appeared to have been endemic to such establishments. Parisian police censured taverns for the "clang

---

[4] Alexander Parks Moore, *The Genre Poissard and the French Stage of the Eighteenth Century* (New York, 1935). See Chapter Three for a further discussion of the genre and these authors.

[5] Nicolas-Edme Restif de la Bretonne, *Les Nuits de Paris*, in *Les Oeuvres de Restif de la Bretonne* (Paris, 1930-1932), 1:140-144.

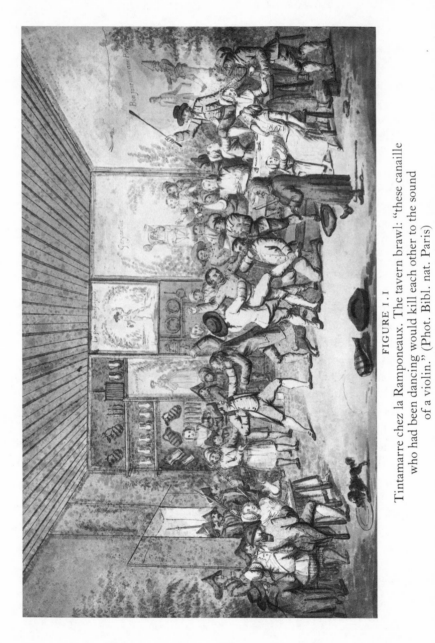

FIGURE 1.1

Tintamarre chez la Ramponeaux. The tavern brawl: "these canaille who had been dancing would kill each other to the sound of a violin." (Phot. Bibl. nat. Paris)

of epees and of saber blows, the frightful swearing and cries of 'murder' and calls for the nightwatch with which all the neighborhood is alarmed occasioned by the fights and brawls that often break out."[6] "These places have become caverns of debauchery," the jurist Fréminville warned, "which . . . occupy Justice in imposing the law on them. . . ." He cited a judgment of the Parlement of Dijon that embodied "all the principles of ancient ordinances" concerning taverns: "people commit in cabarets . . . infinite excesses, . . . hold offensive discourse, accompanied very often by blasphemy . . . fight and mistreat each other, and from that arise an infinity of disorders and lawsuits that ruin families."[7] Like Mercier the police were concerned about the canaille using taverns for their recreation and for refuge. Regular injunctions against "suspicious people and vagabonds" frequenting taverns were reinforced with constant patrols by the police at night and after the curfew.[8]

More than the reputation of a marginal institution is at issue here. The danger and disrepute associated with taverns extended to the customers and their behavior. Mercier's judgment of taverns, an attitude shared by much of his elite audience, effectively trivialized an important aspect of popular culture and its institutions and so managed to blur the line between laboring classes and dangerous classes.[9] Whereas Mercier and Restif portrayed the violence as mindless and indiscriminate, the police described it as depraved and criminal.

[6] A[rchives] N[ationales], Y9538, 22 September 1757.

[7] Edme de la Poix de Fréminville, *Dictionnaire ou traité de la police général des villes, bourgs, paroisses et seigneuries de la campagne* (Paris, 1771), pp. 104-106.

[8] See, for example, any one of dozens of reports by police inspectors making "night visits" in B[ibliothèque de l']A[rsenal], Arch. Bastille, Ms. 10133.

[9] See Louis Chevalier, *Laboring Classes, Dangerous Classes in Paris during the First Half of the Nineteenth Century*, trans. Frank Jellinek (Princeton, 1973), for the classic comparison of laboring and dangerous classes. He points out, pp. 6, 60-61, that Mercier "drew up the rules" for describing criminality, yet argues that his *Tableau* lacked the obsession with crime common to works in the nineteenth century.

Nearly all linked it to drunkenness in some way. This equation of taverns with violence, crime, and debauchery forms the basis of an elite rejection of popular culture. Not only did such a portrayal ignore the overwhelmingly peaceful uses of taverns that permitted the daily fellowship of hundreds of thousands of men and women, but it distorted the very nature of the disorder that did erupt, from time to time, in taverns. To rectify this portrayal, the historian must discover evidence from other sources, yet ironically the populace left a record of its own behavior and attitudes in few places other than the very criminal archives that chronicled their misbehavior. To these we must turn then, both to glean information about peaceful sociable behavior and to understand the real nature of popular disorder in taverns. But what better way to begin an analysis of taverns than by confronting the phantoms of plebeian degeneracy that haunt the institution?

If taverns truly offended against law and order to the extent suggested, then Parisians were fortunate indeed to have a police force so well equipped to protect them. The Parisian police provided the state with a precocious supervisory body, the object of both admiration and disapproval throughout Europe.[10] Agents of the police circulated frequently through the city in pursuit of refuse, immorality, sedition, and crime. The police prided themselves in being able to keep track of subversive authors, foreigners, and criminals. They boasted of their knowledge of the Parisian underworld.[11] Police magistrates, the commissaires, also offered help to the rest of the Parisians, taking their complaints and depositions in forty-eight offices located throughout the city. A nightwatch and guard of increas-

[10] Pierre Deyon, *Le Temps des prisons: essai sur l'histoire de la délinquance et les origines du système pénitentiaire* (Lille, 1975), pp. 75-76; Alan Williams, *The Police of Paris* (Baton Rouge, La., 1979), p. xvi.

[11] Williams, *The Police of Paris*, p. 109, notes the usefulness of this claim to the police's image and cautions skepticism. See also Richard Cobb, *The Police and the People: French Popular Protest, 1789-1820* (London, 1970), pp. 14-45, for a discussion of police informants during the revolutionary period.

ing size and efficiency added their main force to protect those in danger and to bring miscreants before a magistrate. The police's function went well beyond patrolling the streets, of course, but clearly their duties allowed them to deal frequently with public drinking places and with the men and women who went there.

The identification of taverns and their patrons with violence and crime should have left some mark on the judicial records, both in the criminal records and in the files of the commissaires themselves. The extensive judicial archives of eighteenth-century Paris offer a means to analyze this violence and yield, at the same time, an abundance of information about popular culture. These archives can show whether the tavern's disrepute was warranted. There is always the risk with such documents of overemphasizing the disreputable, aberrant aspects of a problem, but there is little choice. Few documents provide such a faithful rendition of the people's own voices or offer such detailed evidence about their daily life.

Without doubt taverns witnessed brawls, drunkenness, fights over cards, thieves and cutpurses, much as the police maintained. Yet paradoxically, the judicial archives of the old regime provide a more balanced verdict of popular behavior in taverns than did Mercier. These archives suggest that violence was certainly a part of tavern comportment, but such violence was neither as frequent nor as indiscriminate as contemporary writers were suggesting. Much of the popular disorder in taverns could not properly be called criminal.[12] Rather the archives reveal the rivalries and tensions of self-respecting people who resorted to violence for reasons of status, reputation, and

[12] Farge and Zysberg, "Les Théâtres de la violence," p. 984, call it "banal violence . . . which arises from all the acts and gestures of daily existance" in contrast to "criminal violence" or "heinous crime." Antoinette Wills, *Crime and Punishment in Revolutionary Paris* (Westport, Conn., 1981), p. 108, finds in the court cases that survived into the Revolution that "half of the cases of 'violence' brought to trial in the Revolution were declared not to be crimes at all, simply street fights. The accused were acquitted or freed with a warning."

power. They demonstrate as well the extent to which honor motivated men's behavior in taverns. This depiction does not refute the existence of disreputable taverns or customers, for there are important limitations on what even the police learned about crime, but it does balance the picture. Such a balance may make it possible to see beyond the violence and to discern the peaceful, sociable uses of taverns that violence occasionally interrupted. To do so, it is necessary to understand the nature of violence and crime in taverns and the process by which this crime came to the attention of the judicial system.

THEFT

The police associated crime particularly with theft, and most of the cases that actually appeared before the criminal courts concerned a robbery.[13] Although taverns were accused of countenancing many kinds of criminal behavior, the court records might suggest that theft was a problem there as well. For when these courts were presented with an incident in a tavern, it was often a theft; and anyone relying on the records of these courts to study popular culture might well dismiss taverns as dens of thieves.[14] Yet the absolute number of such cases was insignificant: scarcely half a dozen per year in the records of the extraordinary criminal court out of 200 thefts heard by that court in most years, and two score cases in the records of the ordinary

[13] Steven G. Reinhardt, "Crime and Royal Justice in Ancien Régime France: Modes of Analysis," *Journal of Interdisciplinary History* 13 (1983):444-446.

[14] Based on a reading of all of the documents of the grand or extraordinary criminal court in the years 1721, 1731, 1741, 1751, and one-half of those in 1761, one-half of the 38 cases occurring in taverns that were heard before the extraordinary criminal court involved theft. More than one-third of 57 cases occurring in taverns heard before the petit or ordinary criminal court involved theft. The records of the ordinary criminal court go back only to 1760, except for one liasse of fragments, so the analysis of this court is based on three of twelve liasses in both 1761 and 1771.

criminal court out of about 1,000 thefts each year.[15] It is essential, rather, to investigate the massive number of complaints and preliminary cases that never went to court, which survive in the archives of the police commissaires. When considered in the context of all of the incidents taking place in taverns that were seen by commissaires daily in Paris, theft in taverns appears quite unusual. In a sample of 932 incidents in taverns that came to the commissaires' attention (including 95 cases that later went to criminal courts), theft accounted for only 13 percent.[16] Obviously, few Parisians went to taverns expecting to have their purses, or throats, cut. The frequency of theft in taverns was not significant, when compared either with the number of thefts elsewhere in the city, or with other activities in taverns. Whether taverns were actually the headquarters for cutpurses, however, is a different question and one that receives special consideration elsewhere in this study. The point is that they were rarely the scene of such crimes.

The most obvious target of a thief in a tavern was actually the tavernkeeper himself. Although historians looking back from the nineteenth century judged that "it was much less rare to see tavernkeepers lend a hand to crimes than to find themselves vic-

[15] See Petrovich, "Recherches sur la criminalité," for total figures on the extraordinary criminal court. Farge, *Vol*, p. 114, shows that theft played a much larger role (72 percent) in cases before the extraordinary criminal court as a whole than they did among tavern cases. See Farge and Zysberg, "Les Théâtres de la violence," p. 986, for total figures in the ordinary criminal court.

[16] This study is based on a sample of 1,216 cases found in the records of the extraordinary and ordinary criminal courts, the minutes of the commissaires, several registers of the nightwatch, and several files of police inspectors. With few exceptions, all of these records would have passed through the hands of the commissaires, although the vast majority would have gone no farther than that. The cases are drawn fairly evenly from nine years ending in "1" between 1691 and 1771, although few of the records from the courts or the nightwatch survive from before 1751. The analysis in this chapter excludes 284 cases that gave evidence about use of taverns but did not actually record an incident in a tavern. The remaining 932 cases document some criminal or violent event in, or just outside of, a tavern. See Appendix for a discussion of these records.

tims," the reverse in fact seems to have been the case.[17] Utensils, napkins, mustard pots, and plates were too easy to remove. A café owner found that a silver spoon was missing at the table of two of his regular customers, a pin seller and the man's brother-in-law, a soldier. They insisted that they did not have it, and the soldier became so incensed that he "went out to the street to find some stones" with which to "break everything in the shop." But the owner searched them and found it in the pin seller's pocket, whereupon the man broke down, crying, "I am an unfortunate, I deserve to be killed."[18] Everyone knew that owners were forced to leave their shops momentarily vacant whenever they fetched wine from their cellars, and thieves occasionally profited from the opportunity. Customers enjoyed access as well to a tavernkeeper's domestic space and effects, since the upstairs rooms in taverns could serve as public rooms by day and bedrooms by night.

Of course, some customers stole from each other as well. A laundress drinking with several other women spied one of them pocketing a handkerchief from the basket of clothing and loudly accused her. The other woman desperately asked to be excused, offering to sell her body for the accuser.[19] A customer discovered he had lost his purse and complained to some soldiers with whom he was drinking. They all tried to find it and finally searched each other, only to discover that the victim's own cousin had the purse in his pocket. "You would even take your cousin's money," one of them cried, challenging the thief to a duel. "You are a scoundrel who has debased my company." The thief was killed in the street outside of the tavern.[20] The

[17] Michel and Fournier, *Histoire des hôtelleries*, p. 342; Petrovitch, "Recherches sur la criminalité," p. 255, also notes that the profession appearing most often among the victims in the extraordinary criminal court was the wine merchant, but Farge, *Vol*, p. 129, finds that theft of alcohol claimed a small percentage (10 percent) of total theft of food.

[18] AN, Y10086, 24 October 1741.

[19] AN, Y10226, 18 November 1760.

[20] AN, Y10993b, 1 May 1751.

indignation expressed by the thief's companions was not simply the outrage of the victim but the disapproval of self-respecting men. Although judicial cases concerned with theft in taverns occurred relatively rarely, they remind us that most customers were not thieves and viewed theft with horror.

A master wheelwright named Boucher recognized how sensitive his peers felt about the accusation of theft. He had assembled with several colleagues, men he called friends, at a tavern in their neighborhood. Boucher says they drank some bottles of wine and, "to pass the time more agreeably," and with "unanimous consent," they had played at quoits. At the end of an amicable game, however, Boucher found that he had lost one of the coins with which he had been playing and began to look for it. He emphasized in his testimony that he had looked behind chairs at a distance from the tables where they had been playing and drinking, but one of his companions noticed and asked what he was doing. He claimed that he replied, "It is a coin (an *écu* of 6 *livres*) with which I was playing that has become invisible; nevertheless I do not suspect anyone." He did find it on the floor and said to his companions, "You have heard, messieurs, that I did not ask any of you for my écu, nor disturb any of you from the table because we are all honest men [*honnêtes gens*]." But the master harnessmaker replied "in a tone not at all joking" that Boucher was not an *honnête homme*. Boucher called him a blackguard [*jean foutre*] and the harnessmaker "in spite of the company," had gone to complain to a commissaire.[21] Presumably the man complained about abusive language, but he may also have objected to the implied accusation. Certainly a merchant objected to it when he brought suit against a colleague for having "insulted his honor and reputation and accused him of taking a *louis d'or*," and he demanded a "reparation for the said accusation of theft."[22] Even the suggestion of theft involved men's honor, as Boucher realized.

[21] AN, Y15643, 4 July 1751.
[22] AN, Y14066, 10 July 1741.

As many as half of the accusations of property crimes were between people who knew each other, however, and many accusations reveal a history of property disputes. The merchant who complained of having been robbed by a couple with whom he was drinking admitted that his assailants had taken two vests from him for past debts that he owed them. He objected still that "they were wrong to pay themselves in this fashion."[23] The cry of "thief" went up when cardplayers cut through a dispute by grabbing the money on the table, or when a journeyman took his drinking companion's watch from him, "saying he would not have his watch back until he paid for the wine."[24] If the perpetrator thought he had a right to the money, the case might have to be settled before the law. A mirrormaker said he was simply playing a joke on his friends, "to laugh and divert himself," when he hid their clothes as they swam, but they accused him later of robbing them.[25] Friends accused each other of petty theft and were sometimes justified. There seems to have been a certain amount of mistrust, even among friends and acquaintances, that existed just below the surface of comradeship.

Theft in taverns might also be anonymous, of course; people picked each other's pockets even there. But a recent study of such crimes finds that only a few took place in taverns.[26] More often the thief identified a victim in a tavern from the money he showed while paying, and relieved him of his wallet out in the street or the alley. Taverns provided the opportunity of seeing a man's purse, and if a customer had drunk too much he was less likely to be careful. What could be easier than to accost the victim on his slightly uncertain way home at night? Yet other customers might come to his aid. Three domestics testified to

[23] AN, Y15180, 2 August 1751.
[24] AN, Y10139, 30 January 1751; Y10227, 14 March 1761.
[25] AN, Y11626, 22 August 1691.
[26] Patrice Peveri, "Les Pickpockets à Paris au XVIIIe siècle," in *Revue d'histoire moderne et contemporaine* 29 (1982):18, gives a detailed discussion of where pickpockets plied their trade and finds only 7 percent stealing in taverns.

having followed a customer out of a tavern because they were worried about his safety. He had shown his purse too freely in the tavern and was clearly not sober enough to defend himself on his way home. In the end they barely managed to rescue him from several soldiers who had marked him out in the tavern.[27]

The assailants were often soldiers, perceived by their contemporaries as violent men. Despite the reputation of soldiers, it was journeymen and day laborers who figured most prominently (58 percent) among men accused of theft. Yet they also complained most frequently of theft, suggesting once more a certain familiarity between victim and perpetrator. On the other hand a relatively large number of men accused of theft could not be identified by occupation, because the plaintiff did not know who had accosted him or did not recognize the assailant. Such anonymous assailants were much more common in cases of theft (23 percent of the assailants) than in other kinds of incidents (14 percent).[28] Some prostitutes also seem to have made a habit of robbing their clients. Again this would not have occurred in the tavern, but only after a visit to the tavern had revealed the client's purse. Women in taverns were generally accused of theft proportionately more often than men (24 percent of female defendants compared with 9 percent of male defendants).

The question of whether taverns offered asylum to criminals cannot be answered directly from the criminal records. By their

[27] AN, Y10145, 19 August 1751.

[28] Soldiers make up 11 percent of the accused. The figures are based on seventy-six men complaining of theft and ninety-one men accused of theft whose occupations were identified. Journeymen and day laborers provided only 40 percent of those complaining of theft, but plaintiffs from these occupations were more likely to complain about theft (18 percent of the time) than those from other occupations (10 percent of the time). Because defendants were often identified only by the plaintiff or witness in these documents, the lack of identification for some was more a result of their anonymity rather than any inherent obscurity of social condition. I have no reason to believe they were significantly different from the defendants whose occupations were known, and so do not include them in the figures.

nature these documents focus on criminal events, those that were reported at least, and do not probe much beyond. Thus they can assure us that taverns were not often the scene of crimes but cannot preclude the presence of unsavory people. A different source, the records of police patrols and of the police court, offer a better idea of the clientele. Commissaires and police inspectors made "night visits" several times a week looking for "vagabonds, beggars, suspicious people, and persons accused of theft."[29] To this source we shall return in the last chapter. For the moment, the criminal documents can shed light on the behavior and motives of those involved in a reported crime or incident.

VIOLENCE

If theft did not often trouble taverns, violence appears to have been endemic. More than one-quarter of the adjudicated violent crimes in late eighteenth-century Paris was committed in taverns or on their doorsteps: more violence took place there than in all other interior spaces of the city combined.[30] The real problem with taverns, then, was personal violence: fights and arguments, murder and mayhem. But this should not be exaggerated. The fights could be brutal, and there are numerous stab wounds reported in tavern brawls, but murder was quite unusual—little more than 1 percent of the cases taking place in taverns ended in murder. Nor does the tavern's prominence as a location of reported violence translate into a large absolute number of cases that appeared in the commissaires' records. The amount of reported incidents of violence and theft in tav-

[29] BA, Arch. Bastille, Ms. 10129, is devoted to just such patrols in 1750 and 1751. There are other reports for different years scattered throughout the Bastille archives and the series Y. See Chapter Six for further discussion.
[30] Farge and Zysberg, "Les Théâtres de la violence," p. 987. The figure is actually 29 percent. The Petrovich group, "Recherches sur la criminalité," p. 217, also finds 29 percent of its few cases of violence taking place in taverns.

erns, if we assume that the surviving archives retain most of the reports, was scarcely two per day, in a city with several thousand taverns and six hundred thousand inhabitants. Perhaps taverns also figured prominently in cases that were not reported, although it seems more likely that altercations in public drinking places would have been brought to the police's attention more often than those in private. In any case, the real significance of violence in taverns lies in the nature of the public disputes that took place there.

Tavern patrons stand accused of indiscriminate violence and of drunken, irrational, random aggression. The evidence for these charges is based, however, on the impressionistic accounts of a disdainful elite. Police records can offer independent evidence about the kinds of violence reported to the authorities. Again, this evidence is impressionistic, for reported violence reflects to some extent the prejudices of the police—namely, what they were willing to hear—as well as biases based on the wealth, rank, and ambition of the plaintiffs. But the picture revealed by police reports is valuable because it is so different from that of a Mercier or Restif, despite the similarity in prejudice between the police and elite authors. We can discover a very different world of tavern violence and comportment with the police records, which, while not refuting the standard condemnation, serves as an important corrective.

Violence figured prominently in the incidents taking place in taverns that came to the attention of the police. Of 932 tavern cases drawn from the judicial archives (see Appendix) nearly three-quarters involved verbal or physical assault (see Table 1.1). The rest of the cases included theft (13 percent), disturbing the peace or *tapage* (4 percent), fraud (3 percent), and a miscellany of police patrols and unspecified reports (8 percent). Although there appears to be a tendency away from violence, particularly verbal abuse, and toward theft over the course of the century, this trend is more apparent than real. The figures for the last three decades include far more evidence from the

TABLE 1.1
Crimes and Disorders Reported in Taverns

	1691-1711 (%)	1721-1741 (%)	1751-1771 (%)	Total for All Crimes (%)	Total for Violent Crimes (%)
Violence					
Verbal	20	15	11	14	19
Physical	36	38	29	33	44
Disturbances	3	2	6	4	5
Toward owners	15	16	18	17	22
By owners	8	8	3	6	7
Toward and by owners	1	2	2	2	3
Fraud	8	2	1	3	—
Theft	5	13	17	13	—
Miscellaneous	4	4	12	8	—
TOTAL (N)	245	234	453	932	710

Note: Percentages here and throughout have been rounded off to the nearest integer and thus do not always add up to 100.

criminal courts and from the nightwatch, both of which focused more on theft than on issues of violence.[31]

The tavernkeeper himself was a principal target of what looks at first glance to have been random violence. He complained of assault or abuse in one-sixth of all the tavern incidents; 22 percent of all the violence in taverns was directed at him. It might be a drunken customer demanding too much drink, or a fellow tavernkeeper expressing his rivalry in a burst of invective. The disputes between owner and patron involved more than simple bad temper, however. Most embodied con-

[31] Without the evidence from criminal courts and the nightwatch, the figures for the first sixty years change but little. These records make up 38 percent of the last thirty years, however, and without them the figures for theft decrease to 11 percent and verbal and physical assault increase to 13 and 32 percent, respectively. Over one-third of the tavern cases that went on to the extraordinary and ordinary criminal courts involved theft, whereas theft in taverns accounted for only 8 percent of the commissaires' tavern cases.

tests over payment for, and access to, drink and space. In a further 7 percent of tavern violence, patrons brought complaints against the tavernkeeper, and another 3 percent had complaints leveled simultaneously against owner and customer. Nearly all these disputes were expressions of popular claims to control of the tavern, whether explicitly in customers' complaints or implicitly in their abusive behavior, and are considered at greater length in the discussion of popular perceptions of taverns in Chapter Six.

Most of the violence occurred between customers. Indeed two-thirds of the customers who complained to the police about anything happening in taverns had been assaulted by another customer. This violence often amounted to little more than an offense to someone's dignity or honor. An important fraction (one-fifth) of the personal violence in the records went no further than verbal abuse, though such slander and insults were vividly resented. The largest category of violent incidents (44 percent) involved physical assault between customers. Clearly the tavern could be a rough place, but the kinds of violence revealed by the sources are far more deliberate than the police's rhetoric would lead us to believe, provoked less by savage passion than by calculated considerations of honor and reputation. The image of tavern customers portrayed by the police or by Mercier simply missed a whole range of contentions and ignored a significant portion of those involved in tavern violence.

The men who brought this violence to the police's attention, the plaintiffs in cases of tavern violence, belonged to a different world than the criminal one conjured up since then (see Table 1.2). More than half of the men (62 percent) complaining of violence in taverns identified themselves as artisans of various rank, many of them (35 percent) master artisans or shopkeepers. A smaller number (12 percent) belonged to a heterogeneous mixture of liberal professions, bourgeois, *négociants*, a few nobles, and even fewer clerics, grouped under the heading "elites." Nearly one-half (47 percent), then, of the plaintiffs

CHAPTER ONE

TABLE 1.2
Social Standing of Men Involved in Tavern Violence

	Plaintiff (%)	Accused (%)
Elite	12	8
Shopkeeper	11	7
Master artisan	24	19
Artisan	12	13
Journeyman	15	20
Day laborer	12	13
Domestic	7	8
Soldier	8	11
TOTAL (N)	416	561

Note: Disputes with tavern keepers are not included.

appear to have come from the propertied or self-employed levels of society. Unfortunately these records, like so many others from the old regime, do not make clear what the exact status and condition of an individual really was. Plaintiffs gave their profession and usually their status in a guild, if they belonged to one (that is, journeyman, master, garçon, or marchand). Most were probably telling the truth; they were, after all, men coming forward voluntarily before an officer of the law who might even make an independent investigation of their complaint. But without information about wealth, it is rarely possible to be certain that a master artisan, for example, really was propertied and independent. Studies of the Parisian economy emphasize the disparities that existed within the ranks of masters belonging to one guild, and between the masters of different guilds.[32] These records will not reveal the wealth of their informants but they can shed light on attitudes and aspirations

[32] Adeline Daumard and François Furet, Structures et relations sociales à Paris au milieu du XVIIIe siècle (Paris, 1964); Richard Mowery Andrews, "Social Structures, Political Elites and Ideology in Revolutionary Paris, 1792-1794: A Critical Evaluation of Albert Soboul's Les Sans-culottes en l'an II," Journal of Social History 19 (1985):71-112.

36

that, although harder to quantify, may be equally precious in establishing a person's place in society.

Assailants were roughly similar in status, if somewhat less elevated. Artisans of different ranks constituted 60 percent of the accused as well, but employers and elites made up only 34 percent. Assailants were generally identified, however, by the plaintiff or a witness, making their status somewhat less certain. The assailant was known to the plaintiff in most cases, but there are occasions on which he was identified simply as "wearing the clothes of a worker." The social profile of men in these records looks reasonably similar to that found in other studies of criminality, although assailants in taverns came from the self-employed or leisured levels of society more often than those accused of violence throughout Paris.[33] A small number of plaintiffs and accused were women (about 11 percent), who are difficult to identify socially. Some gave their own occupation,

---

[33] The figures for social structure of plaintiffs and accused are complicated by the existence of some 7 percent who were both; that is, there were a few cases in which men filed a complaint against each other. I have treated each pair of suit-countersuit as a single case to avoid giving double weight to these incidents. But the principals in these cases are included in the figures for both plaintiffs and accused.

For a comparison with the Parisian population as a whole, see Chapter Three, note 21. The social structure of those involved in tavern violence can be compared to those involved in violence found throughout Paris by Farge and Zysberg, "Les Théâtres de la violence," p. 988. The figures for plaintiffs in the two studies are reasonably similar, yet a problem with comparing these two sets of figures arises from Farge and Zysberg's inclusion of violence directed at tavern keepers—a category of violence that is not considered in this chapter. If Farge and Zysberg's tavernkeepers are excluded from the list of plaintiffs, the proportions change, at which point the similarities begin to fade, and plaintiffs in taverns appear somewhat higher in status than plaintiffs in general. The disparity between accused in the two studies is even more striking. Violence in Paris as a whole was far more the fault of the lowest classes, the salaried employees and workers, than it was in taverns. The reasons for this may be partly due to the different levels of the judicial process from which the two sets of figures are derived. Whereas Farge and Zysberg rely solely on the records of the ordinary criminal court, the bulk of this study comes from the less formal commissaires' archives, where many cases did not go as far as a court hearing.

others mentioned only the profession of their husband. Women did not fit comfortably into the tavern, as I attempt to explain elsewhere, nor did they have much of a role, except as dependents, in a society of honor. Thus the following analysis is based on male behavior, unless otherwise noted.

The similarity between plaintiffs and accused gives an idea of the kinds of violence that were being reported. Disputes were far more likely to erupt between social peers than between different classes, as other studies of early modern violence have emphasized.[34] At the same time, the plaintiffs and accused who gave their age (only 11 percent in all) suggest an interesting disparity between victims and assailants. While the majority of defendants were young (79 percent were less than thirty-six years of age and 64 percent were less than thirty-one), their victims were generally older (64 percent were more than thirty years of age).[35] The evidence is too thin to support the thesis that generational conflicts underlay many of these contentions, and yet a number did in fact pit young men out of power, for example in a guild, against their elders who had power.

Most of the disputes found in taverns, then, were no crapulous conflict of the destitute; this was no beggars' banquet as Mercier so disdainfully describes it, but rather the fellowship and discords of men who claimed to have honor and reputations and who worked diligently to protect them. As a study of violence throughout Paris at the end of the old regime noted about the people involved: "far from being 'marginals,' most seem

[34] Based on 440 victim-assailant pairs in cases of personal violence, where the occupation of both is known, only 26 percent opposed a master artisan, or those with higher status, against someone with lower status (of which four-fifths were assaults by the lower-class individual).

[35] The figures for age of defendants are practically identical to those Farge and Zysberg found for their total sample. The number of plaintiffs who gave their age was quite small (only 43), yet the 545 witnesses (discussed in greater detail in Chapter Three) who gave their age were closer in age to plaintiffs than to defendants.

very much a part of the popular classes."[36] Nor was the law reserved for the elites; most plaintiffs were laboring men. Such people turned to the nightwatch less to control their own passions than to rectify a perceived injustice. Or they went directly to the commissaire himself, for even the laboring classes were willing to use the mechanisms of the judicial system in their own interest.

Whether a plaintiff came on his own or with the guard, the commissaire had the complaint written up. If the malefactor had been brought by the guard, the commissaire could send him to jail, usually the Châtelet, to await further action. Otherwise he advised the plaintiff to retire and plan to continue the case through the formal channels of the courts. He could agree to prosecute the case at the government's expense if it affected public security, but few offenses in taverns were treated in this manner and most had to be pursued at the plaintiff's expense as a "civil party."[37] The commissaire might also attempt to resolve the issue in his own chambers. What percentage of plaintiffs insisted on pursuing their cases is not known, but it is clear that many of the complaints that can be found in the archives of the commissaires did not show up before either of the criminal courts.[38]

---

[36] Farge and Zysberg, "Les Théâtres de la violence," p. 988. Yves Castan, *Honnêteté*, p. 90, also argues that "we can admit the banal composition of the 'criminal' population as a sample of the global population from which it was drawn."

[37] See André Laingui and Arlette Lebigre, *Histoire du droit pénal* (Paris, 1979), 2:90, for discussion of partie civile. Reinhardt, "Crime and Royal Justice," pp. 445-449, points out that 100 percent of the verbal assault and damage to property and 96 percent of the "non-fatal physical violence" treated in the provincial courts he studied were "private cases"—that is, partie civile.

[38] The *Encyclopédie méthodique: Jurisprudence* (Paris, 1789), 9:564, notes that "[the commissaires] can amicably arrange disputes and quarrels in their offices, otherwise they ought only to forbid the parties to slander and misbehave, and to send them to appeal [se pourvior]." Christian Romon, "L'Affaire des 'enlèvement d'enfants' dans les archives du Châtelet (1749-1750)," *Revue historique* 270 (1983):86, agrees that "very often these complaints did not go beyond the commissaire's hôtel." If 29 percent of Farge and Zysberg's 265 plaintiffs in 1770 can

Most of the incidents brought to the commissaire were considered sufficiently petty by the state that the costs of adjudication had to be borne by the plaintiffs. Such private cases that did go on might become very expensive, as witnesses were called and paid for time lost at work, but the result of the trial was likely to be satisfactory. Criminal procedure gave several advantages to the plaintiff, particularly in affairs handled by the ordinary court where the accused could not even confront witnesses against him. His best defense lay in bringing a countersuit. In the end, the penalty inflicted on the aggressor was usually minor—a reparation rather than a punishment. Private cases that came before the ordinary criminal court were considered nonafflictive—that is, their punishment would be a fine and a "prohibition to speak or speak ill of the plaintiffs," or at worst the printing and posting of a sentence throughout the city, but no "humiliating" punishment, such as branding, banishment, or the galleys, was appropriate.[39] Such penalties were reserved for the infrequent incidents involving death or serious injury, and for the endless stream of theft and crimes against property. But if the courts did not consider a fine technically "humiliating," it was galling enough to the loser, and the winner could flaunt his verdict at his enemy as a public vindication.[40]

The winners of such court orders used the possibility of pub-

---

be considered as involved in tavern violence, then we can compare that figure of 77 with the 78 tavern plaintiffs from only 14 commissaires, a little more than one-quarter of the total, found in the commissaires' archives in 1771.

[39] AN, Y10732, 18 February 1701. Yves Castan, *Honnêteté*, pp. 71-74; Reinhardt, "Crime and Royal Justice," p. 444. Steven L. Kaplan, "Note sur les commissaires de police de Paris au XVIIIe siècle," *Revue d'histoire moderne et contemporaine* 28 (1981):669-689, points out that cost of initiating a plainte, theoretically 3 livres, was often less.

[40] See Yves Castan, *Honnêteté*, passim, for an extensive discussion of the use of complaints to settle disputes of honor. Nicole Castan, *Justice et répression en Languedoc à l'époque des lumières* (Paris, 1980), p. 49, points out that the amends imposed by law on the guilty party included a public declaration before witnesses to the court clerk.

lishing and posting the case as a way of escalating tensions and of enhancing their victory. Such a strategy provoked a number of fights, as in the case of two scrapmetal dealers who insulted each other "wherever they met," and finally brought the matter to a head in a tavern. They loudly exchanged insults and the guard had to be called in to keep them from attacking each other. In the ensuing depositions that each filed separately before a commissaire, the metal dealer, LeRoy, claimed that his opponent accused him of having invented and forged a court order, which seems to have been the basis of their fight. The other complained that LeRoy threatened him with posting the court order on the street corners.[41] To make a case public in such a manner was extremely damaging to the loser, and so was generally reserved for serious offenses.[42] Yet flaunting the possibility in taverns, as happened in several cases, was already a step more public and therefore more provoking.

Wounded honor urged a man on to seek "authentic reparation" through the agency of the law, but there were factors deterring him from an open break before the law. The cost of justice presumably dissuaded a wine merchant, the Sieur Savinos, from pursuing a complaint against a customer. The guard had brought them both before a commissaire, and both had made a complaint, "but considering that the said complaint would involve them in a suit [a *procès*]," they dropped the charges.[43] Friends might step in to reconcile those involved in a dispute, like the master shoemaker who wished to "make himself a mediator and reconcile [two other shoemakers who were fighting] being both his friends." But in response, one of them named Thire "took his pencil, wrote on a piece of paper 'Biquet is a

[41] AN, Y12990, 26 September 1771.

[42] According to Williams, *The Police of Paris*, p. 33, "Printed [police] sentences were invariably intended as exemplary punishment" and not the usual action of the court. He cites the Lieutenant General of Police noting that "this printed sentence is regarded as a more severe punishment than a fine."

[43] AN, Y12990, 22 August 1771.

scoundrel,' signed it, and said 'This is how I certify that he is a scoundrel.' " At this, the peacemaker lost his patience and, "ripping up the piece of paper, told [Thire] he was a madman."[44] Thire does appear a bit unbalanced, writing his little "certificate" on several occasions, but the mediator's exasperation was due at least partly to Thire's unwillingness to make peace. And of course Biquet finally swore out a complaint against Thire's insults. Historians of crime have become increasingly aware of the mechanisms for settling disputes short of a court trial, though such settlements are rarely recorded and thus elusive.[45] Parisians could settle out of court through a desistance (*désistment de plainte*), which generally entailed the payment of some reparation. Such desistances were probably the fate of many of the complaints that were brought to a commissaire but never went to court.

The problem of whether to make a plainte was taken out of the hands of some people by the untimely arrival of the guard. An important minority of the cases involving taverns (21 percent), particularly those dealing with brawls and with conflicts between wine merchants and customers, came first to the attention of the guard, which then brought the antagonists before the commissaire.[46] The guard consisted of fifty-seven squads of seven men each, either posted at stations throughout the city or

[44] AN, Y14195, 26 July 1751.

[45] See N. Castan, *Justice et répression*, pp. 16-48, for a lengthy analysis of the arbitration mechanisms available in city and country. Alfred Soman, "Deviance and Criminal Justice in Western Europe, 1300-1800: An Essay in Structure," *Criminal Justice History* 1 (1980):14, reports that in a sample of conflicts resolved by notaries in seventeenth-century Paris, roughly "three-fourths of the acts explicitly refer to judicial proceedings already begun." Thus many of the conflicts that ended before a notary in the eighteenth century might be expected to appear in the commissaires' archives as well, where judicial proceedings began. He also notes, p. 17, that the "Parisian notaries' role as infra-judicial arbiters had sharply diminished" by the eighteenth century.

[46] The fraction of watch and guard cases was 21 percent overall but until 1731 the percentage was less than 10. It remained at between two and three times that percentage in the following years.

patrolling the streets.[47] Most were on patrol in various quarters, day or night, stopping suspicious people and breaking up fights, but many incidents came to the attention of those at the guardpost either through "public clamor" or by messenger. Then the guard would arrive to arrest the thief or hothead and bear him back to the commissaire. Other studies of the police point out that the populace had little love for the guard and would occasionally come to the rescue of a thief or vagabond in their clutches, yet their prisoners were as likely to be artisans disputing with each other or with the wine merchant.[48] In that case their prisoners might take the opportunity of their visit to the commissaire's office to make a formal complaint before him.

If bringing a complaint to the commissaire entailed the costs of adjudication, then we are unlikely to observe the poor in these records as frequently as their participation in violence might warrant. The reports of the men of the guard, however, provide a slightly more comprehensive observation of tavern violence. What they discovered while making their rounds was often quite fortuitous, and when they were asked to intercede, it was usually at the request of observers or the tavernkeeper.[49] If anything, the watch probably reported more about the behavior of the lower classes, to judge from a report about a "sergeant major of the watch" who, on discovering a merchant butcher being detained by his men at their guardpost for taking part in a tavern disturbance, "and [in the words of the butcher]

[47] See Williams, *The Police of Paris*, pp. 71-84, who says that the squad was less then twelve men until 1771 and that guardposts were only created in 1720.

[48] Arlette Farge, *Vivre dans la rue* (Paris, 1980), pp. 188-190; Farge and Zysberg, "Les Théâtres de la violence," pp. 994-997.

[49] An ordinance of 17 October 1698, in Arch.Préf.Pol., Fonds Lamoignon, ordered all tavernkeepers to inform their local commissaire of all "brawls, quarrels, disputes, and differences" immediately so that he could prevent the "bloody fights and murders and other deadly accidents that one sees happen most often after unimportant quarrels that are easy to quash at their start." Tavernkeepers do appear to have made the effort to notify the guard in many cases.

TABLE 1.3
Social Standing of Plaintiffs by Type of Case for All Cases

	Plaintiffs Who Go Directly to Commissaire (%)	Plaintiffs Brought by Watch (%)	Total
Elite	12	15	77
Shopkeeper	10	10	60
Master artisan	25	17	141
Artisan	12	10	70
Journeyman	14	19	96
Day laborer	13	8	75
Domestic	7	15	50
Soldier	6	8	40
TOTAL (N)	494	115	609

seeing that it had not happened between soldiers but between bourgeois which obliged him to tell his men to free the [butcher]."[50] There was some difference then between the conscious decision of a plaintiff to make an issue of a dispute before a commissaire, perhaps hours, even days after the event, and the complaints arising from the guard surprising a brawl. The guard encountered a higher percentage of complaints by tavernkeepers and a lower percentage of slander than did the commissaire, for the guard's role was more to protect people from physical violence than to defend their honor, but otherwise their caseloads were fairly similar. Given the differences then in the way the two different kinds of procedures worked, it is interesting that the plaintiffs who availed themselves of the two methods should be so similar in social status (see Table 1.3). Defendants dragged in or mentioned by the guard were also members of the lower class slightly more often (74 percent) than when plaintiffs initiated the case (67 percent). If domestics and journeymen were proportionately most likely to avail themselves of the guard and not go directly to the commissaire, the day laborer was least likely to. This similarity suggests that

[50] AN, Y10732, 22 March 1701.

the commissaire's records miss less of "real" violence than the cost of adjudication might suggest.

The judicial archives certainly confirm the violent nature of this society. Most students of popular culture have remarked on this fact, yet it is difficult to be sure just how representative such behavior was since the evidence relates most often to cases of egregious violence. If, on the surface, this violence seems to be what Mercier was warning us about, a closer look reveals a jealous, agonistic world in which men competed for honor, status, and power.[51] Even the stories of extreme violence, such as the murder of an artisan named Chenard, may instruct us, nevertheless, about the range of such behavior and the patterns that violence might take. A party of six Parisians, most of them horse dealers, had assembled in a tavern south of Paris on a Thursday afternoon in early summer. There they drank in the garden, and one of them joined a dance that was going on in a different part of the cabaret. At the dance, however, the young man, a butcher's assistant, ran into an acquaintance, a man "known in the faubourg St. Antoine for insulting and fighting all those he judges apropos without cause or reason." The two seem to have exchanged insults, for the butcher's clerk returned to his party saying he had seen the man, Chenard, and had arranged to meet him at five in the morning on the moat of the Bastille "to fight with fists." His friends told him he was wrong to have gotten into an argument and asked what had caused the dispute. Chenard, he said, had claimed to be stronger than he, but he "could fight two like Chenard." The company "remonstrated unanimously that Chenard's bravado did not merit any attention and would not harm his reputation or his bravery." The call for restraint, however laudable it seems, looks rather naive in the light of other examples. A challenge was far more

---

[51] For a discussion of the term "agonistic" and a superb illustration of an agonistic society, see Weissman, *Ritual Brotherhood*, pp. 27-35. See also J. G. Peristiany, ed., *Honour and Shame, The Values of Mediterranean Society* (Chicago, 1966).

likely to be accepted, "to mark his bravery" as one man explained when brought by the guard to the commissaire.[52]

As the group was talking, however, Chenard came up to their table. According to a witness he appeared a bit "drunk [*pris de vin*]." Another of the company, Duplessis, scolded Chenard for planning to fight and noted that "fisticuffs [*les jeux de main*]" always led to hard feelings among friends.[53] But Chenard said he was not afraid of danger, that "he was strong and vigorous," and he challenged Duplessis to "fight together until one received the first hit." Duplessis agreed, and the two moved away from the others to the end of the garden and began to fight. The "combat" was soon over; after exchanging blows, Chenard admitted, "I do not want to fight any more," and asked, "Is that what you want of me?" Duplessis, known as Mongros, was the stronger.

The ritual combat was over and, according to one witness (one of Mongros' companions), the two went back to the table and drank amicably together. Another witness testified, however, that Mongros was not satisfied with Chenard's admission of defeat and answered, "No, I am going to your table to drink some of your wine." In this second version, the drink after combat was not a pacifying toast of friendship but rather a triumphant gesture, as the victor helped himself to the spoils of the defeated. The second witness was probably closer to the truth, for the hostilities proceeded to escalate.

Mongros' company started to leave shortly after the drink. They claimed that, on passing Chenard's table, Chenard had called to the butcher's boy "till tomorrow, at the agreed place." The young man replied he would be there, but Chenard continued, "if you don't show up you're a jean foutre," and added other insults. At that, he and several others of the party threw themselves upon Chenard and beat him up.

[52] AN, Y11933, 31 July 1751. He and his opponents—both guards of the general provost of money—were sent to prison by the commissaire.

[53] "Jeux de main" could also refer to "exchanging light blows for fun," although that definition seems too mild for this contest; see *Petit Robert*, s.v. "jeu."

Other witnesses, less interested in avoiding blame, made the attack on Chenard sound more deliberate. They described Mongros going up to Chenard's table and helping himself again to some of Chenard's wine. Chenard protested, saying, "What, you beat me and you come again to drink my wine?" and added, "I can handle you, but against six I cannot defend myself." But at that, three or four of the six attacked him, hitting him with their fists, their feet, and a cane. When Chenard finally fell down, they proceeded to jump up and down on his stomach and to beat him on the head with the cane.

The witnesses were under no illusion as to what was happening. Several tried to intervene, protesting that it was "shameful to assassinate a person thusly," and "shameful to see a man thus mistreated." Two of Mongros' companions fled as the fight began, one saying, "My forces fail me, I cannot see a man assassinated like that," and the other, "The act is unworthy, I am leaving." One of the witnesses went to find the guard, but the sergeant claimed he was tired and did not want to come. He finally detailed three men to follow the witness back to the cabaret, but when they arrived almost an hour later everyone had left. One of the assailants had carried Chenard outside, telling him he was going to find someone to dress his wounds, but instead had left Chenard by the side of the road and fled. When the guard could find no one in the cabaret, they left.

The witnesses were considerably more sympathetic than the guard and went off in search of Chenard. They found him along the road to Paris being comforted by his mistress. They heard him say to her, "I die for you." All of them carried him to a house nearby where he was bled and left to spend the night. Then, the witnesses found Chenard's parents in Paris and told them the news of their son. His parents arranged to have him transferred back to Paris, but he died the next day, from internal injuries it seems.[54]

Such violence suggests the extremes of brutality on the one

[54] AN, Y10146, 30 September 1751.

hand and ritual on the other that encompassed the manifestations of conflict in this society. The combats and the tests of
strength, as with Duplessis and the assignation at the Bastille,
were arranged like a duel in which men measured themselves
against each other, although some of their companions considered their bravado "quarrelsome."[55] Passions could be aroused,
however, and turn murderous. There is a possibility that Mongros and his friends had deliberately provoked and killed
Chenard, perhaps for past quarrels that are hinted at. Yet the
execution was so crude, so brutal, that it seems less planned and
more a result of rage. In the extreme case, then, of violence
manifested in the tavern, men might beat each other to death.
But tavern brawls very rarely led to murder.

Most conflict was neither merely "quarrelsome" nor murderous, but fell into a broad category between these two points.
Tavern brawls started because of a misunderstood remark, an
unfriendly glance, an argument. Men fought with whatever
weapons came to hand, although occasionally they would rush
home and return with a sword.[56] Men's anger was slow to cool;
if an assailant was thrown out of a tavern, he might wait for
hours to assault his enemy out in the street. An historian of violence in southern France during the old regime has pointed out
that the absence of weapons in a fight, or the use of weapons
found spontaneously at hand, signified unpremeditated violence to jurists of the period. Thus he finds at least three-quarters of the violence he studies to have been "ill-considered

[55] Jacques-Louis Ménétra, *Journal de ma vie: Jacques-Louis Ménétra, compagnon vitrier au XVIIIe siècle*, ed. Daniel Roche (Paris, 1982), p. 319. Roche comments that "the fight with fists or with canes became a regulated duel."

[56] In theory domestics and laborers were not allowed to carry weapons of any
kind, and no one was allowed to carry firearms; see Williams, *The Police of Paris*,
pp. 221-222. In fact, all kinds of people are found with swords, as well as knives
and canes. Many people fought only with feet and fists, perhaps an early form of
savate, which Chevalier, *Laboring Classes*, pp. 423-424, suggests was common
among Parisians.

crimes of passion."[57] The use of weapons was probably no more common in Paris, but most tavern violence can be considered unpremeditated only in a certain sense. Although physical assault often erupted spontaneously out of a confrontation, Parisians in taverns generally confronted each other with deliberation. The physical violence thus attended the dispute much as an afterthought, but the evidence points to the premeditation of many of the disputes.

Drunkenness also may have provoked some of the violence, or so the police hinted, and several historians have argued since then.[58] Obviously tavern customers were drinking alcohol, and obviously some had drunk too much, but what that implies is less obvious. French jurisprudence offers some clarification with the legal ramifications of drunkenness. Most jurists agreed that drunkenness tended to lessen culpability, because it implied that a crime was not committed in cold blood, but some referred also to the sixteenth-century injunction that declared drunkenness an aggravating factor.[59] A master candlemaker, accused of having stolen two "parasols" from a tavern, insisted in a "humble supplication" to the court that he was "drunk

[57] Julius Ruff, *Crime, Justice, and Public Order in Old Regime France. The Sénéchaussées of Libourne and Bazas, 1696-1789* (London, 1984), pp. 78-79. He refers to "sticks" (used in 27.1 percent of his cases) as a weapon hastily chosen, but Parisians appear to have used sticks and canes, which were serious weapons, in much the same way that nobles used swords.

[58] Wills, *Crime and Punishment*, pp. 153-155, claims that "The single most frequently recurring problem the poor cited as the cause of their involvement in crime was . . . drink. . . . Many of the accused came before the commissaires in a drunken state." Ruff, *Crime, Justice, and Public Order*, p. 81, on the other hand, simply asserts that "alcohol exacerbated any disputes that erupted in the taverns" and notes those cases where alcohol was present. N. Castan, *Les Criminels*, pp. 199-202, says about tavern brawlers in the south of France that their habit of drinking quantities of weak wine left them vulnerable to the effects of a switch to brandy. But those places serving brandy in Paris, the cafés and brandy sellers, actually suffered less personal violence, proportionately, than other kinds of disorder.

[59] Pierre François Muyart de Vouglans, *Les Loix criminelles de France dans leur ordre naturelle*, new ed., enl. (Paris, 1780), 1:14.

49

[*yvre*] and without reason when he was arrested and did not know what he was doing, which renders him absolutely excusable."[60] In practice, however, the plea of drunkenness was rarely used. Only 7 percent of the defendants were identified as somehow intoxicated, and almost none of the defendants had said it about himself. Instead the wine merchant or the police had remarked on one-half of the drunken defendants and a further one-third were so described by the plaintiff himself (who would thus be mitigating the guilt of his own assailant). Most of the references to drunkenness came from the second half of the eighteenth century, when police cases suggest either a growing alcohol problem or an increasing willingness to talk about it.

Police treatises and records give some indication of tolerance for drunken aggression, but the role of alcohol in violence can perhaps best be summarized as ambiguous. A master engraver had encountered a journeyman clockmaker, whom he described as "drunk [*pris de vin*]," coming by a tavern on the place Dauphine and "strongly insulting" another master engraver. "Instead of paying attention to the insults," however, the victim left, "seeing that the said [journeyman] was drunk." The engraver telling the story ran into the journeyman a bit later and "from charity led him to his home since he was entirely drunk," but the journeyman drew a sword and wounded him, at which the engraver brought a complaint to the police.[61] The account indicates a certain latitude allowed the drunkard's behavior but does not suggest that the plaintiff was reticent to identify the drunkenness or that the drunkenness mitigated the final assault. Anthropologists caution that the disinhibiting effects of drink arise less from the chemistry of alcohol than from the conventions of social attitudes toward drunkenness. Thus each society decides for itself what kinds of behavior it expects

[60] AN, Y9668, 28 December 1761. The man had been imprisoned (to await trial) despite his drunkenness, which all the witnesses commented on, but I do not know whether his plea led to a pardon.

[61] AN, Y10732, 15 August 1701.

from people influenced by alcohol, and they in turn tend to conform to this model.[62] French attitudes are not clear, however, and indeed the subject of drinking and drunkenness requires a lengthier discussion in a later chapter. Drunkenness, in any case, sanctions a certain amount of aggression rather than actually provoking it. To understand the violence, there must be a greater awareness of the social and personal tensions that preceded it.

Despite the appearance of spontaneity, much of the violence involved long-standing conflicts, increasingly revealed by witnesses and additional investigation. The commissaire Trudon (from the quarter of the rue St. Antoine) uncovered just such a feud in the instance of a simple tavern brawl that had been stopped by the nightwatch. The sergeant of the watch had brought the two men, a secondhand-clothes merchant and a locksmith, to the commissaire's office, where the merchant had made a complaint. They had been drinking at separate tables, he explained, when the locksmith began to insult him, for no evident reason, calling him a knave, a jean foutre, and similar abuses. The plaintiff made no response, "except to say that he was not a knave for having sold him iron rods for which he was still owed 17 *sous*." At that the locksmith jumped on him, grabbed his collar, and knocked him down with several blows.

If Trudon had any suspicion that this was merely the denouement of an old quarrel, the witnesses called during the next two days confirmed it. According to one, the locksmith had offered the clothes merchant a drink when he had come in, which the merchant had refused, but they had joked and laughed together. Then the merchant had proposed a wager, claiming that the locksmith was shorter than one of his companions. When

---

[62] Craig MacAndrew and Robert Edgerton, *Drunken Comportment: A Social Explanation* (Chicago, 1969), esp. pp. 83-99. See William Taylor, *Drinking, Homicide, and Rebellion in Colonial Mexican Villages* (Stanford, 1980), pp. 63-72, for a brilliant illustration of some of these ideas, particularly of drunkenness as "time out."

the men were measured, the merchant lost the wager, but then refused to pay for a pitcher of wine, saying that the locksmith ought to buy it because he still owed the merchant the 17 sous. This exchange had provoked the fight. Another witness pointed out that even before the wager the merchant had reminded the locksmith of an "ancient quarrel they had had together and told him that, in the quarrel, the locksmith's wife had taken him for the locksmith."[63] This cryptic hint is as far as the testimony goes, but it is enough to suggest that even the tavern brawl cannot be dismissed as indiscriminate aggression. There are deeper and more elaborate motivations to many, perhaps most, of the contentions that moved from the tavern to the commissaire's records.

A considerable number of the fights were merely the culmination of a long series of encounters and disputes. Depositions rarely give more indication than that of the antecedents to an argument, making it all too easy to interpret such documents as spontaneous, even random, outbursts of aggression. Certainly such outbursts occurred, but the fact that most antagonists knew each other and that almost half were drinking with each other suggests a history behind the antagonisms. Men with grudges, or "ancient disputes," took up their quarrel when encountering each other in a tavern, or when a rival followed his enemy to a tavern and confronted him there.[64] A plaintiff spoke of the "results of an animosity that [the assailant] had maintained for a long time against the plaintiff." His enemy "had not ceased to insult and slander him each time they met, and finally . . ." the dispute had come to a head in a tavern where the two were drinking.[65] The assailants of a journeyman carpenter told him, as they beat him, that "it had been a long time that they owed him and that they had only brought him with

[63] AN, Y15055, 31 March 1751.
[64] AN, Y10993b, 21 February 1751. See also Y12416, 1 January 1751; Y11218, 26 December 1731.
[65] AN, Y15348, 3 February 1751.

52

them [to dine at a guinguette] to accommodate him thusly."[66] A
fruit seller in the company of half a dozen of his colleagues
drinking in a tavern near the Châtelet had turned to one of them
and said, "you are a jean foutre." The response of the second
man, Charlois, was rather curious: "I have however an honest
wife, and you have one whom I respect a great deal, and do not
speak of mine." "I bet you are going to get angry," continued
the first, Panin, "[but] let's drink instead." But as they were
paying the bill, Panin punched the other in the neck, saying
"you (and switching from *vous* to *tu*) are a knave, it has been a
long time that we have meant to do this, we must finish it here."
Charlois then grabbed him by the neck and hit him twice. Even
after their friends had broken up the fight and told Charlois to
leave, he waited outside in the street for them to come out and
followed them up the street trying to continue the fight with
Panin.[67] In the words of a surgeon who had just been insulted
"loudly and in the presence of a number of people," this was
just the "continuation of several disputes that he has had with
[the defendant—another surgeon] in different meetings."[68]
Thus the tensions that divided and gave form to a community
lie at the root of many of the disputes, and addressing these tensions is an essential step before we can understand the role of
taverns in popular culture.

Disputes could go on indefinitely, festering until the contenders found themselves in a tavern before a suitable audience.
A master *tabletier* returning from work with an account book
under his arm had gone into a café where he found a colleague
who insulted him. The man had told him that he had the "air
of a collector, that he wore clothes with gold buttons and was
not careful about paying his debts." He threatened to throw
him into the street and make him ask for pardon on his knees,
but the plaintiff simply left the café before a fight started. A

[66] AN, Y12308, 10 July 1701.
[67] AN, Y11228, 19 March 1741.
[68] AN, Y10993b, 24 November 1751.

week later he was drinking at a tavern near his home when the colleague came in with two other master tabletiers. The plaintiff asked if the man "was still angry and still wanted to throw him in the street and make him kiss his ass." The two got mad and started to fight but were separated. When the plaintiff sat down, however, his assailant hurled a pot at his head.[69] Similar scenes occurred regularly in taverns, generally ending with the two contenders being separated. It is perhaps not unfair to wonder whether such intervention, acting as an expected limit to violence, was not one of the advantages of fighting in a crowded place like a tavern. Other customers usually made an effort at least to intervene, unlike the passivity with which Chenard's assault was greeted. The willingness of some witnesses may have been due to their familiarity with the tavern and the contestants, whereas Chenard was out of his neighborhood.[70]

Some testimony indicates a cold-bloodedness about violence, an acceptance of the need to fight in certain circumstances, that appears quite deliberate. A surgeon's assistant, who "blocked the dance floor" at a suburban tavern, was finally pushed off the floor by a postillion who had paid for the dance. The postillion later claimed he did not know the other, but the violin player who was there "daily to conduct the dances" said they both came "quite often." After the dance, the postillion, who made the complaint, boasted that he followed the surgeon out of the room, "took him by the collar, dragged him out into the street and gave him several blows with a cane." The surgeon had warned him "you [*tu*] will pay me for this" and the next day arrived at the tavern with a band of surgeons' assistants whom he told "if the postillions come in the cabaret they will pay." The postillion did indeed come that evening with a few other postillions and encountered his opponent who said, "you [*vous*]

[69] AN, Y13376, 31 January 1751.

[70] Gregory Hanlon, "Les Rituels de l'aggression en Aquitaine au XVIIe siècle," *Annales, économies, sociétés, civilizations* 40 (1985):262, also remarks on the intervention of witnesses, which he finds in roughly three-quarters of the cases.

remember what happened yesterday; we must finish the thing today." The postillion agreed, and several dozen surgeons' assistants attacked him and his small band. In the end neither the postillion nor the violin player made any mention of physical damage from the fight, and the complaint claimed simply that the postillion's hat had been taken from him, borne away perhaps as a trophy.[71] A hat performed a similar service for the rival of a merchant pork seller. The merchant had met other pork sellers as he entered a tavern, one of whom took his hat and urinated into it. The incident allowed the two to vent a long-standing feud.[72]

If this description brings to mind the image of the canaille killing each other to the sound of the violin, the difference is that the postillions were establishing their public status, their claims to a public arena, and their alliances through a martial contest. This was very much a part of popular culture, and the only thing the postillion could complain about was the theft. Men came to blows in the course of arguments over their wives, their reputations, and their honor. "The ultimate vindication of honour lies in physical violence," an anthropologist of European societies reminds us.[73] The savagery of the violence should not obscure the important fact that much of it served to defend men's vital interests.

The contestations that erupted in taverns frequently grew out of disputes based on work and the rivalries of corporate life. They reveal how deeply guild colleagues might be divided over guild issues and how ferociously they might pursue each other in legal disputes. The election and powers of the elected guild officials [*jurés*] were of capital importance. Several cases brought charges of electioneering, a breach of guild regula-

---

[71] AN, Y9668, 9 December 1761.

[72] AN, Y10851, 19 July 1741.

[73] Julian Pitt-Rivers, "Honour and Social Status," in Peristiany, ed., *Honour and Shame*, p. 29.

tions, and, worse, of buying votes.[74] A case accusing a shoe-maker of attempting to buy his colleagues' votes listed a dozen shoemakers who had been approached, and five of the seven witnesses described the infractions taking place in different taverns. The defendant and his accomplices would invite their colleagues to a local tavern and offer them money or try to pay for the expenses incurred at the tavern. The accused seemed to seek out their colleagues in taverns, as if preferring to meet on neutral ground.[75]

A fight in a café among a dozen sheathmakers further illustrates the powers of the juré. They had attended the swearing in of new masters at the hôtel of the procureur du Roi, after which a group of them had retired to a café for coffee and liqueur. They were found there by a second group centered around a master named Daubancourt, whose younger brother had just been made a master. The brothers insulted the plaintiff, who as juré had blocked the promotion of the younger brother. But now the office of juré had passed to friends of the Daubancourts and they were there to gloat over their triumph. After insulting the plaintiff and his friends, they followed him into the street and beat him up.[76]

The guard broke in on another such fight and brought one of the combatants back with them to the commissaire's office. After the guard interrogated him and took down his responses, it became obvious that the "dispute was only an argument between men of the same profession [and] that there had been no tumult or *rixe* or anyone wounded," so they released the man. He stayed, however, to make a formal complaint against half a dozen master cauldroners, his colleagues and jurés of his guild. The plaintiff had been invited by one of them to come for a

[74] AN, Y11626, 12 December 1691; Y12107, 4 August 1701; Y12115, 23 March 1711; Y15449, 14 October 1751, are examples. These cases are included in the category of "fraud" in Table 1.1.

[75] AN, Y10732, 20 September 1701; Y12107, 4 August 1701.

[76] AN, Y10732, 27 July 1701.

drink at a nearby tavern, where another master cauldroner had joined them, and they had each consumed a quart, "without having any trouble." They were then joined by four jurés of the guild who had been talking in the tavern and the group drank another four bottles of wine. When the time came to leave, however, the jurés suggested that the plaintiff pay the whole expense because "having been received by the guild he had not yet done anything for it and besides when he was with his jurés he ought always to pay." At the plaintiff's refusal they further charged him with owing them a feast for having an apprentice begin in his shop. The plaintiff denied owing them anything except his share of the bill, whereupon they attacked him with canes and candlesticks. He was making a formal complaint of all this to the commissaire but above all feared their "threats to make him a formal visit [as jurés] and cause him trouble."[77] Disputes of this kind clearly involved power and access to power, and the power of the juré was the highest to which most artisans could reasonably aspire. Such disputes could factionalize a whole guild and thus are more prominent than the more common forms of conflict that usually divide colleagues.

Even among salaried workers, with no access to corporate power, violence revealed the importance of corporate identities, as well as the prominence of disputes based on work. A group of journeymen bakers who encountered a group of journeymen brewers in a tavern beyond the barriers quickly fell to fighting over an incident the day before in which a brewer's cart had blocked the way of a baker's cart. The quarrel was soon stifled, but as the brewers left an hour later, they were attacked by several dozen journeymen bakers, who beat up one of them, a soldier of the French Guard who had been drinking with the

[77] AN, Y12337, 31 July 1711. See Steven Laurence Kaplan, "The Character and Implications of Strife among the Masters inside the Guilds of Eighteenth-Century Paris," *Journal of Social History* 19 (1986):631-647, for more on fights among guild masters.

brewers, so severely that he was left for dead. Three-and-one-half months later the soldier with three of his friends from the Guard lured one of the bakers into a cabaret near the baker's lodgings where they practically beat him to death.[78] As the tale of the eighteenth-century journeyman, Ménétra, makes clear, journeymen used collective violence to reinforce their solidarity and identity.[79] But the soldier's tale reveals the kinds of feuds that could provoke violence as well.

The competition for work precipitated some of the tension that spilled out into violence in taverns. It provoked the "hatred" of two journeymen roofers against one of their colleagues and led them to assault him one evening in a tavern. The plaintiff, Delaville, had gone to a local cabaret after hearing vespers with another roofer. His assailants were also drinking there and one of them came up to his table to speak to him. Delaville "presented him with a glass of wine, which he drank," but the man began to insult the plaintiff as well as his "bugger of a master," who was employing Delaville in the roofing of the Invalides but had refused to give work to the other two. The plaintiff had objected that they ought not to speak that way about someone who was absent and pointed out that the entrepreneur had been giving him work for years. His assailant, joined now by the other, told him to go to the devil and called the entrepreneur a "bugger of a Prince of Orange." They then proceeded to beat Delaville so soundly that he was unable to work for three weeks.[80] Thus the beating effectively "solved" the problem of preferential employment by putting the man out of action. A master locksmith's journeymen expressed their "jealousy against a German journeyman" whom he had hired

<hr />

[78] AN, Y10147, 28 October 1751; Y10993b, 23 August 1751.

[79] In Ménétra, *Journal*, p. 320, Roche notes that "fights . . . are linked to a particular mode of sociability where aptitude for violence mixed with the capacity for solidarity. They are the public staking of honor."

[80] AN, Y13037, 26 November 1691.

by luring the foreigner to a tavern to beat him up. This "jealousy" was the traditional desire of Parisian workers to control their own labor market.[81]

Competition for a job worth 7,000 to 8,000 livres drove a master ribboner to violence against a colleague. The ribboner, Adam, was so "jealous of not having had the enterprise that he has not ceased denouncing the said Cousin [his rival], saying that his merchandise and his work are not according to the art." This dispute had already led to a suit before the consuls of Paris but now spilled over into a criminal case when Adam assaulted the rival and his wife while drinking with them at a tavern. The wife had challenged him for "decrying her husband" and Adam had responded by accusing her of being a bankrupt thrice over and hitting her.[82] One has the suspicion, in this case, that the wife was trying to provoke the man, perhaps in order to add a criminal case to the other legal battles.

The resort to violence might well have been a calculated decision by one or both antagonists, whether to aggravate a quarrel or to employ the rituals of a duel, but violence seems often to have escalated inadvertently out of a deliberate confrontation. Jurists in old-regime France recognized a dual nature of physical violence, or "real injury" (*injure réel*) as they called it. The physical harm done someone, on the one hand, counted as grounds for complaint. Thus those who were severely injured by an assault could claim reparation for wages lost, medical expenses, damages, and so forth. On the other hand, violence could be a matter of honor as well, an offense to one's dignity; "a blow is very insulting," as one deposition put it.[83] Although plaintiffs made no attempt to distinguish, it seems that many of

[81] AN, Y14334, 20 June 1771. See David Garrioch and Michael Sonenscher, "*Compagnonnages*, Confraternities, and Associations of Journeymen in Eighteenth-Century Paris," *European History Quarterly* 16 (1986):38-40, for a discussion of Parisian workers' attitudes toward non-Parisian journeymen.

[82] AN, Y15238, 19 July 1731.

[83] Muyart de Vouglans, *Les Loix criminelles*, 1:316. AN, Y10083, 10 June 1741.

the blows suffered by plaintiffs offended their reputations as much as their bodies. Honor was most often at issue, at least in cases that originated in taverns.

SLANDER

Because of the public nature of the tavern, insults and slander lay at the root of most of the violence in taverns. The charges of slander also reveal a clientele of men who were fighting not in drunken rages but to defend their honor or discredit a rival. Some verbal assaults were damaging enough to warrant a complaint on their own, though most were merely a prelude to physical assault. Insults might be little more than name-calling, which was provoking enough, especially if "repeated in order to insult."[84] Verbal injury then shaded into more serious forms of slander. Yet the distinction was not terribly clear, either in practice or in law. Jurists differentiated between insult (*injure*) and slander (*calomnie*) but defined *injure* broadly enough to include any verbal abuse meant to harm another. They recognized factors such as place, time, and social status, which might have exacerbated the gravity of insults.[85] Popular complaints referred most often to verbal violence as *injures*, but again there was quite a range in the nature of this abuse. Certain phrases appeared frequently: jean foutre was a favorite, and

[84] AN, Y10726, 1 July 1691; Y11626, 21 October 1691; see also Y. Castan, *Honnêteté*, pp. 41-43; 141-145.

[85] According to the *Encyclopédie*, 35 vols. (Paris, 1751-1780), s.v. "injure," "for speech to be considered insulting [injurieux], it is not necessary that it be calumnious, it need only be defamatory." Muyart de Vouglans, *Les Loix criminelles*, 1:312, defines injure verbale as "all outrageous remarks that are held against the honor and reputation of another. . . ." He describes calumny (1:239) only in the context of bearing false testimony in trials. He also discusses (1:314-318) the circumstances that affect the gravity of injuries. A "public place" is one such aggravating factor, although he defines this as "such as in a church, during divine service, or at the palace of the Prince, or at judicial courts in session. . . ." Elsewhere (1:20), he includes "places that are dedicated to faith and public safety," and "houses of debauchery, in gaming académies and forbidden places."

bougre de gueux, *foutu coquin*, *fripon*, and variations on these themes were regularly employed.

In addition to many of the standard insults that came before the commissaire, there were the more original, and more outrageous, insults that referred to specific aspects of the plaintiff's business or sexual practices. Several friends drinking at a tavern one morning in winter turned to conversation about a mutual friend who was not present. One of the company, a maker of edge tools, mentioned that the absent man, the plaintiff of the case, owed him money for work done in the past. The others, however, assured him that they knew the plaintiff as a "steady man," a very "honnête homme." On being so corrected, the toolmaker declared that the plaintiff "passed for an honest man" but in fact had had an affair with his niece and had actually made her pregnant. He made these statements as "something certain and indisputable." To this more precise and more scandalous charge the others had no response, and were clearly shaken in their esteem for the plaintiff. One went to him the next day to report, and to be reassured.[86] A man who has been called a bougre de chien, or a jean foutre has a complaint to make, but a man who has been called a *banqueroutier*, or a "pimp who sells his wife and sleeps with his niece," has some explaining to do.[87]

Sexual themes figured prominently in slander. A charge of sexual impropriety or any question about a wife's reputation touched men's honor as closely as a calumny against their business reputation or honesty. Indeed the two seemed to be linked at times. A cookshopkeeper accused several of his colleagues of being pimps and of running a brothel, which "insults against the honor and reputation of the plaintiffs . . . he repeated several times in the presence of people who were in the tavern."[88]

[86] AN, Y10993b, 26 February 1751.

[87] AN, Y12950, 13 July 1751. The plaintiff was a procureur at the Parlement of Paris.

[88] AN, Y15228, 11 June 1721.

A wife's reputation was sufficiently central to a husband's honor that it was perilous to raise the subject even in jest. A journeyman gunsmith, in one case, made the mistake of thinking that friendship allowed familiarity. He had been drinking with some friends in a café one evening, and at the table next to his sat two young men and a married couple who were his neighbors. The wife left with one of the young men, and the journeyman "began to joke about the neighbor letting his wife leave with the young man, not thinking to offend because he and the neighbor knew each other particularly." But the man "had not wished to hear teasing on this," and challenged the journeyman to step outside. There in front of the café they fought "with feet and fists" until the guard came along and arrested them.[89]

Similarly, two artisans from the faubourg St. Antoine complained separately of an argument they had. They shared a drink and played *boulles* together in a tavern near both of their lodgings and one, a shoemaker, teased the other, a master currier, about his age. He must be "out of shape for some things," he said, but the currier assured him that he could "well accommodate a *jeune fille*, and that the shoemaker's wife could be a witness to that." As the shoemaker reported it, they had been discussing "a joyous matter," but the currier had had the "imprudence to make some indecent remarks." The currier claims he had merely responded to the shoemaker's teasing in kind and had been called a "jean foutre" and a "bougre de gueux . . . which was repeated." The currier did not reply, but "had only taken some people from the company as witnesses." The mention of the shoemaker's wife had evidently turned the conversation from a "joyous matter" to an "indecent discussion."[90] Men could be teased, but not about their wives.

The preoccupation with male honor and reputation pervades these documents. Complaints of verbal violence in taverns,

[89] AN, Y10993b, 6 June 1751.
[90] AN, Y10993b, 9 September 1751.

much of it leading to physical violence, most often originated with a challenge to someone's honor, and the defense of reputation motivated men from all levels of society. Sexuality, particularly a man's ability to control his wife's sexuality, counted heavily in their definition of honor, but more often the subject was professional. A reputation for honesty, for paying one's debts, or for working with the necessary skill and assiduity came up frequently as the prize for which men fought. A secondhand-clothes merchant had bought another clothes merchant a glass of brandy, "treating him" because of a "good dream" the other had boasted of, only to be called a "foutu gueux" and to be accused of stealing merchandise nightly from other clothes merchants. Because these "calumnies had been said in the presence of several persons known to the plaintiff," he went off to find the guard to complain.[91] Similar allegations "were intended to dishonor and tarnish the reputation" of a sawmiller, who was being slandered by a wood merchant he knew. The plaintiff was finally provoked into legal proceedings by their meeting in a tavern where the merchant said "among other things that he [the plaintiff?] had old hands that he would not change for new ones, meaning to suggest to people in their company that the plaintiff was capable of dishonesty." The miller demanded an "authentic reparation for these insults and slanderous imputations."[92]

The letter of a master basketmaker, André Delavarenne, insisted on the gravity of this kind of slander. His enemies were waging a campaign to destroy him, he wrote to the lieutenant of police, led by his "capital enemy" the present head of his guild of basketweavers. This man, Felix de Bassin, was "doing everything possible to ruin his reputation and commerce," and was organizing factions within the guild that met in taverns to hound the plaintiff and have him "hung as a usurer." They had

[91] AN, Y12990, 30 October 1771.
[92] AN, Y11697, 22 May 1771.

taken him to court already and had won their case but continued to pursue their vendetta against him. Delavarenne had finally been provoked into writing his complaint to the police by the events that had taken place earlier that evening. Bassin and others of the guild had met at a tavern near the plaintiff's house for a party. They were celebrating the feast of the kings, with the kings' cake from which one lucky participant would "draw the king" (the bean or coin baked into the cake that identified the king) and with shouts of "the king is drinking" whenever the "king" touched his glass. Delavarenne charged them with using the occasion to slander and insult him in his absence, "holding him up to derision because of the advantage they had over him." Then, "not content to fill themselves with wine," they had piled into a carriage "bottles in hand and their pipes in their mouths" and had driven through the neighborhood and past the plaintiff's door shouting "the king drinks" and "pub-licizing" their derision of the plaintiff.

At that, Delavarenne had gone to a commissaire of his quarter to make out a formal complaint. The commissaire, L'Abbé, had gone himself to the tavern near the plaintiff to "make certain" of the party and, on finding the men that Dela-varenne had accused, had drawn up a deposition. Thus, in an upstairs room of the widow Caille's tavern, L'Abbé found a square table, around which sat ten masters of the guild, two of their wives, and six children, all eating and drinking. What was wrong, these men asked, with making merry as they were doing? They were there to amuse themselves and to "draw the king." Delavarenne in response concluded his letter by point-ing out that the "truth of these assemblies and feast of the kings that Bassin and other masters had held in taverns" was to ruin his reputation and commerce.[93]

The facts of the complaint were largely confirmed in the fol-lowing weeks of the investigation by the witnesses, all masters

[93] AN, Y12548, 18 January 1701.

TABLE I.4
Social Standing of Plaintiffs Involved in Verbal or Physical Violence

	Verbal (%)	Physical (%)
Elite	11	12
Shopkeeper	12	10
Master artisan	40	19
Artisan	12	12
Journeyman	8	18
Day laborer	11	12
Domestic	4	8
Soldier	2	10
TOTAL (N)	101	315

of the guild, brought in to testify. They spoke of Bassin and others taking them to taverns where they had slandered Delavarenne and talked of posting [*faire afficher*] the sentence against Delavarenne in the market place. In this case, as in others, men were pilloried in taverns as effectively as in the stocks.

A purely verbal injury, of the kind directed at Delavarenne, contributed only 19 percent of the judicial cases of violence taking place in taverns, whereas 44 percent added bodily injury (physical assault) to insult. (The other one-third of the cases embroiled customers with tavernkeepers and are not considered here.) Men complaining of verbal offense belonged far more often (52 percent) to the ranks of guild masters and shopkeepers, like Delavarenne, than did men complaining simply of physical assault (29 percent) (see Table 1.4). An additional 11 percent might be called elite. Only 35 percent of the plaintiffs in this kind of case were employees. A majority, then, of those who complained of verbal injury were the equals of Delavarenne in social status or perhaps even more respectable. In contrast, only 40 percent of those complaining about physical violence belonged to the possessing classes. The possessing classes in general constituted a larger percentage of those complaining about insult than about any other crime. They would seem to have a greater sense of their own reputation and a greater ability to persuade the police that it was worth defending. A common attitude at the time and since seems to be that the lower classes were somehow innately more violent, but surely some of the disparity in suits must be due to their expectations of adequate judicial revenge for a mere verbal affront.

Delavarenne's opponents are in many ways typical of those accused in these archives. More than one-third of those accused of engaging in verbal violence only were master artisans and nearly one-half were either master artisans or of higher rank. Only 30 percent of those accused of physical violence belonged to the possessing classes, though the number of their peers who complained of such violence was proportionately less as well. Verbal assault between men of different social rank occurred relatively rarely (23 percent).[94] The assailants discovered in these archives, those accused of assault or slander, were scarcely less respectable than their victims. Indeed, their assaults and slander were often provoked by the same sense of reputation and ambition for power and status that inspired the complaints against them. It is important to realize, too, that these aspirations, which emerged in their most articulate fashion from the middle ranks of society, were shared by the laboring poor who enjoyed less access to institutional sources of status and honor yet who evinced a strong sense of reputation and standing among their peers and their own communities.

The participants in Delavarenne's case were respectable, though probably not wealthy, and powerful, though only within the microcosm of their guild. Their contention, never specified, clearly revolved around the tense competition for power within the guild, power on a small scale to be sure, but

---

[94] The figure is based on forty-eight dyads, or pairs of plaintiff-accused, for which the profession is known for both people in a pair.

power that could lead to the ruin of a competitor's reputation and business. We have only to consider the journal of Ménétra or other cases in the police archives to find the same fierce struggle for power within guilds. This power was achieved through the votes of the master artisans, and thus required the political skills of a ward boss and the ability to build coalitions and factions and to do so clandestinely. The background to much of this activity was the tavern, the meeting place of factions and cabals, the arena in which one destroyed one's enemies and the stage on which one celebrated the triumph. The tavern was a constant focus of such activities, whether they were the quarrels within a guild, between colleagues, among neighbors, or even within families. These quarrels are the recurring theme of the judicial archives.

"Rivalry and jealousy of commerce" were said to be the motive for a master vinegarmaker, Deberque, "long fomenting the ruin" of two colleagues, according to their complaints. They accused Deberque of "plotting with others and caballing in the community to render them suspect, to dishonor them and to remove them if possible, but if not to turn them into members who were not irreproachable." Deberque, they claimed, "based his defamations on impostures that he took pleasure in uttering in taverns."[95] Slander like this was clearly aimed at the power and position of the two masters, both of whom were senior members (*anciens*) of the guild. The attack focused on their honor and reputation (irreproachability) as their most important assets, which indeed they were for most men.

Salaried laborers used the language of honor less often in these records than did their social superiors. Jurisprudence of the period makes it clear that the courts would have been skeptical of any such claim.[96] Yet even day laborers and unskilled

---

[95] AN, Y12177, 6 March 1771.

[96] Yves Castan, *Honnêteté*, p. 85, remarks on this subject, "It was established in justice that [the poorest class] had a thick skin and it was inadmissible that its members could complain of an insult, calumny or inconsequential blow. . . .

workers claimed to defend their honor and reputation. A journeyman mason accused another of having "tarnished his reputation," but this the other denied and insisted that he was an
"honnête homme."[97] Two day laborers asserted that they were
"honnêtes gens" in a complaint they had brought against a beggar for assaulting them in a tavern.[98] The complaint of a market porter sought to defend his "reputation and that of his colleagues" against the "public injuries" of a coachman who was
causing a "great scandal in making it seem that the plaintiff and
his colleagues had committed some reprehensible action."[99]
The issues at stake might well seem more trivial than those
among guild members. A tavern waiter was moved to violence
against a customer's "insults"; they had been arguing about
hunting and the customer accused him of "never having killed
anything except bedbugs in his life."[100] Yet this too involved a
man's prowess and reputation. Workers would also assert their
dignity against their betters. Several butcher's assistants drinking together in a local tavern were disturbed when the merchant
for whom one of them worked came up to them and insulted his
assistant. "Where is the key to the scalding house," he wanted
to know, adding that the assistant was a cheat and ought to be
hanged. Another assistant objected that "he believed that there
were no cheats in his company." At that the merchant called
him a cheat as well and attacked him, for which the victim
brought a suit against the merchant.[101] Men of all ranks felt
compelled to defend their business ethics, their sexual behavior, their wives' virtue, and their professional honor.

The tribunals' attitude did not suffice, however, to convince the populace [les
petits gens] of their lack of honor and, principally in cities and towns . . . complaints of insult and light violence became more and more frequent." See also
Muyart de Vouglans, *Les Loix criminelles*, 1:318-320.

[97] AN, Y15238, 29 July 1731.
[98] AN, Y13238, 15 August 1751.
[99] AN, Y12115, 6 November 1711.
[100] AN, Y14174, 6 September 1731.
[101] AN, Y12100, 11 June 1691.

Men's professional honor required them to defend the honor of the whole guild. When a carriagemaker discovered some saddlers drinking at a table near his, he announced that all saddlers were bankrupts, that all of them wore the "green hat" (a penalty for bankrupts), and that it was enough that one was a saddler to be a bankrupt. Despite the saddlers' protestations, the man "repeated the same invectives" and added that "there was a very great difference between master carriagemakers and master saddlers." In fact there was very little difference between the two professions and their very similarities led to jealousies and outbursts of this kind.[102] The saddlers subsequently complained to a commissaire "as much for themselves as for their community because of the insults uttered in the presence of several people."[103] While it may seem odd to take serious offense at such an extravagant libel, bankruptcy was a grave charge, particularly in a society that relied so heavily on credit and the faith that debtors would pay creditors. As a consequence, bankruptcy figured prominently in the lexicon of slander.[104] Such an accusation led to a massive investigation, bringing in scores of witnesses, to clear the name of a wine merchant. He had left town on business for several weeks, and the rumor quickly spread that he was leaving town to avoid paying his creditors. The investigation revealed an elaborate campaign to slander the man, waged, not surprisingly, in cafés and taverns.[105] Because the tavern was such a public place, the rumor quickly gained wide currency.

The public character of taverns meant that statements made in front of others, even when the subject of the slander was not present, became a matter of honor, and had to be avenged. Reputations had an existence independent of a person's presence or

[102] Franklin, *Dictionnaire des arts*, s.v. "charon."
[103] AN, Y14944, 21 June 1731. See Y12307, 20 June 1701, for a similar tirade by a chiffonier against the community of vuidangeurs.
[104] N. Castan, *Les Criminels*, p. 255.
[105] AN, Y9903, 15 May 1781.

of his feelings. Several witnesses testified to having told someone that "it is not good to speak ill of someone not present."[106]
In other cases, individuals, usually men of some standing,
complained about insults spoken in the presence of others in the
cabaret.[107] A café owner protested to two customers who were
discussing a man that he knew, "They ought not to speak of
people not present." At the same time, the owner's wife had
gone to fetch another customer, a "*compère*" of the café owner
and an acquaintance of the absent plaintiff. "*Compère*, listen
how they are calling M. Caron (whom the witness knew) a fripon and a coquin."[108] Caron was sufficiently upset that he went
to the café the next day and interviewed various customers who
had overheard the conversation. Several suits described ven-
dettas waged by spreading slander "around the town [*dans le
monde*] . . . and publicizing such indecent talk in taverns."[109]

The violence here is no more than verbal violence, yet deadly
enough in its aim of ruining a colleague. A verbal injury was a
very serious offense to these people; men gave and received
them with care and attention. The insult or slander defined the
relation of two men or parties to each other. It attempted to
damage men's standing, their "honor and reputation" in a public context. As a master tabletier complained about two companions who had slandered him in a tavern, "they had sought
all along the occasion to destroy him."[110] Such slanders were not
just a form of violence but often a form of economic aggression
as well. The secondhand-clothes merchant accused in a tavern
before his acquaintances of nightly theft saw these "calumnies
. . . [as a] serious offense to his honor, and his reputation (and

[106] AN, Y13888, 22 October 1701. The sentiment is echoed by two day laborers, Y9657, 28 December 1760.

[107] AN, Y15228, 11 June 1721; Y12356, 14 August 1721.

[108] AN, Y15449, 2 December 1751.

[109] AN, Y12925, 11 October 1741.

[110] See AN, Y14066, 11 September 1741; Y12925, 11 October 1741 for the
phrase *honneur et réputation*. Y13387, 27 March 1761.

his *crédit*)."[111] His *crédit* referred equally to the confidence he inspired and to the credit he needed to do business, for his ability to attract customers and suppliers and to find the loans and credit so essential to business was inextricably linked to his reputation. A man's reputation was, after all, his public asset, his public persona. A public attack on that persona, and the subsequent defense before a magistrate, were actions on an elevated, public plane; to the extent that they dealt with power, whether in guilds or in the community, they were political actions as well. Anthropologists recognize the existence of "local-level politics" in which people can compete for public goals and power quite independently of governing structures.[112] Surely some, though far from all, of the contentions in taverns make sense in that context. An historian of Parisian artisans has also suggested that verbal abuse in public places, particularly the tavern, aimed at defining both the ideal artisan and an ideal relation between employer and employee. Here, too, public abuse is seen as political, or perhaps protopolitical, as it prepared the way for the revolutionary discourse of the sans-culottes during the Revolution.[113]

The uniquely public character of any public drinking place explains much of the prominence of cases dealing with slander and reputation in the judicial records relating to taverns. Plaintiffs frequently noted that they were insulted "publicly" or "in the presence of the people who were in the taverns."[114] The insults that a customer in a tavern "had repeated publicly several times, with menaces while holding his cane . . . are too atro-

[111] AN, Y12990, 30 October 1771.

[112] See, for example, Marc J. Swartz, Victor Turner, and Arthur Tuden, eds., *Political Anthropology* (Chicago, 1966), pp. 4-8. See also Marc J. Swartz, ed. *Local-Level Politics* (Chicago, 1968), Introduction.

[113] Michael Sonenscher, "Les Sans-culottes de l'an II: repenser le langage du travail dans la France révolutionnaire," *Annales, économies, sociétés, civilizations* 40 (1985):1100-1101.

[114] AN, Y10726, 1 July 1691; Y14066, 26 April 1741; Y11626, 30 October 1691.

cious and scandalous, having been said publicly, for the plaintiff to remain in silence."[115] A gardener concluded his complaint by saying, "This insult is more dishonoring to the honor and reputation of the plaintiff for having been proclaimed [*publiée*] loudly and publicly in a cabaret in the presence of numbers of people."[116] The gardener's assailant, his brother-in-law, had actually visited him at home and insisted on going to a tavern to settle a dispute. The man seems deliberately to have sought the publicity of a confrontation in a tavern. The fact that people were present to witness the incident as well as the fact that it happened in a tavern made it a public event. Several complaints describe women storming into taverns and "loudly" attacking the plaintiff, "causing the neighbors and passers to assemble" and "even bringing people to put their heads out the window."[117] Thus public calumny in taverns might spill out into the street and involve the whole neighborhood. On the whole, however, slander was less likely to become street theater than it was to remain the vicious allegations made before one's drinking companion. If an insult was "repeated several times in the presence of people who were in the cabaret," it could not be passed over lightly.[118] As another plaintiff put it, "These are insults spoken publicly in a public place."[119] By being a "public place," the cabaret transformed events that happened there into public affairs, and it became harder to settle the matter privately.

The tavern may indeed have been a privileged arena for contests concerning one's reputation. Without looking systematically at disputes outside of taverns as well as inside, it is difficult to prove such a statement, and no study has yet addressed the issue. It is clear nonetheless that taverns figured prominently as

[115] AN, Y12115, 28 December 1711.
[116] AN, Y11933, 21 December 1751.
[117] AN, Y14009, 7 August 1732; Y14527, 17 October 1731.
[118] AN, Y15228, 11 June 1721.
[119] AN, Y14518, 4 June 1721.

a stage for such attacks on reputation. Men gathered there with their peers for recreation and business and participated in the symbolic exchanges that publicly articulated their social relations. Taverns were thus the most obvious place to launch an assault on a rival's honor. Of course, insults in taverns were more likely to be witnessed and thus stand up in court, but the public nature of the tavern and the presence of witnesses do not seem to have deterred slanderers. To the contrary, it seems that those wishing to destroy an enemy's reputation deliberately sought the public arena of the tavern in which to make their attacks.

A confrontation, whether for debts or for past grievances, was peculiarly satisfying on the stage of a tavern floor, with the other customers from the neighborhood as an audience. Antagonists even saved their denunciations of the other party for the public forum of a cabaret. A master locksmith was well aware of that fact when he charged a master carpenter of "seeking since yesterday the means of meeting the plaintiff and for this purpose had followed him into a cabaret." There, "in the presence of several persons," the carpenter had called the plaintiff a "dishonest man, a fripon, a thief," and had repeated this "several times in the presence of several workers in order to discredit the plaintiff."[120] Another man made a point of shouting "*Au voleur!*" at his enemy when the two met in a tavern.[121] On another occasion a surgeon had been asked to join several of his colleagues at a tavern near his home, but one of them had become so abusive that the plaintiff had moved to sit with people that he knew at a nearby table. The defendant, whose "fury had increased to the point where he could not control his words," had yelled that the plaintiff's wife "had herself bedded by his employees." The plaintiff had been "obliged to arm himself with all imaginable patience to support such insults to which he

[120] AN, Y11626, 30 October 1691.
[121] AN, Y11933, 28 December 1751.

73

could only weakly respond."[122] The plaintiff concluded that the scene had been premeditated and pointed out that "such things said in a tavern and by a colleague are more than sufficient to harm his reputation."

Thus violence in taverns expressed many different kinds of hostilities and tensions, some provoked by a chance word or a misunderstood song, others that lay deeply embedded in the rivalries of guild and neighborhood life. Rather than finding it strange that drinking companions should have fallen out, or that enemies should confront and even seek each other in taverns, we must recognize that the nature of so many of these disputes, concerned as they were with honor and reputation, naturally lent itself to the public forum of the tavern. Reputation is a public trust, a public persona, and it is dealt with publicly by others. The tavern was the appropriate location for these public contests.

ONLY a tiny percentage of tavern customers appeared before the commissaire, of course. Most drank peacefully, but even those who fought might escape the patrol or felt they could make no claim to the sentiments of honor and reputation that inspired the complaints examined here. The tavern customers and the attitudes they expressed clearly cannot be expected to represent all the others in taverns. What about the prostitutes and vagabonds accused of theft, the unemployed who tried to cheat the tavernkeeper, or the soldiers who assaulted civilians? This was a society, after all, with perhaps 10 percent of its population living on the margins, a "floating population" that existed precariously and at times, no doubt, illegally. These documents probably miss much of this lowest level of Parisian society. The complaints in these documents expressed too much dignity, and too much concern for that dignity, to be applied plausibly to the marginal population. Although the social pro-

[122] AN, Y10993b, 24 November 1751.

file of plaintiffs and accused in tavern disorder looks much like the rough outlines of Parisian society, the *marginaux* remain very much in the shadows of what is known about the city's population. Thus their place in the commissaires' archives that deal with taverns is clearly underrepresented. Certainly they are far less conspicuous in tavern violence than they are in the enormous number of crimes of theft that occupied the majority of the courts' time and energies. Perhaps these *marginaux* could not afford to drink as often as more established Parisians and thus frequented taverns less often. Or perhaps authors like Mercier were right that the taverns were teeming with such "dregs of the populace," in which case they managed somehow to escape the clutches of the guard, the nightwatch, and the police patrols. The police were fated not to find them or record their activities, and we can only speculate on their habits and practices.

If the judicial archives consulted here do not refute the fears of the police, except indirectly, they do reveal an important aspect of tavern behavior and clientele that the police appear to have ignored in their preoccupation with crime and criminals, particularly with theft and thieves. With more evidence, the obsession with theft in taverns can be dismissed as an exaggeration. It is not possible to refute the existence of thieves and criminals in taverns but at least we can balance that depiction with an image emerging from the judicial archives of a world of artisans and others intent on protecting their honor and objecting vividly to any slander or insult. The commissaires' own records of tavern life allow us to discover the laboring classes there, rather than the dangerous classes. Their accounts of verbal and physical violence reveal a theater in which honor and reputation were assiduously cultivated and publicly defended.

Two. The Purveyance of Drink

It is a bit incongruous that the mayhem and passions just recounted took place in the spartan shops of simple businessmen. The tavernkeeper was, after all, a retail merchant attempting to make a living purveying food and drink. He could not have welcomed the disorder that attended his business, yet must have recognized that he was selling more than just comestibles. By selling space to their customers, taverns provided an arena in which patrons could pursue their disputes, their friendships, and much else. Customers came for both the drink and the space, and to understand the institution we have to consider how the tavernkeeper supplied both, for his ability to secure wine for his customers and to provide them with a place to drink conditioned the social function and culture of taverns.

Parisians enjoyed a wealth of public drinking places in their city: nearly 3,000 in all by the middle of the eighteenth century, or roughly one for every two hundred inhabitants. Indeed the purveyance of alcohol may almost be said to have been one of the primary economic functions in Paris, for the 1,500 wine merchants outnumbered the membership of all but four other guilds. If the 380 *limonadiers* who owned cafés, several hundred guinguettes circling the city, the unknown numbers of beer sellers, and those fruit sellers and grocers who sold beer and brandy were added to this group, then the sellers of drink exceeded all other individual occupations.[1] The trade in alcohol

---

[1] Jean-Joseph d'Expilly, *Dictionnaire géographique, historique, et politique des Gaules et de la France* (Paris, 1768), 5:420. He also lists 640 épiciers and 321 fruitiers, but not all operated taverns. Jacques Savary des Bruslons, *Dictionnaire universel de commerce* (Copenhagen, 1761-1765), 2:424, gives the same figure for wine merchants in 1725. Jacques Saint-Germain, in *La Reynie et la police au grand siècle d'après de nombreux documents inédits* (Paris, 1962), p. 298, puts the number of limonadiers and brandy distillers at 250 in 1674; and p. 293, notes that a census of 1670, found in the Collection Delamare (BN, Ms. fr. 21695,

clearly played an important role in the economic and social life of the city. By the eighteenth century the people of Paris had learned to rely on the tavernkeeper not only for their daily wine but for their entertainment as well. For in addition to purveying alcohol, the tavern furnished space that provided a location for sociability and for public life. The manner in which these vendors of alcohol presented their wares, the conditions of sale, and the sophistication of the retail network determined Parisians' access to drink. Equally the structure of space in taverns, the arrangement of rooms, tables, and counters, and the creation of an ambience shaped the comportment of customers who drank there and the nature of their sociability.

Although most tavernkeepers ran establishments of modest size and rude appearance, the trade in alcohol in Paris was quite sophisticated and increasingly complex. The city's enormous appetite for wine stimulated an elaborate logistical network to supply it. Merchants poured wine into Paris from all over the northern half of France and turned to places even farther afield during the century before the Revolution. The number of public drinking places increased significantly during that same period. More importantly, the kinds of shops selling alcohol diversified dramatically, both in their wares and their decor. The introduction of new kinds of drink, some of them nonalcoholic, and the surge in the state's taxation of wine led to the creation of distinct institutions in which these drinks were sold. Merchants used the opportunity to experiment with different decorations and arrangements of their space and to attract a different clientele. These changes, abrupt and sweeping as they were, provide an opportunity for analyzing the dynamics of Parisian public drinking. Such an analysis must begin, however, with

---

fol. 270), lists 1847 cabarets. A similar list for 1684 found by Jacques Dupaquier, *La Population rurale du bassin parisien à l'époque de Louis XIV* (Paris, 1979), pp. 210-211, gives 1872 wine merchants and 300 limonadiers and brandy distillers.

the legal and economic distinctions that organized the drink trade.

The state distinguished drinking establishments by the kinds of alcohol they sold and the conditions under which the alcohol was sold. The privilege of selling wine belonged to the guild of wine merchants alone, whereas the master limonadier sold coffee and shared the right to sell brandy (*eau-de-vie*), with the master distiller, the grocer (*épicier*), and the *vendeur d'eau-de-vie*. Beer sellers belonged to no guild and were often men and women who claimed some other professional identity. Parisians must have been aware of the intense rivalries and scrupulously guarded monopolies that distinguished the several guilds selling alcohol and the shops in which they sold it, but their daily vocabulary emphasized the underlying similarities. Parisians in the eighteenth century used the term *cabaret* to refer loosely to any establishment that sold alcohol and offered a place, with tables and chairs, in which to drink it. They perceived a drink shop of any kind as a unique social space in the urban landscape and appear to have used the different kinds of establishments almost indiscriminately, appropriating the space for their recreation and leisure and as a place to assemble or do business. Although I refer to all public drinking places as "taverns" in the same general manner throughout this study, it is important to clarify the sources of diversity.

The wine shop, known originally as the *taverne*, was the most ancient of the various drinking establishments. Wine merchants and *taverniers* can be found in the thirteenth-century *Livre de metiers*, though the guild was not officially recognized with letters patent until 1587. The statutes required that the health and quality of the wine must be protected by its practitioners. Also, the guild of wine merchants, like other guilds, expected its members to maintain a standard of personal morality, but this was a particularly crucial standard for wine mer-

78

chants because "public safety finds itself threatened by the retreat [they] can give to certain suspicious persons."[2]

The guild had long distinguished between wholesale and retail merchants. The wholesale merchant could not sell in quantities of less than a quarter of a *muid*, which was the standard
measure in the Parisian region, equalling 288 *pintes* (quarts) or
268 liters. The retail merchants (*marchand de vin en detail*) and
taverniers could not sell in quantities of as much as a quarter
muid and sold most of their wares by the pot or pinte.[3] Both
wholesale and retail merchants were equally constrained in
their use of merchandise that they had brought in from the
provinces, one-third of which was obliged to be sold at the central wine market. By the fifteenth century, the guild had added
a further retail outlet, the cabaret. The cabaret enjoyed, in
principle, the right to provide customers with "seats, tablecloths, and plates." The taverne and the retail wine merchant
sold wine *à pot*—"in other words, to take out."[4] In all likeli-
hood, tavernes also gave customers a place to drink, yet an important treatise written at the beginning of the eighteenth century maintained that the taverne avoided the excesses of the
"odious" cabaret because the taverne's wine was "to be taken
home" and consumed "in the family with its normal meals."
The distinction between the cabaret selling *à assiette* and the tav-

---

[2] The wine merchants were awarded letters patent in December 1585, although Parlement did not register the letters until 27 June 1587. See Edit du
Roi, 1585, in *Pièces diverses concernant les marchands de vin de la ville et faubourgs
de Paris* (Paris, 1626-1762), Pt. 1, p. 1; François Olivier-Martin, *L'Organisation corporative de la France d'ancien régime* (Paris, 1938), p. 206; and Duchesne,
Code de la police ou analyse des règlements de police. 4th ed. rev. and enl. (Paris,
1767), 1:218.

[3] Marcel Lachiver, *Vin, vigne et vignerons en région parisienne du XVIIe au
XIXe siècles* (Pontoise, 1982), pp. 19-20; Savary Des Bruslons, *Dictionnaire de
commerce*, s.v. "vin." Delamare, *Traité de la police*, 3:718, claims that taverniers
and retail merchants employed essentially the same business methods but were
distinguished by the "fortune" of the retail wine merchants.

[4] Dion, *Histoire de la vigne*, p. 482.

erne selling *à pot* involved the right to serve food (hence the plate), but the right to seat customers was also implied in this distinction and may well have been the principal cause of jealousy by the taverniers.[5]

Whatever the reason, the taverniers gradually came to demand the rights of the *cabaretiers*. This right the cabaretiers paid for, in higher taxes, but taverniers accepted the higher taxes in return for the advantages of selling "with plates." Thus they requested, in 1680, to be allowed to provide seating and tables for their customers, in return for paying the higher tax.[6] With the government's acquiescence, the legal distinction between taverne and cabaret essentially disappeared, though the government insisted that tavernes could not be known as cabarets. As late as the eighteenth century, the difference between a taverne and a cabaret still had some meaning, if only that the taverne was considered more vulgar.[7] Yet by the eighteenth century most commentators agreed that the distinction was no longer important because there were no tavernes left. Furetière's *Dictionnaire universel* in 1727, for example, noted that no one made the distinction any more and demonstrated the

[5] Delamare, *Traité de la police*, 3:718-719.

[6] Arch.Préf.Police. Fonds Lamoignon, lettres patentes, 29 November 1680. The letters patent noted that the taverniers claimed to have had the right "for all time" to "provide tables, seats and tablecloths," with the permission of the tax farmer, and that this had not been detrimental to the cabaretiers "because only the menu peuple went to tavernes." Still the king explicitly granted them this right, along with the right to buy wine outside of the 50-mile limit. An edict of 12 July 1707 permitting wine merchants to give drink in their houses and cellars presumably extended the same right to them. See François Isambert et al., *Recueil général des anciennes lois françaises depuis l'an 420 jusqu'à la révolution de 1789* (Paris, 1821-1833), 20:523.

[7] *Encyclopédie*, s.v. "taverne," "however the word *taverne* connotes some idea less respectable [honnête] and more base than cabaret; the main reason for this is that taverne is more commonly used in the edicts and in the public discourse against drunkards [*ivrognes*]." Savary des Bruslons, *Dictionnaire de commerce*, s.v. "taverne," also notes that "the word tavern is more insulting than cabaret, when one reproaches someone with frequenting these sorts of places."

point by mixing up the two words.[8] Indeed judicial records suggest that as early as the 1690s the word *taverne* had disappeared from popular vocabulary. Thus the simplicity of popular usage mitigated the theoretical complexity of the wine guild's organization.

The nomenclature actually current in judicial records suggests that the traditional, legal distinctions within the guild of wine merchants were fading into obscurity in the face of fundamental changes in the organization of the drink trade. With few exceptions, witnesses in judicial cases spoke of all wine shops as cabarets, and the owners of these establishments nearly always identified themselves before the police as wine merchants (marchands de vin).[9] A cabaretier in contrast was almost certain to be the owner of an establishment outside of the city, exempt from the guild's regime. There is reason to believe that many wholesale merchants also owned taverns and ran them either directly or indirectly through a tenant. Thus, even the nominal distinctions between wholesale and retail had become blurred. The tavern was becoming so widespread, in fact, that the word cabaret came to refer to the shops of beer and brandy sellers as well—for example, *cabaret à bière*. It is difficult to explain this process of merging with any certainty, but two events that occurred more or less simultaneously toward the end of the seventeenth century might have influenced it. At this time, Parisians witnessed the emergence of two new drinking institutions, the guinguette and the café; each was sufficiently unlike the wine shop that the distinctions between different kinds of wine shops may have lost their significance.

[8] Antoine Furetière, *Dictionnaire universel* (La Haye, 1727) s.v. "cabaret." In fact, confusion over the distinction was widespread. Both Savary des Bruslons, *Dictionnaire de commerce*, s.v. "taverne," and the *Dictionnaire de Trevoux* (Paris, 1752), s.v. "cabaret," made the same reversal.

[9] Savary des Bruslons, *Dictionnaire de commerce*, 4:1216, also notes this practice.

The first of these new institutions, the guinguette, lay outside of the city's boundaries. There had actually been taverns in the outskirts of Paris for centuries. Ever since the crown had begun to tax wine entering the city, it is safe to assume that taverns established themselves just outside of the tax boundary. But the state chose in the 1670s and 1680s to extend the boundaries of the taxed region and to increase the wine tax. The government raised the wine tax several times during the seventeenth and eighteenth centuries, enough to double the price of cheap wine early in the eighteenth century and to triple it by the Revolution.[10] As the tax increased over the course of the eighteenth century, the growing disparity between the cost of wine inside and outside the city enhanced the guinguette's appeal. The guinguette could sell wine for a half or a third its cost in cabarets.[11]

After the tax boundary was extended in 1674 to include the city of Paris and its principal faubourgs of St. Antoine, St. Martin, and St. Denis, most of the guinguettes clustered in the areas north, east, and south of Paris where the tax barriers lay closest to the city: the Porcherons, Nouvelle France, la Courtille, and Vaugirard. Guinguettes were so numerous in these areas that they gave contemporaries the impression that no one lived outside the city except wine sellers. In fact, the *taille* records indicate that roughly one in four of the taxpayers living around Paris did indeed sell wine. In 1771, twenty of the par-

[10] See Dion, *Histoire de la vigne*, pp. 503-525, for discussion of taxes and a map of barriers; also Lachiver, *Vin, vigne et vignerons*, pp. 257-261, on taxes.

[11] Lachiver, *Vin, vigne et vignerons*, p. 267, cites 4 to 5 sous per pinte at guinguettes and 12 to 15 sous in Paris. Account books of wine merchants in and outside of Paris, however, suggest a rather less remarkable gap in price. The cheapest wine that appears in account books of guinguettes at several times during the century was 6 sous per pinte, whereas the pinte often sold in urban taverns for as little as 8 sous. Variations in price and quality over time make direct comparisons almost impossible, but Lachiver's price ranges are evidently too broad; see Arch. Seine, D5B⁶ 2854 (1712), 248 (1716), 754 (1717), 2704 (1721), 965 (1722), 5775 (1726), 3103 (1727), 657 (1740), 1430 (1750), 4453 (1752), 6210 (1764), 2783 (1764), 3343 (1769), 3847 (1772), 1240 (1777).

ishes lying closest to Paris contained a little over four hundred households selling wine, although not all of them should be considered guinguettes. Not all of the wine sellers (in those parishes where the amount of wine sold was recorded) were listed as running "cabarets," and some who were sold almost no wine. Nearly one-quarter of the establishments in parishes with sales figures sold less than 10 muids (26.8 hectoliters) of wine per year, and probably lacked facilities for public drinking. Only a small fraction of households (roughly one in ten) sold over 100 muids (268 hectoliters) of wine in a year, which was probably only average for taverns in the city. Ramponeau's famous guinguette, the Tambour Royal, which has served as a model of this institution to the present, was actually one of four or five of the largest sellers of drink in the suburbs (selling 292 muids).[12]

Although similar to urban taverns in that they provided wine, guinguettes were essentially different establishments by the middle of the eighteenth century, offering distinct kinds of leisure and entertainment. The cheap wine at guinguettes supposedly prompted drunken orgies among the populace every Sunday. "It is at [the suburb of] la Courtille that the *peuple* consecrate Sunday to drink and libertinage," claimed Mercier.[13] The guinguette also offered other attractions that appealed to urban customers. Located outside the city, guinguettes had the space for much larger rooms and gardens. They encouraged dancing inside and out, and games on the lawns. The location of the guinguette added to its appeal, for in its

[12] AN, Z¹ᴳ 343A, (1771); 343B, (1771); 350, (1773) *Rôles de tailles*. All but two dozen of these taverns could be found in ten parishes closest to Paris. The roles for Department Two (including Montmartre, La Chapelle St. Denis, Aubervilliers) do not exist for 1771, so 1773 was taken as the closest year with information. Even in that year, the lists for Montmartre do not give figures for the amount of wine sold. The average amount of wine consumed in Paris was roughly 240,000 muids, of which the majority was probably sold by 1,500 cabarets. See Chapter Four for a further discussion of wine consumption.

[13] Mercier, *Tableau de Paris*, 2:140.

physical separation from the city it developed a unique ambience that took advantage of the space, the tranquillity, and the "freedom of the countryside."[14]

In the eighteenth century, guinguettes sought to become the popular arena of Parisian entertainment and leisure. Their success, particularly among the laboring classes, was so great that they quickly became a symbol of popular culture. These guinguettes captured the imaginations of visitors and Parisians alike.[15] "To see Paris without seeing [the guinguettes of] la Courtille . . . is like seeing Rome without seeing the Pope," was the refrain of a popular poem.[16] A tourist in France before the Revolution (who had come to Paris "out of pure curiosity") made a special trip to the guinguettes of the Porcherons suburb (where alas he was robbed) to see the sight "about which he had heard so much."[17] These new wine shops were never so numerous as the traditional taverns in the city. Yet guinguettes had considerable importance in eighteenth-century culture, and their prominence in recent studies on popular culture far outweighs their relative numbers. Some historians even suggest that guinguettes had replaced cabarets as a center of laboring-class recreation by the Revolution.[18] When the government jeopardized many guinguettes by extending the tax boundary again, just before the Revolution, the move provoked riots and attacks on the taxmen and their stations.[19]

At roughly the same time that changes in the tax barriers in-

[14] The phrase "freedom of countryside" is found in a caption to one of the engravings of Ramponeau's tavern in the BN, *éstampes* collection.

[15] Savary des Bruslons suggests, in his *Dictionnaire de commerce*, 2:197, that "some believe the word *guinguette* comes from ginguet, which means small wine, because that is all that is sold in these sorts of taverns" (quoted in Alfred Franklin, *Dictionnaire des arts, métiers et professions exercé dans Paris* [Paris, 1906], p. 377).

[16] Jean Joseph Vadé, *La Pipe cassée*, in *Oeuvres de Vadé* (Paris, n.d.), p. 12.

[17] AN, Y9787, 16 October 1771.

[18] Lachiver, *Vin, vigne et vignerons*, p. 261.

[19] Dion, *Histoire de la vigne*, pp. 518-522.

creased the numbers and renown of guinguettes outside the city, the café was emerging inside the city. The first café appeared in Paris in 1672 and rapidly gained popularity in the following decades. [20] Its arrival coincided with the introduction of several new kinds of drink to Paris, particularly coffee from which it took its name. This new drink, however, was not quite to Parisians' taste. Little more than a novelty and patronized mostly by foreigners, the first café did not do well. Nevertheless, the king granted the rights to sell coffee in cafés to the limonadiers, a guild of lemonade sellers, and the guild quickly grew. While such exotic concoctions as coffee played a crucial rule in the café's unique identity, the increasing popularity of another relatively new drink, eau-de-vie or brandy, added equally to the café's appeal. The French were distilling brandy even before the Dutch made it into an international commodity in the sixteenth century, but Frenchmen considered brandy largely as a medicine until the seventeenth century. By the end of the *grand siècle*, the inhabitants of Paris had recognized its other attractions and were drinking it regularly. [21] The limonadiers gained the right to sell brandy and a variety of liqueurs along with coffee and other nonalcoholic drinks, and this newly popular form of alcohol helped to ensure their success. Certainly it was the right to sell brandy that embroiled the limonadiers in fighting for the privilege with other guilds selling

[20] J. Leclant, "Le Café et les cafés à Paris, 1644-1693," *Annales, économies, sociétés, civilisations* 6 (1951):1-14. The limonadiers were created en jurande in March 1673, though they did not receive their statutes until January 1676. They were joined with distillers and brandy merchants into a single guild in 1676. Dion, *Histoire de la vigne*, p. 603, observes a connection between the two new institutions of the guinguette and the café: the first cafés appeared on the left bank at points most remote from guinguettes. This implies, however, that cafés and guinguettes were functionally interchangeable, which I dispute.

[21] R. Delamain, *Histoire du cognac* (Paris, 1935), pp. 29-30, portrays brandy as popular with the lowest classes in the seventeenth century, but "a taste for brandy developed especially at the end of the seventeenth century and quickly spread among the leisured classes."

brandy. One serious rival, the distillers' guild, combined with the limonadiers to form a single guild.

The guilds of grocers and vinegarmakers, however, continued to dispute the café's right to sell brandy, as well as the right to serve it at tables. Again the issue of seating was practically as important as the monopoly on what could be sold. In 1705 the king reaffirmed the rights of all rivals to sell brandy, but restricted the right to sell at tables to the limonadiers alone. But in 1744 the Parlement felt called upon to reconfirm the rights of vinegarmakers and distillers to sell brandy "wholesale and retail in their shops even in little glasses or in cups," and "recognized their right to seat those to whom they sold drink at tables."[22] Cafés shrugged off the competition. By 1704 the number of master limonadiers had become "so numerous" and unwieldy that the king took measures, temporarily, to restrict the guild's growth.[23] His restrictions were soon lifted, and the

[22] An ordinance of 1677, Arch.Préf.Pol. Fonds Lamoignan, makes it clear that people drank at the shops of brandy sellers. An arrêt of Parlement in 1697 told the limonadiers to stop bothering vinegarmakers who sold brandy in "little glasses at their counters and tables." The déclaration of 24 November 1705 was intended to clarify the edict of July 1705 which had denied apothecaries, vinegarmakers, and épiciers ("and all others having a shop") the right to sell coffee, in powder or as a drink, or any liqueurs or fruit in brandy, or to make and sell chocolate in tablets or in rolls, and to give brandy to drink in their shops. But since the épiciers and the others claimed always to have enjoyed this right, the king allowed them to sell brandy en détail, even to give brandy to drink in their shops, as they had done before the edict of 1705, but "those who drink it there cannot seat themselves at a table [s'attabler] in the shop" (Arch.Préf.Pol., Fonds Lamoignon, déclaration du Roi, 24 November 1705). The arrêt of 7 September 1744 is in Arthur-Michel de Boislisle, ed., *Lettres de M. de Marville au ministre Maurepas* (Paris, 1896-1905), 1:233. The limonadiers shared the right to make and sell brandy and liqueur with the épiciers, apothecaries, druggists, vinegarmakers, distillers, and faianciers; they shared the right to sell beer with brewers, faianciers, candlemakers, fruitiers, and many resellers. See Savary des Bruslons, *Dictionnaire de commerce*, s.v. "liqueurs," and "bière."

[23] An édit du Roi of December 1704 abolished the guild of limonadiers and replaced it with a special office of coffee and liquor sellers. This edict was revoked in July of the following year, but the king tried essentially the same thing

number of cafés in Paris continued to grow—to nearly three hundred in 1716 and well past a thousand by the Revolution.[24] The various guilds selling drink were attended by several kinds of semiprofessional competitors. An unknown number of bourgeois exercised their privilege to sell wine of their own cultivation without paying any tax on it. This right extended only to wine grown on the seller's property, and it had to be sold "*à huis coupé et pot renversé*"—in other words, through the doorway, without entering, and to take out. A royal ordinance at the end of the fifteenth century stressed the fact that the privilege "did not mean the right to sell *en assiette et taverne* [that is, to seat customers in one's house] since running a taverne is a base profession. . . ."[25] The privilege frequently led to abuses, however, as bourgeois tried to sell wine from other sources or let someone without the privilege sell it for them. The benefits of providing space with the wine were sufficiently attractive that tax agents complained of doormen and porters using their masters' privilege to set up taverns at the gatehouses of *hôtels particuliers*.[26] The letters patent of 1680 that extended the privilege of seating to tavernes also explicitly denied bourgeois the right to offer tables. Yet by 1724, a royal declaration an-

---

in September 1706 and did not revoke this second edict until November 1713 (Arch.Préf.Pol., Fonds Lamoignon).

[24] Fosca, *Histoire des cafés*, p. 14, gives the figure of 1,800 by 1788. The *Tableau général des maîtres distillateurs, limonadiers et vinaigriers de Paris pour l'année 1789* (Paris, 1790) gives a figure of 1,890 members in the guild, but since this number includes vinegarmakers the number of cafés was obviously less—one-third less if the ratio between limonadiers and vinaigriers of a century earlier still held. Roche, *Le Peuple de Paris*, p. 258, cites 2,800 cafés near 1780 but that must surely be a misprint. In contrast Mercier, *Tableau de Paris*, 1:227, puts it at 600 to 700 in 1782, which seems too low.

[25] Dion, *Histoire de la vigne*, p. 481.

[26] See AN, G⁷1178, Ferme générale des aides, 1689-1699, for complaints by tax agents. An arrêt du conseil d'état of 24 January 1705 (in Arch.Préf.Pol., Fonds Lamoignon) complained of "suisses, portiers et autres domestiques de plusieurs hostels et maisons" who sold wine en détail.

nounced that, despite the efforts of the wine merchants' guild to hinder bourgeois in this commerce, and despite "having obtained several decrees that authorized them" in this hindrance, the king would nevertheless authorize bourgeois to provide seats and tables, but not napkins, plates, or food.[27] The king finally solved the problem in 1759 by abolishing the fiscal privileges of bourgeois winemakers altogether.[28] The police also complained of wine cellars selling *à bouchon*, that is by putting a bush or branch over their door. This sign denoting a drink shop had been universal in the Middle Ages, but by the eighteenth century "ordinary cabarets" had signs like any other shop. The *bouchons* (the word also meant tavern) kept to side streets and suffered a particularly low reputation in the eyes of the police, though they were not outlawed.[29]

Cafés also faced competition; the humble street vendors of brandy retailed alcohol, but their stands could scarcely count as public drinking places. The street vendor was allowed to sell only brandy, on a table 2 feet by 1 foot, with a small portable tent flap to protect it from the elements. His wares were limited to two 2-quart pitchers and his cups could only be of pewter. His table could not be within ten houses of a café. Such street vendors clearly looked nothing like the café, but café owners used their political muscle to keep the vendors as marginally competitive as possible.[30] Café owners shared the right to sell beer with brewers, potters, candlemakers, fruit sellers, and others known as "resellers" (*regraitiers*). The beer trade seems to have been more loosely regulated, and had grown to six hundred sellers by 1789.[31]

---

[27] *Pièces diverses*, Pt. 1, p. 98, déclaration du Roi, 28 September 1724.

[28] Dion, *Histoire de la vigne*, p. 482.

[29] BN, Ms. fr. 21709, fol. 71 (Coll. Delamare), ordonnance de police, 27 February 1725.

[30] Arch.Préf.Pol., Fonds Lamoignon, arrêt de Parlement, 1 July 1678.

[31] Savary des Bruslons, *Dictionnaire de commerce*, s.v. "bière." The *Tableau général des maîtres distillateurs* lists 317 "persons who have paid the sums fixed

A Parisian had the option, in the end, of drinking coffee and tea at the café, brandy and other liqueurs at the café or a number of other shops, wine at a cabaret or outside the city at guinguettes, and beer at numerous shops set up by artisans with a little extra money and enterprise. There were probably almost three thousand of these drinking places by the middle of the century and closer to four thousand by the end of the century.[32] Thus Parisians had easy access to public drinking places in most parts of the city, particularly if they did not care about the kind of beverage they were drinking. All of these establishments shared a fundamental similarity in offering a place to gather, although significant differences in decor and ambience distinguished one type of institution from another. Of course, the accessibility of drinking establishments also depended on where they were located. Having a map of taverns would be very useful for this study, but a comprehensive map of taverns is very difficult to draw. With the disappearance over the last two centuries of practically all eighteenth-century fiscal records from Paris, the most obvious sources of information no longer exist. There are, instead, several indirect methods that offer a partial vision of the geography of the alcohol trade.

A solitary tax record from the middle of the century does appear to document many wine shops and has been used by several historians in their discussion of taverns.[33] A map of taverns (in this case of cabarets and cafés) drawn from this record reveals a considerable density of drinking places in certain sections of the

by the déclaration of 19 December 1776 for the retail of brandy, beer and cider," and 288 individuals who sold beer and cider alone.

[32] In 1789, the number of beer, brandy and cider sellers was 655, and the number of cafés was probably around 1,200, according to the *Tableau général des maîtres distillateurs*. Roche, *Le Peuple de Paris*, p. 258, estimates 2,000 wine merchants in the same decade.

[33] BN, Coll. Joly de Fleury, Ms. 1273-1280, taxe des pauvres; Léon Cahen, "Communication sur les marchands de vin et débitants de boissons à Paris au milieu du XVIIIe siècle," *Bulletin de la société d'histoire moderne* (6 March 1910):109-111.

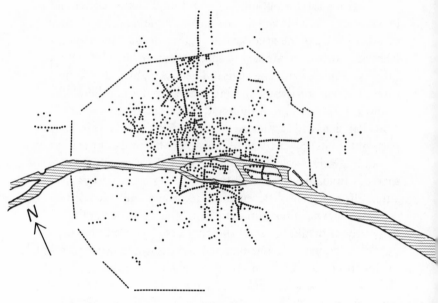

FIGURE 2.1
Map of taverns in Paris in the mid-eighteenth century.

city (Figure 2.1). The area of les Halles and the place Maubert drew scores of wine merchants and cafés, as did the two islands. Dozens of other shops clustered along the river banks and on the major streets of the city. Cafés appear to have sprung up in a roughly similar, if much less dense, pattern. The eastern part of the city is noticeably sparser in drinking establishments than the middle and west, although the records for some of the eastern parishes are unreliable. The figures for taverns in the faubourg St. Antoine are hopelessly inaccurate, for example, as the evidence from other sources demonstrates.

Indeed this tax record presents serious problems, as its users have noticed.[34] The date of its information is uncertain, al-

[34] François Furet, "Structures sociales parisienne au XVIIIe siècle: l'apport d'une série fiscale," *Annales, économies, sociétés, civilizations* 16 (1961):939-958.

FIGURE 2.2
Map of taverns in judicial cases.

though some entries have been verified for the 1730s. Unfortunately the names of the wine merchants and limonadiers mentioned in the record do not match any of those found in the judicial records, even back as far as 1691. Some of the parishes recorded no taverns at all, where clearly some must have existed.[35] Furthermore, although the tax records generally identify occupations, at least in most parishes, knowing the location of a wine merchant is not the same as locating a tavern. Some wine merchants, particularly the larger businessmen, lived separately from their taverns and cellars, of which they might

[35] For example, the parish of St. Médard. Furthermore, Saint-Germain, *La Reynie*, p. 293, reports 199 cabarets in the faubourg St. Antoine, where the taxe des pauvres lists barely a dozen, and far more in the faubourgs St. Germain (204), St. Marcel and St. Victor (162) than are identified in the taxe.

have several. This explains, I believe, the cluster of wine merchants on the Ile St. Louis, a pattern that is not matched by the judicial records. Their proximity to the wine market, the *halle au vin*, suggests that these shops may have been storage cellars or the establishments of large wholesale merchants. Nor is it clear which fruit sellers, grocers, and vinegarmakers served alcohol on their premises. Thus, this map cannot claim to provide a comprehensive geography of public drinking places, although it can give a rough idea.

A map of those drink shops involved in judicial cases, either as the scene of an incident or mentioned in testimony, offers a different perspective than the previous map, though it is similar in many ways (Figure 2.2). Taverns (mostly cabarets and cafés and a few beer and brandy shops) clustered along the main north-south axis of the St. Denis and St. Martin streets in the north and the rue de la Harpe and the rue St. Jacques in the south. The areas along the river, particularly on the right bank, were also quite dense. The intersection of these two axes, at the Ile de la Cité and the St. Jacques de la Boucherie parish, contained the highest percentage of taverns, with the exception of the area around les Halles. Such a pattern conforms to the population centers of highest density, as well as the distribution of the poorest parishes (those with the lowest tax rates).[36] This map is a composite, in that it provides the location of taverns from nine different decades between 1691 and 1771; thus, it corresponds only loosely with reality at any given moment but it reveals important patterns. Public drinking places of every kind were found most in the center of the city, along the river, around the markets, and in a corridor running north through the middle of the Right Bank to its suburbs. These were the laboring sections of the city. These areas, along with concentrations of taverns on the Left Bank and in the faubourgs where

[36] See Rudé, *The Crowd*, pp. 242-243, Appendix 2, for population density; and Furet, "Structures," pp. 948-949, for a summary of the information in the taxe des pauvres about rich and poor sections of the city.

the laboring population was growing, identify the nature of the taverns' principal customers. The maps suggest the importance of the laboring classes as patrons of taverns. At the same time the pervasiveness of taverns reminds us that they were accessible to all social groups.

THE LOGISTICS OF SUPPLY

The wine merchant's counter lay at the end of a long, complex, and highly commercialized supply system. The wine trade brought wine from nearly all parts of the country, indeed from all over Europe, which poured into the huge Parisian market to serve its vast demand. From the humble lands of the *vigneron* to the hands of the humble Parisian artisan, the wine passed through the ministrations of the *commissionaire*, the wholesale wine merchant, the *jaugeurs de vin* at the docks of Paris, and finally the retail wine merchant, who might then lease the wine to a *garçon marchand de vin* or cabaretier. The bulk of the wine coming into Paris traveled a relatively modest route from either the Orléanais, Champagne, Burgundy, or the Parisian basin, though not from the city's immediate vicinity. Parisian wine merchants were forbidden to buy wine within 20 leagues (some 50 miles) of the city.[37] Winegrowers from this zone could bring their wine into the city, but a recent study of the area dismisses this possibility because of the prohibitive entrance taxes.[38] The wine from around the city fed the guinguettes instead, and the city wine merchants turned to the area just outside 20 leagues.[39]

[37] This limit was imposed by an arrêt of 1577; see Dion, *Histoire de la vigne*, pp. 497-499.

[38] Lachiver, *Vin, vigne et vignerons*, pp. 274-275.

[39] See ibid., pp. 272-276, for more detail about the wine going to guinguettes. The cellars about which he has information appear to have been filled overwhelmingly with local wine. The guinguettes whose inventories I have consulted all filled their cellars primarily with wine from beyond the 50-mile limit: AN, MC, XXVIII-323, 23 August 1751; LXVI-489, 14 September 1751; Arch.

The bulk of the Parisian wine supply derived chiefly either from the area south of the city, including Orléans and some of the Loire, or from the vineyards stretching south from Dijon to Lyon. Paris is said to have consumed all of the wine produced by the Orléanais, for example, and four-fifths of the wine produced in the Beaujolais.[40] Much of the wine from farther up the Rhone River and from Burgundy came to Paris. Bordeaux and the Mediterranean region sent relatively little wine to the city in the eighteenth century, although the devastating weather at the beginning of the century forced Paris to turn increasingly to the south for its supply.[41]

The records of what was a carefully regulated trade have mostly disappeared, but a fragment from the beginning of the eighteenth century suggests something of this commerce. A register of some of the wine (6 percent of the total) arriving at the city's ports for tavernkeepers testifies both to the reach of the Parisian market and to its heavy reliance on local supply. During the three years from 1702 to 1705, a majority of the wine (57 percent) appears to have originated in the area around Orléans and Blois. One-quarter of it came from east of the city, either in the Champagne or around Auxerre. The rest had been produced along the Seine, the Loire, or the Saône Rivers.[42]

Much the same geography of supply emerges from the inventories of a number of Parisian wine merchants, which give some sense of what lay in their cellars and what they were sell-

---

Seine, D4B⁶ 15-715, 1755. The cellars of the Image de Notre Dame in the Porcherons were being furnished by a commissionaire: AN, Y15238, 26 December 1731.

[40] Dion, *Histoire de la vigne*, pp. 563-567, 587.

[41] Ibid., pp. 325-330.

[42] Marcel Lachiver, "L'Approvisionnement de Paris en vin," *Mémoires de la féderation des sociétés historiques et archéologiques de Paris et de l'Ile de France* 35 (1984):277-287, draws this analysis from AN, Z¹ᴴ 337, déclaration et lettres de voitures pour les vins, 1702-1777, but cautions that the document identifies the origins only of the boatmen transporting the wine and not of the wine itself, though he argues a reasonably close connection between the two.

ing. The list of one wine merchant's purchases in 1737 shows 5 percent (by value) from Orléans and 20 percent from Blois, less than 100 miles from Paris. More than one-half of his purchases came from Anjou and Tours, regions along the Loire River that figured sporadically in other accounts. This merchant's acquisitions from 1739 contained nothing but a wine identified as "auvergne" (presumably meaning "auvernat," the word commonly used around Orléans for the pinot noir grape), whereas his purchases in 1731 included wine from Languedoc and Sologne.[43] More than one-half of another merchant's deliveries in 1731 were from the Orléanais, and a further 20 percent came from Tonnerre, near Auxerre.[44]

More generally, a majority of the wine, by value, in a sample of two dozen tavernkeepers' inventories, had traveled a relatively short distance.[45] Orléans provided almost one-quarter (22 percent) of the wine. Only 2 percent was listed as coming from Blois, but much of the wine not specifically identified or identified only as red, black, or white (18 percent of the total value) was probably from the area between Blois and its neighbor, Orléans, and other environs of Paris.[46] The wine called "auvernat" was also from the Orléans region and figured prominently (7 percent) in merchants' cellars. The auvernat vine en-

[43] Arch. Seine, D4B⁶ 2-101, 17 March 1740. See Dion, *Histoire de la vigne*, pp. 159, 558-571, about "auvernat."

[44] AN, Y15238, 8 July 1731.

[45] AN, MC, XXVIII-219, 24 October 1730; XXVIII-323, 23 August 1751; XXVII-180, 3 February 1731; XXXVIII-387, 6 February 1751; XXVIII-221, 24 April 1731; XLVI-329, 4 October 1751; VII-279, 7 September 1751; CII-290, 12 January 1730; XXVIII-23, 7 May 1694; LXVI-484, 1751; Arch.Seine, D4B⁶ 5-222, 1743; D4B⁶ 15-715, 1755; D4B⁶ 10-488, 1752; D5B⁶ 248, 1716. The calculation is made by value because the plethora of volume measures would have required lengthy computations to arrive at a standard volume, and even then a similar volume size could differ from one place to another.

[46] The wine identified in several inventories simply as "noir" may refer to pinot noir, a grape common throughout northern and western France. A wine identified as "gros noir," popular among tavern keepers because it gave color to other wines mixed with it, was produced in the region around Blois. Dion, *Histoire de la vigne*, pp. 566-568.

joyed a good reputation until the eighteenth century, when so many wine producers turned to coarser, more productive vines, which they continued to call auvernat.[47] The vineyards around Auxerre, including "Chably" and known also as basse Bourgogne, sent 5 percent, and those of Champagne produced 3 percent of the wine. From a little farther afield, Burgundy supplied 14 percent of the cellars' total. To the south of that, the wines of Mâcon, which included at this time the wines of Beaujolais, provided 12 percent. The rest of the wine was from Languedoc (3 percent of the total), from a smattering of Loire valley regions, and even a little from Roussillon, but nothing from Bordeaux. A study of the Parisian wine trade from the end of the century shows a continuation of the predominantly regional nature of the wine supply.[48]

Red wine was far more in evidence in these cellars than white, a reflection of popular preference.[49] Wine merchants were even accused of dyeing their white wines to meet the enormous demand. The age of the wines in these inventories is rarely given, but we may assume that they were less than five or even four years old. The inventories describe wine as "old" after as little as two years, although the value of such wines had not yet declined. Wine did not keep well at this time beyond two or three years.[50] Some inventories consequently describe one or two barrels of spoiled wine, "good only for vinegar."

The problems of storage discouraged merchants from building an inventory. The volatility of wine prices may also have ar-

[47] Ibid., pp. 254, 558-564.

[48] Louis Bergeron, "Paris dans l'organization des échanges intérieurs français à la fin du XVIIIe siècle," in Pierre Léon, *Aires et structures du commerce français au XVIIIe siècle*, Colloque national de l'Association française des historiens économistes, 4-6 October 1973 (Lyon, 1975), pp. 241-242, 256.

[49] Lachiver, *Vin, vigne et vignerons*, p. 116, also notes the rarity of white wine.

[50] Henri Enjalbert, "Comment naissent les grands crus," *Annales, économies, sociétés, civilizations* 8 (1953):320-321. Lachiver, *Vin, vigne et vignerons*, p. 115, points out that new wine was preferred to old and was generally more expensive.

gued against speculative buying. Composite prices recorded by Labrousse show jumps of as much as 100 percent from one year to the next in the price of wine; "the cyclical fluctuations [of wine prices] are . . . superior to those of all other products." Thus the wines in 1751 inventories were roughly 80 percent more than those in 1731 inventories, but prices proceeded to drop by almost 40 percent in the following five years.[51] The wine merchant, Blin, complained in his bankruptcy statement of 1759 that the 200 barrels of wine he had bought in 1754 "instead of increasing, diminished" in value and cost him 3,800 livres.[52] The intermediate price trend was relatively stable until the 1760s when it moved into a consistently higher range.

The inventories also reveal the range of quality in various cellars. The cheapest wine in most cellars was a "red" of some unspecified origin, worth 55 to 65 livres per barrel (demi-muid), or 41 to 49 livres per hectoliter, in 1751. The "black," the Burgundy, auvernat, and Chablis were roughly the same amount. The Mâcon and Orléans wines were some 30 percent more expensive, and the wines of Roussillon and Languedoc were 60 to 100 percent costlier. The bulk of a cellar obviously consisted of the cheaper wines that were aimed at a more popular clientele. Yet the dearer Orléans and Mâcon wines had a substantial place in most inventories, and cellars often contained small amounts of more expensive wines, such as Champagne, to serve a more refined palate. Such a range cautions us from envisioning the tavern customer as uniformly poor.

The cost to the customer allowed the wine merchant a relatively modest profit. With his cheapest wine selling generally at 10 sous for a pinte in 1751, he received 144 livres for a muid that might have cost him 110 livres or more. The cost of the pinte in a cabaret ranged from 8 to 12 sous, tending in the long

[51] Claude-Ernest Labrousse, *Esquisse du mouvement des prix et des revenues en France au XVIIIe siêcle* (Paris, 1933), 1:269-276.

[52] Arch. Seine, D4B⁶ 21-1020, 29 November 1759.

run to increase slowly over the century, but advancing and re-treating many times over the course of a decade.

The wine came to Paris from the wine-producing regions in several ways. The wine producers or vignerons brought it themselves, if they lived near a river and were not too distant from Paris. The father of Restif de la Bretonne, for example, made the trip himself, taking his own wine and that of some of his neighbors down the Yonne River to the Parisian wine mar-ket.[53] A whole community of boatmen worked the Loire River and the canal between Orléans and the Seine River to supple-ment the ventures of vignerons.[54] The other rivers leading into Paris were equally conduits for wine from the east and south. The other way for wine to arrive was through the commerce of wholesale wine merchants in Paris. These men worked through contacts in the wine regions to buy the wine and bring it back themselves. Often such merchants were sons of the region in which they bought their wines, relying on family networks to do business.[55] One Parisian wine merchant recorded debts owed to his older and a younger brother, who were both boat-men on the Loire.[56]

Merchants also worked through agents, or commissionaires, in various regions to acquire wine. The commissionaire in the seventeenth century was little more than an agent of the wine merchant but he had become increasingly independent in the eighteenth century, making purchases on his own account. By the end of the century he acted essentially as a separate inter-mediary between the growers and the merchant. This position

[53] Dion, *Histoire de la vigne*, p. 552.

[54] Several lists of debt refer to voituriers par eau or maître mariniers. See Arch. Seine, D4B6 3-147. AN, MC, XXVIII-176, 19 February 1721, gives an example of a contract between a voiturier par eau of Amboise and three wine merchants of Paris for three boats of wine taken from Blois to the port of St. Paul in Paris, at a price of 18 livres per barrel.

[55] Bergeron, "Paris dans l'organization des échanges," p. 241; J. P. Panouille "Le Quartier Maubert, St. Severin," thèse de maîtrise, Paris, 1970.

[56] Arch. Seine, D4B6 2-107, 28 April 1740.

gave him considerable power in the market and over the financially more vulnerable growers. Just as his greater capital gave him leverage over the grower, his superior knowledge of the local market yielded an advantage over the Parisian merchant. A treatise from the end of the century took the commissionaire to task for using his power to distort prices.[57]

The accounts of a commissionaire from Beaujeu, just south of Mâcon, in 1765 outline the scale of one such enterprise. The man, Teillard, transported 2,348 barrels (4,400 hectoliters) of the 1764 Beaujolais harvest to Paris, or roughly 3 percent of the total wine trade in that direction. Although the accounts do not specify, he undoubtedly moved the wine with carts across the 40 kilometers of land separating the Beaujolais vineyards from the Loire River, at a cost of 4 livres per barrel. From the town of Pouilly on the Loire, the wine then traveled by water up the Loire, through the Canal de Briare, and up the Seine to Paris. At little more than twice the cost of the land voyage (9 livres 10 sous), the boat trip took twenty times longer (six weeks versus two days). The cost of such a trip was not negligible. When the wine arrived in Paris, Teillard sold it to more than two hundred customers, most of whom bought only one or two barrels. Bourgeois, monks, several doormen of great princes (acting perhaps on behalf of their masters), and many others stocked their private cellars with Teillard's merchandise. Most of his wine, however, was sold to two dozen wine merchants of various ranks. A few of these were clearly large-scale merchants (négociants), who bought several very large consignments. The rest were tavernkeepers, who came regularly—once every month or so—to buy two or three barrels.[58]

The account books of wine merchants filing for bankruptcy

[57] François Brac, *Le Commerce des vins, réformés, rectifié et épuré, ou nouvelle méthode pour tirer un parti sûr, prompt et avantageux des récoltes en vins* (Amsterdam, 1769), pp. 10-31.

[58] Georges Durand, *Vin, vigne, et vignerons en Lyonnais et Beaujolais* (Paris, 1979), pp. 93-101.

indicate how important the commissionaires were to the Parisian wine trade. Nearly all of a score of wine merchants declaring bankruptcy prior to 1761 were heavily in debt to commissionaires for wine acquired and shipped to Paris.[59] The average debt at the time of bankruptcy was 2,000 livres, although it could be more substantial (the "amount remaining from 3,000 livres," as one wine merchant indicated). The forty-nine commissionaires listed in these accounts operated out of fifteen cities, most frequently from Orléans (thirteen times), Auxerre and Mâcon (six times each), and from Blois (nine times). All of these cities but Mâcon were neighbors of Paris, winegrowing regions dominated by the powerful and voracious capital. Commissionaires in the other cities undoubtedly dealt in wine from various regions. Clearly the commissionaires in Blois sent more than the small amount of wine listed in the inventories from that region. Those in Auxerre, for example, also handled the wines of lower Burgundy.

While most of the wine supply came from relatively local areas, the short distances these wines had to travel should not deceive us into ignoring the difficulties involved in their transportation. The shipment of any heavy commodity was expensive and time consuming in the old regime, and when it was subject to spoilage, as wine was, the results could be catastrophic. The preferred means of transportation for wine was by water, and indeed access to rivers or canals has been a determining factor in the production of wine. Paris was fortunate in

[59] This statement is based on twenty-eight bankruptcies of wine merchants and cabaretiers through 1771: Arch.Seine, D4B⁶ 1-27, 1695; 1-35, 1695; 1-82, 1739; 2-98, 1740; 2-101, 1740; 2-107, 1740; 2-117, 1740; 3-144, 1741; 3-147, 1741; 3-173, 1742; 5-222, 1743; 7-330, 1747; 7-354, 1748; 7-359, 1748; 10-460, 1751; 10-466, 1751; 10-488, 1752; 14-642, 1754; 14-662, 1755; 14-695, 1755; 15-715, 1755; 19-912, 1758; 21-1020, 1759; 21-1065, 1760; 23-1169, 1762; 23-1198, 1762; 29-1561, 1766; 33-1777, 1768; AN, MC, LXI-385, 16 January 1731. These records include sixteen of the thirty-four wine-merchant bankruptcies that exist in this archive through 1751 and twenty-four of the sixty-six total bankruptcies of wine merchants through 1761.

being connected by water to most of the wine-producing regions of the country. Yet the bankruptcy records are filled with laments about the perils of river transportation. A frequent culprit was low water levels, which could slow down and, in some cases, completely close river traffic. "Left in the canal for lack of water," is the explanation of a merchant's loss of 5,500 livres worth of wine in 1731. He later lost 25 livres per barrel (demi-*queue*, equal to 2 hectoliters), at least one-quarter of its value, from "excessive heat" in 1739.[60]

The "observations concerning losses" written by a wine merchant in 1762 illustrate the risks involved.[61] In 1752 he had purchased wine in the Mâconnais but it had been held up en route "by the heat which had caused considerable leakage." By the time it arrived in Paris the "majority was turning sour and bitter" and he claimed a loss of 8,000 livres. The following year he made purchases in Orléans and Auxerre but left them in storage where he claimed leakage cost him 1,400 livres, one-sixth of the wine left in Auxerre having leaked out.

In 1754 I purchased in Saumur 446 *pièces* [a *pièce* equaled 2 hectoliters] both wine of Anjou and of Chinoius [on the Loire], this wine was forgotten to be sent, either by the fault of the *voiturier* or by the commissionaire, so that these wines were left en route because of the heat and the river not being passable because of low water until June and forced the wine to be offloaded on the way, at Mont Louis and stored, which cost me money, and I had to buy wine in Orléans to make up for it. I reloaded the wine in the winter and sent it to be stored in cellars near Meung where it was no sooner stored away than the vault of the cellar collapsed and crushed 55 barrels.

For this he claimed a loss of 6,000 livres.

The same heat and "low water" of 1752 held up the arrival of wine bought in "several regions" by another wine merchant

60 Arch. Seine, D4B⁶ 2-101, 17 March 1740.

61 Arch. Seine, D4B⁶ 23-1169, 9 January 1762. He styles himself a "marchand de vin en gros" in his *Journalier* but he lists the accoutrements of a cabaret in his assets.

declaring bankruptcy; as a result, all the shipments "arrived at the same time."[62] He could not store them all and was forced to leave much of the wine in the market where "excessive heat" caused considerable leakage—6,000 livres worth. The problem of leakage, especially when the heat made the wood of barrels dry out and contract, was a constant theme of these accounts. "Leakage" of another sort also caused problems. The police sentenced a Jean Laumonier to the pillory for having drunk from barrels that he was transporting from Orléans to Paris for a wine merchant.[63] A jurist maintained that "most boatmen or carters tap the casks in their charge." The problem was serious enough that merchants set aside "a certain number of casks for the provision of the boatmen . . . depending on the distance."[64]

Although the wine's journey from its source to the tavern counter was almost completed when it arrived in Paris, the last step might well entail very complicated financial transactions and business relations. In the simplest case the tavernkeeper himself brought the wine in from its source and moved it directly to his cellar. There are examples of tavernkeepers with such contacts in the wine regions or arrangements with commissionaires, but most of the account books of tavernkeepers show more debts owed to other Parisian wine merchants than to agents in the countryside. In theory the wholesale wine merchant provided much of the wine that retailers sold in taverns, and by law a third of the wine brought in wholesale by merchants had to be displayed in the market place for retailers to buy. Wholesale merchants like the Sieur Gaultier also made special arrangements with retailers so that "when the Sieur Gaultier has wine [arrive] at the port he notifies the witness [a wine merchant in the faubourg St. Antoine] who goes and

[62] Arch. Seine, D4B⁶ 14, 695, 24 July 1755.
[63] Pièces diverses, Pt. 1, p. 278, arrêt de Parlement, 14 January 1751.
[64] Delamare, Traité de la police, 3:548.

chooses what he likes, which is delivered by Gaultier who comes several days later to settle the accounts."[65]

The transfer of wine between wholesale and retail merchant was supervised and negotiated through several layers of royal officials. An official "unloader" (*déchargeur*) took charge of off-loading the wine from boats that docked in Paris and transferring them to a merchant's cart or to his cellar. The fiscal demands of Louis XIV's wars led him to create forty official "rollers and loaders" to perform the latter half of the unloaders' function. The two offices were reunited (but much increased in membership) again in 1703. In addition the financial transactions were supervised by "official [juré] *courtiers*" and "official sellers and controllers of wine" who checked on the quality, quantity, and origin of the wine put up for sale, guarded against fraud, and facilitated contacts between wine sellers and buyers.[66]

According to the statutes of the wine guild, the two operations of retail and wholesale were to be kept separate and to be practiced by separate merchants. The market for this exchange seems to have been unsatisfactory, however, since the spirit and letter of the injunction were so regularly flouted, as wholesalers extended their control over the retailing operation. The easiest way to accomplish this was by lending wine and supplies to a cabaretier who had insufficient capital to begin on his own. Because the flexibility of the guild allowed men to set themselves up with a minimum of capital, wholesale merchants had the opportunity to lend them wine or to put up an establishment to help them get started. The Sieur Henaut, for example, began with only two rooms rented from his mother and the "utensils indispensable to his commerce." Since he had no funds to buy wine, he arranged with a wine merchant to be supplied with sufficient wine and agreed to turn over weekly receipts to him

[65] AN, Y14088, 22 June 1761.
[66] Delamare, *Traité de la police*, 3:553-637.

and to buy from no one else "whatever credit and whatever advantage he might find." He ended the year 3,000 livres in debt.[67]

The practice of running a cabaret in such a manner actually could involve numerous legal problems, for the guild of wine merchants strenuously objected to members owning more than one shop, even if managed by someone else. As early as 1647, their statutes pronounced that "to facilitate trade [*trafic*] and to provide means for poor and modest merchants of the guild. . . . to gain their livelihood, henceforth no merchant will be permitted . . . to have or open more than one *cave* [cellar, or in this context, tavern] in the city and faubourgs of Paris, to sell wine in retail."[68] This meant that merchants who set assistants up to manage extra shops for them were breaking the guild's regulations. Furthermore, merchants were supposed to sell wine only in their "houses of habitation." The guild made exceptions to this restriction only in cases where a wine merchant found himself burdened with too much wine that was in danger of going bad if he could not sell it quickly enough. Then he might be allowed to open a second shop for six months.

The guild faced tremendous opposition to this rule. Both the records of the criminal and police courts and the inventories after death allude frequently to merchants with multiple establishments. Some of these the guild closed, as records of prosecutions reveal, but many unquestionably escaped detection. The case of the wine merchant, Delan, who owned a cabaret on the rue des Tournelles and a *cave* on the rue du Temple, shows how the issue created tensions within the guild. Another wine merchant, a neighbor on the rue du Temple, reported Delan to the authorities, complaining that he "stole the sales on which he [the neighbor] based his subsistence and that of his family." When Delan responded that he needed the second shop to help

---

[67] Arch. Seine, D4B⁶ 2-101, 17 March 1740.
[68] *Pièces diverses*, Pt. 2, pp. 24-25.

him remedy a temporary glut of wine and an inadequate shop, the guards of the guild visited his domicile and found "several rooms and *cabinets* arranged to receive many customers and companies and . . . many customers of different estate, some who were drinking wine at 8 sous [per pinte] and others at 10 sous." The guild made him close the other cabaret.[69]

The practice of establishing multiple cabarets increased, however, in the 1720s and 1730s "to the point that most merchants arbitrarily open *caves* without permission . . . resulting in such a great disorder that one sees daily families ruined by *caves* that open in their neighborhood." In 1739 the guild assembled at its office on the rue de la Potterie, and more than nine hundred members signed a resolution calling for the enforcement of the statute. At this point the guild encountered opposition from the Farmers General, spurred on by certain "ambitious" wine merchants. The Farmers objected that the resolution would diminish sales, and thus their tax revenues, and they petitioned the Controller General and the Lieutenant General of Police to stop the guild. In defense of the resolution the guild argued that "it is not the great number of *caves* in a city, but the multitude of customers that assures the sales, which are always made more securely and more decently in a shop in one's domicile, under the eyes of a merchant [who is] active and vigilant in his commerce." The guild also appealed to the classic guild ideal: many modest merchants "living reasonably from their commerce, each supporting a family of children and domestics, finding the means to pay large rents and large taxes" as opposed to "these large shops [*magasins*] which only owe their existence to the cupidity of some merchants, who would create dearth each year in the midst of plenty by the prodigious quantity of their purchases."[70] Their arguments per-

---

[69] Ibid., Pt. 2, p. 52, sentence de police, 9 January 1756.

[70] Ibid., Pt. 2, p. 37, motif de la délibération faite par le corps des marchands de vin, 26 January 1739; and Pt. 2, p. 77, from the procès verbal de police, 26 September 1753.

suaded the Lieutenant General of Police, but the Farmers obtained an arrêt de conseil to delay the guild. The guild tried again in 1744, and were again blocked by an arrêt de conseil a week later. The guild finally got its way in 1746, yet its officers could still find dozens of infractions fifteen years later.[71]

Under these conditions even merchants' assistants (garçons) could set themselves up with a little bit of money. An assistant named Prieur bought his own furniture and utensils, rented two rooms and several cellars, and found a merchant who would furnish him with wine for which he would pay the wholesale price. Lacking the "quality" of being a wine merchant, however, he agreed to "run the cabaret under the name of" the merchant, even putting the merchant's mark on his own utensils and announcing to everyone that he worked for the merchant. This quasi-independence lasted for a year before the merchant unilaterally closed the cabaret because of some unspecified dispute with "his" assistant. Yet his right to do so was immediately contested in a complaint brought by Prieur to the police.[72] It is difficult to know how common Prieur's arrangement was, for there were hundreds of garçons marchands de vin working "under the name of" a wine merchant, all with varying degrees of independence.

Merchants' assistants gained some leverage from manipulating credit. At any one time a substantial amount of a cabaret owner's wealth could be tied up in outstanding debts that the assistant managing the tavern had granted to customers. Thus one owner felt compelled to bring a complaint against an assistant managing a cabaret for him (though the real nature of the relation is not clear) because the assistant had extended credit without the owner's consent. The assistant had disappeared with the account book, the only record of what the owner could claim from his customers.[73]

[71] AN, Y11247, 16-17 June 1761.
[72] AN, Y14527, 9 September 1731.
[73] AN, Y12025, 24 August 1731.

The account books of cabaret owners reveal some of these business activities, but unfortunately much remains unknown. What is abundantly clear from these books is how constant the granting of credit really was, despite the injunctions against tavern owners offering credit and the difficulties of their collecting on bad debts. The medieval laws of Paris denied tavern owners the right to prosecute clients for money owed them, and eighteenth-century commentators continued to refer to the injunction.[74] That cabaret owners continued to offer credit in such circumstances attests to its usefulness in their business. Accounts show anything from two to twelve customers a day buying on credit, the same names appearing regularly, usually for small amounts. Cabaret owners even lent cash to customers on occasion.[75] A cabaret owner granted credit to a dozen or so of his customers—certainly not the total number who came in to drink. Who was so favored? Most of the customers are identified only by name. The rest run the gamut from servant to abbé but most came, not surprisingly, from the possessing classes. The refusal to grant credit, on the other hand, could jeopardize the business, and even the safety, of the owner.[76]

More importantly, wine merchants used credit to lure customers away from each other, and to keep them coming back. As a cabaret owner chastised a former regular customer for abandoning her cabaret, the customer explained that she had found better credit elsewhere.[77] It was a dangerous game that

[74] Delamare, *Traité de la police*, 3:719. See also Jacques Peuchet, *Collection des lois, ordonnances, et règlements de la police depuis XIIIe siècle jusqu'à 1818* (Paris, 1818), 4:122, in footnote.

[75] See note 11 for examples. There are entries for money lent to customers in D5B⁶ 2854. A master shoemaker "debauching" two journeyman (that is, stealing them away from the service) of a plaintiff took them to a tavern to persuade them. Wishing to start them immediately on wages, he turned to the tavernkeeper to lend him the money: AN, Y10732, 27 April 1701.

[76] See the assault on a tavernkeeper described in Saint-Germain, *La Reynie*, pp. 294-295.

[77] AN, Y10993b, 4 October 1751.

the owner was playing, for the customer had run up a bill and then taken her business to another cabaret. Clearly the process of establishing a regular clientele was crucial to the success of a cabaret, and owners expressed their concern on a number of occasions. The reputation of a cabaret derived chiefly from the quality of the wine, but the friendliness of owners and waiters, the availability of credit, and the kinds of entertainment all figure in testimony as well.

With his reputation in mind, one wine merchant found himself embroiled in a battle with a violin player who wished to play in the man's cabaret. The merchant complained about the violinist's excesses and drunkenness and that of his wife who accompanied him. "Wishing to maintain the tranquillity in his house which is as essential to his commerce as the good company that is staying away through dislike of being always on the verge of seeing a fight break out," he insisted that the man stay away. The man's wife, however, threatened to "spread the rumor that there were killings and assassinations at the cabaret and that they buried people in the garden and that the house was an open brothel and other things to defame his house."[78] Customers warned other tavern owners that bad wine hurt their business and that rude behavior by the waiters "was not the way to attract customers."[79]

The waiter played a crucial role in attracting business, as the complaint of a cabaret owner against another cabaret owner in his neighborhood suggests. The accused had seduced a waiter, Godefroy, away from the cabaret of the plaintiff, where he had worked for a year. This was expressly against the regulations and statutes of their guild, but the wine merchant had done so anyway, said the plaintiff, because he "knew that Godefroy had a perfect knowledge of all the companies ["regular customers" (*pratiques*) is crossed out here] who come to eat and drink at the

[78] AN, Y15180, 18 August 1751.
[79] AN, Y14877, 25 October 1691.

plaintiffs, and of all the communities and other bourgeois to whom he furnishes wine." Thus the malefactor kept Godefroy "with the intention of attracting all these customers, and sent him continually to their houses to solicit them to come or to send for wine at" Godefroy's new cabaret. Godefroy asked a mason in the neighborhood to come and to bring his workers and promised that he would give them "good wine." This the mason refused to do, saying that he was "accustomed [*in-graine*]" to the plaintiff's cabaret. The waiter even stopped customers on their way into the plaintiff's shop, telling them that the wine was better at his new cabaret.[80] The same day Godefroy and his master made a complaint in their turn. The former master had encountered Godefroy taking wine to the priests of the community of St. Cosme, which he ordinarily furnished, and started to abuse Godefroy and took away his pitcher of wine. The former master even took bottles and pitchers away from children who came to Godefroy's new cabaret to request wine. Godefroy also accused his old master of not paying his wages.[81] The dispute clearly reveals the importance of regular customers to a tavern's business.

Taverns found a variety of ways to compete with each other for customers. A woman selling liquor in the rue de la Harpe complained of a limonadier, a "near neighbor," who sent soldiers every evening to insult her and "to oblige the plaintiff to abandon her shop."[82] The wine merchant owning the Trois Bouteilles on the rue Tirechappe was likewise forced to bring suit against another wine merchant who had just erected the same sign over an establishment on the same small street. His adversary had only done this, he claimed, "to attract the plain-

[80] AN, Y14661, 28 August 1691. The guild of wine merchants demanded that waiters moving to a new shop, had to go at least "fifteen shops' distance," cited in Steven L. Kaplan, "The Luxury Guilds of Eighteenth-Century Paris," *Francia* 9 (1981):292.

[81] AN, Y14661, 28 August 1691.

[82] AN, Y14611, 23 May 1691.

tiff's clients."[83] Once again it appears that owners identified customers who "belonged" to them, regulars whose patronage they counted on. The function of the tavern sign clearly lay in distinguishing different taverns from each other. Some, such as the Trois Bouteilles, also managed to announce the nature of the shop, or made a pun on the owner's name, or even blasphemed in an amusing way. Most, however, simply used heraldic designs and religious motifs as mnemonic devices.[84]

It was not uncommon to find more than one tavern on a block, so that tensions of the kind expressed above were fairly ordinary. They tended to be expressed only in certain ways, however. The quality of the wine was obviously a point of rivalry, but the price was not. Competition manifested itself in "reputation cutting" rather than cost cutting. Rivals impugned each others' honesty, the morals of their customers and their establishments, and the health of their wares. A fight between a wife and husband over his leaving a cabaret gave the wife's sister, herself a neighboring beer seller, the opportunity to intercede and to vent her spleen at her rival's establishment.[85] Guild rules could not help here; the two shops did not belong to the same guild. Wine merchants were competing with shops selling other kinds of alcohol, and the differences in drink seem not to have been as important as basic similarities of the drinking place.

The owners of drink shops other than cabarets had an easier time than the wine merchant in obtaining their wares. The café owner could go to the grocer for most of the coffee, chocolate, and spices he needed. The brandies and liqueurs sold at cafés could be made in Paris by merchant distillers, though some

[83] AN, Y12107, 23 September 1701. Duchesne, *Code de la police,* 1:461, points out that it was forbidden for "masters to come lodge too near another in order to steal his customers [*pratiques*] . . . [or] or to take the same sign as his colleague."

[84] See Roche, *Le Peuple de Paris,* pp. 230-231, for a discussion of tavern signs.

[85] AN, Y14056, 10 December 1720.

brandy was imported from the west coast of France. Beer came from Parisian brewers, several dozen of whom operated in Paris, mostly in the faubourgs St. Antoine and St. Marceau. The manufacture required considerable equipment and capital outlay.[86] The source of one café's beer (actually the owner called himself a limonadier and beer merchant) was all from local breweries. His café on the rue de la Huchette took deliveries, in 1722, once every eleven days or so of roughly 5 muids each month, though the number of deliveries decreased from twenty-four in January to only four in December. Nearly all of his beer came from a M. Moreau, a brewer in the faubourg St. Marceau. Another brewer, Torchet in the faubourg St. Antoine, made two other deliveries. The price of a muid of beer fluctuated between 26 and 30 livres, most often for "beer" but occasionally for "red beer" and several times for "white beer."[87] The journal of a brewer, on the other hand, shows sales to a wide variety of people, most of them fruit sellers, candlemakers, and vinegarmakers, who probably then sold the beer in their own drink shops. A few customers, however, such as a joiner and a shoemaker, could have been buying it for their personal use.[88]

The cellars of one café contained seven barrels of brandy, fourteen barrels of beer, and a barrel of vin rozay (rosé?). There was also a barrel of ratafia, the spiced brandy that figured prominently in account books as a very popular drink, and 40 pounds of tobacco.[89] The brandy in this cellar probably formed the basis of a number of spiced concoctions that the limonadier could make in his own shop.[90] The account books of other cafés

---

[86] See *Encyclopédie méthodique: commerce* (Paris, 1783), 2:52, on the supply of brandy. Haim Burstin, *Le Faubourg St. Marcel à l'époque révolutionnaire* (Paris, 1983), pp. 169-174, gives some details about brewers in this quarter during the Revolution.

[87] Arch. Seine, D5B⁶ 5022, 1722.

[88] Arch. Seine, D5B⁶ 694, 1749-1758.

[89] AN, Y11218, 3 June 1731.

[90] Delamain, *Histoire du cognac*, pp. 24-29, notes that most brandy suffered

suggest that more brandy was consumed in a spiced and sweetened form than it was straight. Most of these accounts agree that coffee was the most common drink sold. The café's wares were not cheap. A cup of coffee, in 1755, sold for the same price (4 sous) as a pint (*chopine*) of wine.[91] A cup of chocolate cost 5 sous, a bottle of beer and a pitcher of lemonade the same, and a glass of brandy cost 7 sous. The café might also offer an array of exotic pastries and confections.

Whether the drink was brewed in the shop's basement or crossed the length of France, an elaborate commercial network provided Parisians with access to an array of alcohol and comestibles. Although the laws distinguishing different shops caused a certain amount of confusion, Parisians do not seem to have been bothered by the need to change shops in order to change what they were drinking. Indeed, they seem not to have been very choosy about what they drank, so long as it had not been spoiled. The place, the environment in which people gathered to drink, mattered as much as, or perhaps more than, what they drank. The diversity of drink shops, each serving something slightly different, makes sense if seen in that context. For drink shops used the guild distinctions as a basis for developing their own style of furnishing and decor.

THE SETTING

The tavernkeeper had to concern himself not only with securing a regular supply of wine but also with providing a place in which to drink it. He was selling space—a *mise-en-scène*—as well as the drink. This need to offer a place to sit down and gather played a role in the evolution of the various guilds in-

---

from an unpleasant off-taste and required spices and herbs to be made palatable. See Franklin, *Dictionnaire des arts*, s.v. "limonadier," for a list of some of the spiced drinks that were commonly served.

[91] See Arch. Seine, D5B⁶ 1430 for wine prices and D5B⁶ 1643 for prices at a café, both in 1755.

volved in the purveyance of drink and the squabbles that divided them. In addition to tables and chairs, owners could supply privacy, warmth, even elegance. The arrangement of rooms and tables, the decorations, and the furnishings shaped the behavior of tavern comportment. The decor signaled, furthermore, the social aspirations of the owner and the kinds of clientele he was seeking to attract.

Claude Lardin, a wine merchant from the end of the seventeenth century, left an inventory that reveals some of the cabaret's ambience. At the time of his death, in 1694, he owned a cabaret in the faubourg St. Antoine. If he had been there for more than ten years he would have enjoyed the tax exemptions of taverns outside the limit of the *octroi*, but by 1694 establishments throughout his faubourg were subjected to the tax on alcohol. His business was modest. The tavern was a bit smaller than average, with only four rooms listed and two of these, on the second floor, had beds as well as tables. This is where the family slept when the customers finally left. The rooms were all sparsely furnished, without wardrobes, food boxes, or mirrors. Only two rooms had tapestries, but these were "old." The cabaret contained ten tables listed in the inventory, which is slightly below average, but there is no sign that it was in financial trouble. There were 592 livres in cash at hand when he died, and his wine cellar held a respectable 4,423 livres worth of wine. The wine was almost evenly divided in origin between Orléans, Burgundy, and an unidentified region. The cabaret was in full operation, then, with a little more than the average amount of wine in the cellar, and the kinds of wine that suggest contacts in the provinces.[92]

Claude was survived by a wife and at least two children, both sons, who went on to become wine merchants. The inventories of one of them, Claude Noel Lardin, allow us to chart the fortunes of the family between two generations. As a boy he was

[92] AN, MC, xxviii-23, 7 May 1694.

clearly brought up in the midst of the family business and slept where his father's customers drank. Yet he did not succeed to his father's occupation until ten years after the man's death. The reasons for this hiatus are not clear; perhaps Claude Noel was too young in 1694 to inherit the establishment. More likely his father's cabaret went to a brother, Jean, who in 1731 was also a wine merchant, for Claude Noel evidently acquired his establishment through marriage. He was accorded his letter of admission as wine merchant a mere ten days before he married the Demoiselle Anne Jeanne Elisabeth Pecoeur, the widow of Jean Baptiste Huguet, also a wine merchant. Huguet who had died a year earlier was the son of a *conseiller du roi* and *contrôleur des rentes*, so we may perhaps imagine him a fairly substantial man of business. In any case his widow brought 13,000 livres into the union with Claude Noel. She may also have given him an establishment, for Claude Noel had moved in town, to a cabaret on the rue des Quatre Fils, near the place de Grève, sometime before the next inventory in 1730.[93] The occasion of this inventory was the death of the demoiselle, his wife. There is no indication of her age at that point, but she was still of childbearing age. She was survived by her husband and a brother, Edme LeClerc, also a wine merchant, and by two daughters: Marie Madelaine, aged nine years, and Marie Barbe, whose birth had possibly killed her mother, for she was only two months old at the time of her mother's death.

Despite his personal tragedy, Claude Noel had much for which to be thankful. His cellars held 2,417 livres of wine, roughly one-quarter of it "auvergnat," and about one-fifth each from Mâcon and Languedoc (the rest is identified simply as red). His cabaret in town, the Chesne Vert, was somewhat grander than his father's had been. The two upstairs rooms, one of them "large," no longer mentioned beds or mattresses in them. These could be found in another room, with more pri-

[93] AN, MC, xxviii-219, 24 October 1730.

vacy. The *boutique* (shoproom) had a fountain in it "in which to put water and rinse the glasses," and there were other fountains in the courtyard as well worth a total of 70 livres. The court-yard was behind the boutique and had a table and stools for cus-tomers. It also contained a tub for urinating into. The garden (it is not clear where this was located) looked a bit run down, with a "bunch of old firewood not worth describing and a rotten cradle," but there was a table and chairs there as well and a *cab-inet* off to one side with a table in it. Tapestry now covered most of the walls, over 200 livres worth, and one tapestry of 10 *aulnes* (13 feet) in the "grande salle" upstairs was worth 100 livres alone, though it did not cover the entire wall.

In addition to the house in town, Claude Noel rented a cab-aret, the Petit Saint Jean on the grande rue du faubourg St. An-toine. This establishment was probably as large as his other cab-aret, though the space was apportioned differently. A large boutique contained the counter, with its measures and drawers, a small kitchen formed to the side of the counter by a screen with three curtains, and half of the ten tables in the tavern. The boutique also boasted several copper fountains, a food cup-board, and some 250 pounds of pewter measures (which equaled anywhere from 85 to 125 pitchers depending on how many pintes and chopines there were). Although there was no tapestry, the boutique was graced with a clock worth 30 livre made by the Sieur Blimont, clockmaker of Paris. In addition to the boutique, there was a "little *cabinet*" with a single table that overlooked the courtyard. Above these two rooms were two more much like it. A "large" room overlooking the street held three tables and 24 stools. A hanging tapestry decorated with "great personages" covered all of the walls. Behind this room was a small room containing only one table and a bed with sev-eral mattresses. Presumably the two women who ran this cab-aret for Claude Noel slept here. His two cellars in this house are a bit of a mystery. Between them they held only 400 livres worth of wine plus a number of empty barrels. It is hard to know what to make of his business, except that it must have been fairly successful, for he possessed 16,205 livres in cash at the time of the inventory.

Whatever the fortunes of his two cabarets, Claude Noel did not enjoy them much longer. Some six months after his wife's death he died too, and the orphaned girls' two uncles stepped forward to have the cabarets inventoried again. There was little change in those six months, except in the cellars. The amount of wine in his cellars had jumped to the value of 4,240 livres, of which one-third was auvergnat, one-third Burgundy, and almost one-third white wine.[94]

Inventories after death, like those of Lardin, leave much to the imagination, yet in over a score of examples, there are some consistently recognizable features.[95] None of the cabarets had less than two rooms. Whether there was a second room behind the boutique, one or two above it, or merely a small *cabinet* attached to it, a customer had some choice in rooms. The average and most common number was four rooms—two above and two below. This subdivision of space offered customers the possibility of enjoying a bit of privacy. They could shut the doors of upstairs rooms, although the cabaret owner could send an assistant to peer through a peep hole in the door if he wanted to check on his customers. The existence of private areas within a "public place" provided certain opportunities as well as potential paradoxes.

The boutique itself was clearly the hub of the operation. It contained a wooden counter, outfitted with several drawers and sometimes covered with a lead countertop. Because some merchants may have saved and reused the spilled wine, the police

[94] AN, MC, xxviii-221, 24 April 1731.

[95] In addition to the inventories listed in notes 39 and 45 above: AN, MC, xxviii-222, 5 July 1731; xxviii-320, 24 January 1751; xxviii-323, 6 August 1751; lxi-451, 1 July 1751; xxviii-323, 6 August 1751; iii-901, 26 October 1741; xxxviii-387, 27 January 1751; xlvii-137, 23 December 1751; lxvi-489, 14 September 1751; lxi-385, 16 January 1731; xxviii-176, 9 January 1721.

felt it necessary to warn against the practice of collecting wine spilled on countertops that were made of lead.[96] Wine merchants, who already enjoyed a sinister reputation for adulterating their wine, would not have been helped by the additional charge of lead poisoning. Most boutiques listed a fountain for rinsing glasses with water, and the glasses were usually stored in the boutique in a steel cabinet. The boutique also had the measures, the utensils, and often the food, in a *garde à manger*. From the boutique the merchant sold wine to those who would take it out with them, and from the counter wine was dispensed to customers who drank at the tavern. The merchant spent much of his time behind the counter, guarding the cash box and wine supply and serving patrons. Since much of the drinking was done in one of the other rooms, the counter imposed a certain isolation on the merchant.

The counter played none of the roles that it does in bars, pubs, or cafés today. People spoke very rarely of drinking at the *comptoir*, unless they were drinking in the shop of an épicier, where there might not be any tables and people were not encouraged to linger. But the boutique of an épicier was not really a tavern, nor was it generally called a cabaret, for the point of a tavern was that customers were able to tarry and for this it seems that people needed chairs, stools, and tables. In the few cases where customers drank at the counter it was invariably to talk to the wine merchant behind it. Occasionally his friends could be found drinking at the counter and talking to him or to his wife. Some counters had benches behind them and customers occasionally joined the merchant on this bench. Yet the merchant was separated socially as well as physically from his customers. His friends were usually merchants themselves, or bourgeois. In the poorer taverns, the beer shops, the beer sellers were often wives of artisans. There the social distance between customer and vendor was less, and female customers

96 *Encyclopédie méthodique: jurisprudence*, 10:816-817.

could actually be found sitting behind the counter with the beer seller.[97] In all of these institutions, however, the counter was peripheral to the social space of the room, and it was the tables that imposed the principal conformation on people's behavior.

The table accounts for a number of aspects of social behavior in a cabaret. It helped to define a group, by delineating it from others. Tables directed the attention of those sitting at them inward, away from the rest of the room, and reinforced the insularity and the unity of drinking groups. At the same time, the lack of alternative seating—on bar stools, for instance—meant that single customers had to sit at tables and might be less isolated.

A number of factors point to the privacy of groups drinking in taverns. Because most customers drank from a shared pitcher, it was important to know who, as part of the group, had access to that pitcher and thus would help pay the bill. The bill (*écot*) was owed by the group as a whole. *Écot* became a synonym in popular parlance for the drinking group and for the distance that separated groups from one another. A customer being bothered by a man from another group finally told him to leave him alone: "Drink on your bill, I will drink on mine [bois à ton écot, moi bois au mien]."[98]

Tables could become a source of friction when space was limited. If a small group sat at a large table, it might be forced to share the table with another group. In some cases the two groups deliberately ignored each other; witnesses would stress the separateness of two groups at the same table.[99] Men might also join themselves to a group, sharing a salad, or playing cards, but "after having asked the permission of the *compagnie* [the group]."[100] In some cases, however, two groups fought at

[97] AN, Y15055, 10 September 1751.
[98] AN, Y10083, 10 June 1741.
[99] Two groups sitting at a table, for example, "drank à leurs écot and separately." AN, Y10982, 29 January 1731.
[100] AN, Y14088, 8 December 1761.

the mere suggestion that they be forced to share a table. A plaintiff described himself being put at a table by the tavern waiter but found two other customers also sitting there. Upon asking them to "move to the end of the table and make room, in these terms 'Messieurs serrez la botte'," he was attacked by both customers.[101] The frictions between groups are emphasized by the nature of the sources with which we are dealing, but it is clear that a group's claim to a table was challenged at one's own risk.

Tables indeed are one of the chief clues in an inventory to the status of a wine shop. Some cabarets listed no tables at all and appear to have served wine only to take out. Otherwise the table indicates where customers might be found in a cabaret. The boutique usually had tables in it, as many as three or four, though there is no indication of their size. Most rooms did list chairs, usually upholstered, and stools, usually covered with straw, but many tables also had a bench or two of uncertain size. If there was no bench, the number of chairs and stools per table was between three and five, so these were fairly small tables. The testimony in police records also gives the impression of small tables. Witnesses spoke only rarely of having to share a table with a separate group. If the average table was large enough for four persons, then it was suited to the average group of customers. Rooms generally contained two to four tables, although only iconographic evidence gives us any real indication of their dimensions.

Most of the pictures of Parisian taverns available today show the enormous rooms of a guinguette, usually that of Ramponeau's.[102] There we see over a dozen tables in a room, each long enough to hold a dozen or so customers on each side. These pictures may not have represented the norm, and indeed Ramponeau took pride in the gargantuan proportions of his establishment and advertised its unusual size. Yet the inventory of

[101] AN, Y 10987, 9 January 1741.
[102] Various examples of these engravings can be found at the BN, *éstampes*, and at the Musée Carnavalet. See Figures 3.1 and 3.2.

119

another guinguette in 1751 listed twenty-eight tables in its garden in addition to the thirteen inside.[103] Nor was Ramponeau's the largest establishment, by volume of sales, in his suburb.[104] A picture of what is more likely to have been an urban cabaret shows a very different scene (see Figure 2.3). The shoproom in front has only a counter and the only customers in the shoproom have bottles, which they presumably will fill and take home with them. A door behind the counter leads to a room containing one table around which four men are drinking. The room seems large enough to hold several other tables, but the artist has chosen to leave them out. Thus the proportions of the scene are probably right: the table for four, and the room big enough for two or three tables. Yet the artist wished to emphasize the privacy of the drinking group by putting it alone in a room. In reality the rooms were often more crowded, but the evidence of witnesses betrays a desire to achieve a certain privacy, in the midst of a public space, or at least a degree of isolation around each drinking group.

This picture is also too spare in what it shows of the cabaret's furnishings. Most inventories mentioned tapestries on the walls, some of them running the circumference of a room. The tapestry seems to have taken the place of pictures, of which there is no mention. Many cabaret rooms would also have contained a variety of wardrobes, chests, fountains, beds, and barrels.

The picture does include one essential feature of the furnishings: the measuring utensils. On the shelf next to the wine merchant are the pots that he used to measure and serve wine to his customers. The measures then served as pitchers, which customers took to their tables to pour wine into their own glasses. The measures came in three sizes: the pinte, of 0.931 liters, was slightly smaller than a modern quart. The chopine

---

[103] AN, MC, XXVIII-323, 23 August 1751.
[104] See AN, Z^{1G} 343^B (1771).

FIGURE 2.3
The cabaret. (Phot. Bibl. nat. Paris)

was half that size, and the demi-*septier* was half the size of a cho-pine. One inventory specified their weight in pewter as being 3 pounds for a pinte, 2 for a chopine, and 1½ for a demi-sep-tier.[105] The accuracy of these measures was important to the wine merchant's reputation and to his license granted by the po-lice, who came around periodically to check his measures.

Measures were essential to selling, serving, and drinking the wine. A wine merchant, the widow Demarets, engaged in a judicial battle with a cabaretier who was renting a guinguette from her, and closed down his shop simply by taking his meas-ures away from him. The cabaretier sent his daughter, who normally ran the disputed tavern, to a neighbor to borrow some of his measures. When Demarets found out, however, she forced the neighbor, who was also renting his guinguette from her, to take them back.[106] Every inventory mentioned them, though not all were specific about the numbers of measures, saying only 58 pounds of pewter measures, of fine quality, or 130 pounds of common pewter. One inventory, of a guinguette near Bercy, specified a 12 pintes, 14 chopines, and 8 demi-sep-tiers in his tavern, enough for three dozen groups of cus-tomers.[107] Another cabaret listed 24 pintes, 20 chopines, 6 demi-septiers and 36 glasses, used to serve an establishment of four rooms and twelve tables.[108]

A kitchen and the tools of a kitchen such as a *tourne brochette*, a pan, the andirons, and so forth were much in evidence in in-ventories, although in some cases the "kitchen" was simply the end of the shop screened off from the tables and the counter. In any case it is clear that food was prepared in cabarets, although it is not clear for whom. Inventories included knives and forks, usually in some quantity, so customers obviously ate there. In-deed the stolen utensils provoked more than a few complaints

[105] AN, MC, LXI-451, 1 July 1751.
[106] AN, Y15238, 12 October 1731.
[107] AN, MC, XXVIII-323, 6 August 1751.
[108] Arch. Seine, D4B⁶ 5-222, 6 February 1743.

of theft from cabaret owners. The ability to serve food, with "tablecloth and plate," had long distinguished cabaret owners from taverniers, and was a prized privilege. But a right so jealously sought may not have been much used. The food such as salads, fish, artichokes, and chickens that people in judicial testimony mentioned having eaten generally came from a cookshop or an inn (the *rotisseur* or *aubergiste*) rather than having been prepared by the cabaret owner.[109] Some people brought their dinners from home, others sent the cabaret waiter to the cookshop, although occasional account books reveal meals regularly prepared for customers.[110] At the same time, the guild of restaurant owners (*traiteurs*) brought frequent complaints against cabaret owners who served banquets to large companies of people—a right the restaurant owners claimed.

The interiors of some cabarets were enlivened by designs and paintings on the walls. Cartoon drawings and stick figures adorn the walls above the tables in the few engravings of taverns that we still have. The decorations of one guinguette, the Tambour Royal run by the famous Ramponeau in the Basse Courtille suburb, are particularly crude, little more than graffiti. The depictions include a soldier beating a drum (the tambour royal), a woman off to the side, a dog, a man; all are isolated and shown two dimensionally. Around the figures words are scrawled—identifying, slanging, punning, and rhyming. The words are the key to these scenes, as the complaint brought to the police by a young man named Godefroy makes clear.

Godefroy first heard about the picture from the grocer who was serving him some brandy. The grocer had been told by someone "whom he did not recognize but thought was from the

<hr/>

[109] Nicolas Contat, *Anecdotes typographiques où l'on voit la description des coutumes, moeurs et usages singuliers des compagnons imprimeurs*, ed. Giles Barber (Oxford, 1980), p. 38, describes the trip to buy food, which was then taken to the tavern for a ritual feast, and suggests that wine merchants would have charged too much for the same food.

[110] See, for example, Arch. Seine, D5B⁶, 1712, although even here some entries say "for the rotisseur."

quarter," and who had come in to drink some brandy, that one of the pictures on the wall of the beer seller, Berthaut, who lived on the same street, resembled Godefroy. Godefroy and the grocer went to see for themselves, and the grocer assured Godefroy that the picture did not look like him. But Godefroy took it for a picture of himself, "which surprised the [grocer] since he knew that the figure had been made from the imagination of the painter without an order from Berthaut, the same figure that he had made in other places, without a similar name, and in different guinguettes." Two days earlier a journeyman cabinetmaker had been drinking beer at Berthaut's and had seen the same figure that he had recognized as Godefroy, "having bowlegs like him and playing the violin, which Godefroy did daily on the doorstep of his house."

More importantly the caption under the figure identified it as Godefroy and included some unflattering remarks. The journeyman took this information to Godefroy's mother, a widow of a bourgeois de Paris, who asked him to return and transcribe the words under the picture. He went back and, while he had some more beer, copied the caption: "the Sieur Godefroy hunchbacked, crooked, and misshaped; ready to drink and never drunk; they [?] are like carriages for they are never content, always to drink at the symphony large glasses [of?] brandy; a dog and a beggar." The mother, on hearing this, had an attorney take her complaint to the commissaire of the quarter, charging that "all the people of the quarter who drink at Berthaut's see this figure and read the writing and recognize Godefroy, which is a most palpable affront to him, and because he is interested in seeing such an insult erased he has recourse" to the law.

Among other witnesses who had talked to Godefroy and had testified about the case, there was some disagreement about the nature of the figure. A master sculptor and a bourgeois to whom Godefroy had complained separately about the figure had both objected that the figure did not resemble him. Yes, they had seen it on several occasions, they testified, but after all Godefroy did not have bowlegs, nor did he play the violin. Still, there was the name on the figure, which leant weight to Godefroy's complaint.[111]

Meanwhile Berthaut had complained in his turn, two days later to a different commissaire.[112] He had employed a painter named Raphael to repaint his shop. Raphael was employed most willingly "by the whole quarter," particularly because of his "dangling emblems." The figure that he had painted could be found in "practically all of his paintings in beer shops and guinguettes in the faubourgs." When Berthaut's wife was asked about it, she merely replied that there was more than one Godefroy in Paris. But in fact she did not know how to read or write, and when she learned that Godefroy was a neighbor and that the picture was causing "discussions in the neighborhood," she had it erased.

Raphael's emblems, his childish cartoons, may well be the ones dangling from the walls of Ramponeau's guinguette in the engraving. At least there is reason to believe that Raphael had made the engraving itself, for one copy has "par Raphael fecit" scrawled on it.[113] The fact that the figures on Ramponeau's walls did not have the name Godefroy on them suggests that the incident at Berthaut's beer shop was more than an accident. The Berthaut's, or a customer for that matter, could have added the name out of spite or rivalry, as Godefroy's complaint charged. Perhaps the popularity of Raphael's art lay in the opportunities it offered to any customer to pursue the politics of everyday life in satirical cartooning, and pursue it in a public forum so that the "whole quarter" would soon be discussing it.

However much we can visualize the tavern by relying on iconography and occasional descriptions of witnesses or inventories, we have little information about its effect on the other

[111] AN, Y15055, 12 June 1751.
[112] AN, Y15348, 14 June 1751.
[113] BN, éstampes, Oa 545, vol. 2, p. 7.

senses. No one bothered to describe the tavern's odors, but it could not have smelled much better than the rest of the city. Although there are pictures from the period of people urinating in corners of taverns, many witnesses report trips to the garden or the street "pour lacher de l'eau." When one customer employed a bucket of ashes inside the tavern for that purpose, he was set upon by the tavern waiters.[114] There is little indication in police records of customers being sick or vomiting from too much drink, although again contemporary etchings occasionally show someone vomiting in the background. Then there was the smoke of candles and fires, the reek of spilled wine, the smell of food. What was not so common was the smell of tobacco. Pipes were mentioned very rarely, and visitors from Holland noted that cafés in Paris (with more upper-class clientele) differed from Dutch coffee houses in the absence of tobacco.[115] In one of the few examples of an individual smoking, the customers objected to the smell and forced him to move to a different room.[116] Yet the inventories of several cafés referred to tobacco. The smell of a fire drew some customers in search of warmth, though customers in a more private room upstairs might be asked to pay for their firewood.

Visitors to the city were fond of complaining about the noise in the streets. It must have subsided during the night, however, for the cabaret appeared often enough in police courts for having disturbed people's repose. Neighbors complained of the music, singing, dancing, swearing, shouting, and fighting. One witness was able to identify a defendant as the man whose voice she "heard at nights in the cabaret behind her house."[117]

---

[114] AN, Y12115, 6 December 1711; AN, MC, xxviii-221, 24 April 1731, notes a bucket "à lacher de l'eau" in the courtyard.

[115] J. C. Nemeitz, *Les Séjours de Paris: instructions fidèles pour les voyageurs de condition* (1727), reedited by Alfred Franklin as *La Vie de Paris sous la régence* (Paris, 1897), p. 52.

[116] AN, Y11178, 13 June 1761.

[117] AN, Y14877, 21 November 1691. Neighbors complained of a "party of people playing the tambourine, which disturbed their repose" (Y9538, 8 July

People were certainly loud enough to be heard through the walls, as witnesses could attest, but most appeared to ignore what groups at neighboring tables were saying with little trouble.

As for the sense of touch, the utensils were mostly of pewter, as were the pitchers and occasionally the cups. Some customers drank from glasses, however, as the bills for broken glass attest. Cabarets typically had cupboards full of plates and cups of tin, too cheap to be detailed in inventories. Tables were of chestnut or pine; chairs were simple stools or benches, sometimes with cloth on them, but more often with straw. The adjective "old" described this furniture frequently enough to suggest the cabaret's generally crude appearance.

None of the cabarets described above would qualify as elegant or grand. The furnishings were generally simple, cheap, and fairly sparse. Little more was needed than tables and chairs and the odd cabinet. Tapestries were the only concessions to decoration. Perhaps the largest wine merchants aspired to something more refined, but the cabaret owner appears to have been a relatively modest businessman. Certainly his shop would not have made the artisan feel uncomfortable or out of place.

The establishments of other drink sellers, especially of beer sellers, were often even simpler than the cabaret. The police had to raid a *tabac*, where tobacco and beer were sold, after a man was killed there. They found only two rooms, with three tables in each and marks on the tables where the tobacco was chopped. The cellar held a single barrel of beer.[118] A shop as sparsely furnished and supplied as this one took little capital to operate and so it was not uncommon to find them operated by an artisan's wife in her spare time.

The café is much harder to characterize than the cabaret. The

---

1721). Others complained of singing and trumpets until three in the morning (Y9538, 27 October 1724).

[118] AN, Y14499, 18 December 1691.

café's decor was less uniform, its ambience less predictable, and its clientele, as we shall see later, came from a greater range of social groups. At first glance the café symbolized elite, literate, political society, the haunt of debating clubs, of newspaper readers, of agitators. An anonymous pamphlet in 1700 spoke of the "honnêtes gens" in cafés: "gallant men, flirtatious women, elegant abbés . . . warriors, newsmongers, officers. . . ."[119] Diderot situated *Rameau's Nephew* in a café of the Palais Royal frequented by the hero and other aspiring authors. The artisan Ménétra claims to visit a café with Rousseau—one of the very few trips to a café that the artisan mentions in his journal.[120] Plays, poetry, and stories carefully associated the café with the upper levels of society. The iconography of cafés, though hardly extensive for Paris, reinforces this image of elegance. The customers are well dressed, they are reading newspapers or quietly conversing, and the room is luxuriously furnished with crystal, mirrors, chandeliers, and marble. This is the very picture of serene good taste (see Figure 2.4 and 2.5). The rooms shown in other pictures of cafés display similar objects. This decor contrasts strikingly with the simple, vulgar, often shabby interiors of cabarets. The mirrors of the café reflected elite society in its complacency and its splendor, whereas the walls of the guinguette derided popular society with their cartoons.

Not all cafés enjoyed such luxury or catered exclusively to elite clientele. The poor drank at cafés as well as the rich, though probably not as often (the judicial archives, analyzed in the following chapter, suggest that the middle and upper levels of society were twice as likely to drink in cafés as were the laboring classes). Nevertheless, the laboring classes could indeed be found there, at certain cafés at any rate, and more often late at night than during the evening.

[119] Cited in Fosca, *Histoire des cafés*, p. 14.
[120] Ménétra, *Journal*, p. 219.

FIGURE 2.4
The café. (Phot. Bibl. nat. Paris)

The inventories of cafés, even a small number of them, make
the range of possible decors perfectly evident. The café of Jean-
Baptiste Lemoine, for example, was clearly one of the hand-
somest, with no rival among wine shops. The mirrors on his
walls alone were worth more than the total furnishings of many
cabarets. The counter and ten tables all had marble tops and
were evaluated at 450 livres—more than five times the value of
a counter and tables in a cabaret.[121] A clock in the café cost Lemoine 560 livres, and three chandeliers, of Bohemian crystal
worth a total of 1,500 livres, hung from the ceilings. The coffee spoons and coffeepots were of silver, and the coffee cups of
porcelain. The value of this café's furnishings was probably

[121] The value of the mirrors was 1,500 livres. Tables in cabarets generally cost
between 1 and 2 livres and counters could cost 24 to 70 livres. Arch. Seine,
D4B⁶ 20-971, 23 August 1759.

FIGURE 2.5

Vue intérieure du café de Manouri. (Photographie Bulloz)

four to five times that of the average cabaret, with the difference being a matter of elegance and quality of furnishing rather than size.[122]

Indeed the size of cafés seems to have been somewhat smaller than that of cabarets. Another inventory describes a café near the central markets with an interior as rich as Lemoine's, and all of its eight marble-topped tables, the mirrors, the crystal chandeliers, the marble-topped counter, and two armoires were in a single room. A back room, which contained some tools and measures but no tables, and the upstairs rooms were not in use.[123] Lemoine's café also operated on the ground floor; his inventory describes nothing but personal effects in upstairs rooms. Other inventories reveal little more than a room or two in use, and an average number of seven tables per establishment.[124] Thus, the café's furnishings made it seem more exclusive than the cabaret, yet those that lacked an upstairs room could not offer the same opportunities for privacy.

The wealth demonstrated by some cafés was not shared by all. Some inventories describe cafés similar in many ways to cabarets. The tables and counter of the café owner Jacques Briet were all in wood; there is a single mirror on the wall, the measures are of pewter, and no silver is listed. Little distinguishes this café from a cabaret, except perhaps the fayence pots that served to measure beer. The café on the rue St. Antoine owned by LeRoux was slightly more elegant, but not much. The five

---

[122] Lemoine's furnishings come to 5,850 livres. There were also three "apartments" listed on the floors above, which do not appear to have been public rooms. The value of the furnishings of a Sieur François Brisset's café on the rue St. Martin was 5,366 livres (AN, MC, LXVI-489, 14 September 1751). The master limonadier Lemarchand put the worth of his shop's furnishings at 12,000 livres (Arch. Seine, D4B⁶ 3-163, 27 November 1741). The average cost of furnishings in thirty-one cabarets (see references in notes 45, 59, and 95) was 959 livres. Burstin, *Le Faubourg St. Marcel*, p. 167, has calculated an average of 700 livres for (three?) taverns in the faubourg St. Marcel in 1789.

[123] AN, Y11959, 15 July 1771.

[124] Arch. Seine, D4B⁶ 3-163, 27 November 1741; AN, MC, XXVIII-320, 24 January 1751; AN, Y11218, 2 December 1731; Y11218, 3 June 1731.

tables and the counter were all in wood, the eighteen stools appear "some in good shape, some in bad." Yet he had two mirrors, and the coffeepots and a dozen coffee spoons were silver. In all, the furnishings of this establishment were set at 1,000 livres—no more than the average cabaret.[125]

The development of the café at the end of the seventeenth century attests both to the growing popularization of the cabaret and to the elite's determination to gather separately from its social inferiors. An historian writing about one of the first cafés, the café Procope, noted that Procope "understood that to succeed, the café had to become something other than the popular cabaret. On the walls he hung mirrors, a great luxury at the time, from the ceilings he hung crystal chandeliers, and set out marble tables."[126] The results were evidently successful for he was widely copied. According to the eighteenth-century *Dictionnaire de commerce*, "the cafés of Paris are mostly retreats magnificently adorned with marble tables, mirrors and crystal chandeliers, where numbers of respectable folk gather as much for the pleasure of conversation and to learn the news as to drink [coffee]."[127] They were "often visited," a traveler from the 1720s tells us, "by princes and other great personages."[128] Marble, crystal, and mirrors evidently acted as the primary tokens of a café's social identity, yet several inventories listed nothing more than a mirror or two. Thus it is clearly impossible to assert that all cafés aimed at an elite clientele. The disparity in elegance and ambience must have distinguished the café on the rue St. Antoine from the elite cafés of the Palais Royal, where men of letters came to meet.

Over the course of the eighteenth century, public drinking

[125] AN, Y11218, 3 June 1731; MC, XXVIII-320, 24 January 1751. Furnishings valued at 1,200 livres in a café at the Marché neuf did not include any mirrors or other marks of elegance; MC, XCIII-22, 13 May 1751.

[126] Fosca, *Histoire des cafés*, p. 8.

[127] Savary des Bruslons, *Dictionnaire de commerce*, s.v. "café."

[128] Nemeitz, *Les Séjours de Paris*, p. 51.

places assumed a variety of styles and sizes, yet certain themes can be applied to all of them. The primacy of wine was still clear but no longer unchallenged. New kinds of drink were being served and new institutions emerged to serve them. This diversification provided several opportunities in the evolution of the drinking place. New establishments, particularly the café, took the opportunity to develop a very different style of furnishing and a new ambience in an effort to appeal to a more select audience. Thus the emergence of elegant drinking places may perhaps have manifested a growing desire for social exclusiveness, an elite urge to gather separately and to distinguish elite locations more clearly. Not all cafés achieved this goal. Some cafés were a good deal less than sumptuous, and some were patronized by the poor.

It was not simply the new drinks offered in cafés, the coffee and liqueurs, that set them apart. Artisans drank coffee too and went to places selling brandy that had a very different style from that of the café. The various brandy sellers, all antedating the café in origin, appear to have copied the tavern's style, rather than trying to escape it. This may have been an effort to legitimate their commerce and attract the same clientele as the tavern. Here it would seem that style was used to cover a difference in substance, in merchandise. The guinguette, on the other hand, changed its style without really changing its merchandise. The wine was cheaper but it was still wine and would appeal to the same wine-drinking artisans and to the poor. The guinguette, however, evolved its own style of openness and scale. It appealed consciously to all classes and conditions, presenting itself as a place for the great to rub shoulders with the poor. Yet in the end its clientele was somewhat inferior, if anything, to the tavern's clientele. For the trend in all these institutions was toward greater social divisions, whether intended, as with the café, or not, as with the guinguette.

Regardless of distinctions, all such drinking establishments responded to the universal demand for drink and a place to gather. As with any retail, meeting this demand depended on a logistical chain of differing degrees of complexity. The need for inventory, which in the case of wine merchants was often worth more than the furnishings, and for credit made this kind of retail a risky venture. But the enormous demand produced hundreds of men and women interested in running a tavern, some with little capital or experience. As a consequence, Paris blossomed with public drinking places, each providing a social arena in addition to its wares. The very success of these institutions led, paradoxically, to their appropriation by their customers. For, as the following chapters attempt to demonstrate, the essence of the tavern, once the basic elements of wine and space were provided, lay in its use by the people of Paris for their public sociability.

Three. Customers and Their Leisure

Taverns performed an important social function above and beyond their provisioning role. By providing customers with a place to drink, they created an arena to be appropriated by the populace for its social and communal needs. For public drinking was fundamentally a social act, bringing men and occasionally women together for recreation and association. By giving structure to the popular uses of leisure, to public comportment and sociability, public drinking teaches us about the nature of urban communities and of popular culture. The social significance of taverns depends, as a consequence, on who their customers were and the manner in which they employed this space. Contemporary evidence reveals a disjunction in the perspectives of elite and popular commentators on this basic question. Elite attitudes, noted already in the context of violence in taverns, characterized men and women in taverns as contemptible people on the margins of society and dismissed the institution in the same breath. The experience of daily life embedded in the judicial records, however, offers an alternative expression of the tavern's place in Parisian society. The primary aim of this chapter, and indeed of this study, is to demonstrate that taverns were still, in the eighteenth century, an integral part of popular culture.

The archival evidence of public drinking also sheds light on the growing elaboration of drinking places discussed in the preceding chapter. The old regime seems to have witnessed profound changes in popular culture and leisure, and indeed the roughly simultaneous appearance of both the café and the guinguette at the end of the seventeenth century clearly presaged some shift in behavior. The replacement of one beverage and one public institution at which to drink it with many beverages and a variety of institutions suggests a growing stratification and segregation among drinking places. The emerging distinctions of size, decor, and location between different kinds of taverns further shaped their social functions, attracting certain kinds of customers, at particular times, for different pursuits. The judicial records offer some idea of how Parisians responded to these changes. This evolution in the popular use of taverns over the eighteenth century reveals changes in popular culture as well. Historians point to a growing social and cultural segregation in early modern society, a tendency by the elites, during the seventeenth and eighteenth centuries, to withdraw from contact with popular culture and the populace.[1] And one aspect of this trend was the elite expressions of disdain for popular locations and patterns of recreation.

Literary sources offer a fairly clear model of the transformation in the tastes of literate, and particularly literary, society. They assure us that writers, gentlemen, and the upper classes frequented cabarets before the eighteenth century.[2] Poems and paeans to the cabaret and *taverne* exist in sufficient quantity to allow historians to identify the favorite cabarets of Molière and Ronsard, and some of the drinking places haunted by lesser authors. Writers in the sixteenth and seventeenth centuries were not loath to pen a drinking song or ode to wine. But their descendants wrote no more of cabarets in the following century. With the introduction of the first cafés, literary society abandoned cabarets in favor of the new establishment; "the café, from its birth, is a literary café." Wine is no longer the source of inspiration. Now coffee gives "spirit" to the writer.[3]

[1] Peter Burke, *Popular Culture*, pp. 207-286. Isherwood, *Farce and Fantasy*, passim, argues persuasively that certain forms of entertainment, particularly theaters, attracted a socially heterogeneous audience. I am less persuaded that popular and elite culture were merging.

[2] La Fizilière, *Vins à la mode*, passim; M. Magendie, *La Politesse mondaine* (Paris, 1925), p. 511. Gregory Austin, *Alcohol in Western Society* (Santa Barbara, 1985), pp. 164, 199, has collected some of these sources.

[3] Leclant, "Le Café et les cafés à Paris," pp. 1, 8.

Commentators at the end of the old regime and since have shared this view that the urban wine shop, the cabaret, was a dying institution, its carcass left to the infestations of the lowest dregs of the populace. "Before the establishment of the café," declared an anonymous author in 1787, "nearly everyone went to cabarets. . . . Since their establishment all assemble [at cafés]."[4] "Our ancestors went to cabarets," added Mercier, contrasting them with the cafés of his day.[5] A nineteenth-century historian reported likewise that "cafés, in multiplying, performed a sort of revolution in the habits of the Parisian population; they led, little by little, to disgust with cabarets and drunkenness."[6] Fougeret de Monbron, before the revolution, contended on the other hand that, whereas "formerly our fathers gathered at cabarets, . . . today no one drinks anywhere."[7] Indeed, Mercier and others agreed that even cafés were becoming unfashionable by the end of the century. Cafés "have declined greatly in the last twenty years," Restif announced. "However they will never be so degraded as cabarets."[8]

At the heart of such judgments there appears to be a consensus that public drinking places used by the populace in the eighteenth century, particularly cabarets and guinguettes, were generally quite disreputable. They have enjoyed a poor reputation among scholars since then, relegated to the margins of society and treated as peripheral institutions with an inconse-

---

[4] *Diogène à Paris* (1787), cited in P. Lacroix, *Dix-huitième siècle. Institutions, usages et coutumes* (Paris, 1875), p. 363.

[5] Mercier, *Tableau de Paris*, 1:229.

[6] Honoré Antoine Frégier, *Histoire de l'administration de la police de Paris* (Paris, 1850), 2:211.

[7] Louis-Charles Fougeret de Monbron, *Le Cosmopolite ou le citoyen du monde; suivi de la capitale des Gaules ou la nouvelle Babylonne* (Paris, 1750-1759; repr. Bordeaux, 1970), pp. 160-163. I am indebted to Catherine Lafarge for this reference and for Catherine Lafarge, "Paris and Myth: One Vision of Horror," *Studies in Eighteenth-Century Culture* 5 (1976):281-291.

[8] Restif de la Bretonne, *Les Nuits de Paris*, 1:135.

quential role.[9] Such an indictment commonly argued the tavern's marginality in three ways: socially, they suffered a disreputable clientele; temporally, they were used infrequently and for binges; and physically, they existed in the sordid backstreets or beyond the very edges of the city. Thus the clientele of taverns is routinely identified as the poor, the workers, even the dregs of society. The characterization of taverns generally as criminal, dangerous places contributes greatly, of course, to such an image. The way that Parisians supposedly used taverns provides further evidence of the institution's marginality. Customers are portrayed as going infrequently, except on Sundays or Mondays when they spent all day on a binge. "The extreme indigence of a certain part of the *peuple* has only too often its source in the expenditures made in the cabaret on Monday; every worker takes that day off," Mercier pontificated, but, "they have hardly anything except wine for consolation."[10] Such sporadic use would have been the occasion for excess, then, for the drugged escape of the miserable poor. Anything more frequent, however, becomes evidence of real debauchery, a sign of addiction and profligacy.[11]

The irregular drinking was often linked to the suburban tavern, the guinguette, whose marginality also manifested itself physically. Lying beyond the bounds of urban society, excluded from Parisians' daily life by distance and tax barriers, guinguettes became the haven of the populace, so we are told, who had not been able to drink the expensive wines sold at urban taverns. The prospect of cheaper wine in the suburbs is

[9] Emile Colombey, *Ruelles, salons, et cabarets* (Paris, 1858); Fosca, *Histoire des cafés*; La Fizilière, *Vins à la mode*; Michel and Fournier, *Histoire des hôtelleries*; Saint-Germain, *La Vie quotidienne*; Wissant, *Le Paris d'autrefois*.

[10] Mercier, *Tableau de Paris*, 10:208.

[11] Kaplow, *The Names of Kings*, p. 106; Mandrou, *Introduction*, pp. 302-303. Lottin, *Chavatte*, p. 346, notes that the seventeenth-century artisan, Chavatte, "haunted" cabarets regularly. He worries that this might suggest an "exaggerated penchant for drink," but decides that Chavatte was representative of his milieu.

supposed to have galvanized the laboring classes, according to most accounts of Parisian life, leading to a massive migration to the countryside each Sunday by the city's inhabitants.[12] With a whole day to spend at the end of the week, the poor were free to accomplish their purported goal, that of drinking themselves into a stupor on the untaxed wine outside of the city. This resulted, so it was claimed, in orgies on Sunday and perhaps again on Monday, followed by hangovers and the general dissolution of public morals. According to the Marquis de Mirabeau, "The entire population of Paris leaves the city on holidays [to go to guinguettes]. . . . Half of the people come back drunk, gorged with adulterated wine, paralyzed for three days. . . ."[13] The culprit was cheap wine, evidently, as well as the lower classes' desire for as much or more alcohol as they could afford to consume on a drunken spree. Of the urban cabaret, the neighborhood tavern, the literature on popular culture has much less to say, except perhaps that the populace abandoned it in favor of guinguettes.[14] Likewise, the bourgeois eschewed it in preference to picnics in the park. Thus abandoned by contemporaries and trivialized by subsequent accounts, taverns appear irrelevant to the central issues of urban culture and society.

There are good reasons, however, for reevaluating the tavern's status. Historians are learning to treat elite evidence about popular culture with growing caution, noting that it testifies as

[12] George Rudé, *The Crowd in the French Revolution* (Oxford, 1959), p. 15; Kaplow, *The Names of Kings*, pp. 78-79; Braudel, *Capitalism and Material Life*, pp. 162-175. More recently, however, Farge and Zysberg, "Les Théâtres de la violence," p. 1007, have commented that people went to guinguettes "to amuse themselves, to dance, and not only to get drunk or fornicate as Mercier claims."

[13] Marquis de Mirabeau, *L'Ami des hommes ou traité de la population* (Paris, 1756) 1883 ed., pp. 86-87, quoted in Robert Forster and Elborg Forster, *European Society in the Eighteenth Century* (New York, 1969), p. 81.

[14] Lachiver, *Vin, vigne et vignerons*, p. 261. Braudel, *Capitalism and Material Life*, p. 166, for example, claims that "mass consumption [of alcohol] became general with the establishment of the guinguettes at the gates of Paris," as if the populace drank only there.

often as not to elite perceptions and misconceptions about an increasingly foreign milieu.[15] When a Restif or a Mercier suggested that the cabaret was abandoned in favor of the café, they meant of course that it was abandoned by respectable society. Yet the memoirs of an eighteenth-century Parisian artisan named Ménétra provide a very different perspective. A striking fact about Ménétra is his constant reliance on cabarets and guinguettes for his professional, social, and amorous pursuits. This "journal of my life," as he called it, yields concrete evidence, whether the historian wishes to treat it as largely fact or predominantly literature, of the important role of taverns in the social existence of the Parisian laboring classes.[16] The sheer number of taverns and their economic health also belie the standard portrayal of their demise. Their pervasiveness throughout the city argues as well against their marginality.

The evidence in judicial records of violence in taverns, while ostensibly a further indication of their marginality, suggests instead that taverns played a crucial role in public and communal life. Judicial records also reveal the extent to which Parisians relied on taverns in their daily existence. For the thousands of men and women who left their mark in the judicial archives, as for Ménétra, the tavern continued to be central to their society and communities. These people testify to the importance of taverns in their lives and, as reasonably representative elements of Parisian society, in the life of the city.

The men and women who appear, however briefly, in the judicial records form the basis of this study of taverns and of popular culture. As the chapter on violence has argued, these plain-

---

[15] Burke, *Popular Culture*, pp. 65-76. An example of this approach that I have found particularly illuminating is the treatment of Villermé in Sewell, *Work and Revolution in France*, pp. 223-232. The point is central, of course, to recent studies of witchcraft; see, for example, Muchembled, *Culture populaire*, pp. 287-340.

[16] A reference to drinking in a tavern occurs roughly once in every three pages of his recollections; Ménétra, *Journal*, passim; see also Roche's discussion of Ménétra's behavior, pp. 374-375.

tiffs and defendants came from every level of Parisian society, particularly the laboring classes, and should be allowed to speak for that society. The men and women who availed themselves of the commissaires' services to defend their honor and reputation expressed, by this action, a strong sense of their own place in their communities. The defendants in these archives—those accused of assault, slander, or theft—were scarcely less respectable. Indeed their assaults and slander were often provoked by the same sense of reputation and ambition for power and status that inspired the complaints against them. It is important to realize, too, that these aspirations, emerging in most articulate fashion from the middle ranks of society, were also shared by the laboring poor, who enjoyed less access to institutional sources of status and honor yet who evinced a strong sense of reputation and standing among their peers and their own communities. The plaintiffs and defendants encountered in the preceding analysis of public disorder were also anxious to provide information about their sociability. Their testimony usually attempted to establish the peaceful, sociable nature of their behavior, before it was interrupted by their assailants' attack. Like their evidence about an assault, the image of fellowship they portray is undoubtedly exaggerated, yet it too instructs us about norms and expectations.

As this study shifts its focus from violence to sociability, it can extend its net to include a wider cast of characters. The plaintiffs and accused were not the only tavern customers to make an appearance in judicial archives. Indeed half of the men and women whom the records identified in taverns were neither plaintiffs nor accused but rather bore witness or were simply mentioned in testimony. Few tavern customers appear to have drunk alone; indeed most came to the tavern with two or three companions. These companions—whether they were friends, acquaintances, strangers, or enemies—were nearly always mentioned by the plaintiff in his complaint, though not necessarily identified individually. Because the public nature of the tavern, the presence of peers and neighbors, was central to the aggravation and offense experienced by a plaintiff, he was careful to record the presence of an audience. He might also request the corroboration of witnesses if the crime was serious enough and if he intended to pursue his suit.[17] Witnesses in their turn shed light on the identity of their companions and frequently offered information about their activities before and during their tavern visit.

These people provide further vital evidence about the nature of tavern clients and their culture. Their appearance in the archives resulted not from their own passions but from chance and circumstances beyond their control, thus posing different problems of interpretation than those raised by the actual protagonists. Who could be a witness? Who was willing to be?[18] How independent were either witnesses or those merely mentioned in testimony from the protagonists who registered a complaint? This second cast of characters offers little information about the nature of violence or criminality and indeed they are ignored in most studies of crime. Since this study is devoted as much to sociability as to criminality and to the elements of recreation, social reproduction, and play, the noncontentious patrons of taverns—the bystanders, friends, and witnesses— yield information as valuable as that provided by the contenders.

Plaintiffs obviously turned first to companions and friends as witnesses, yet witnesses were not solely a reflection of the plaintiffs' associates. Nearly two-thirds of the witnesses had been sitting separately from either plaintiff or accused. Because the

[17] One plaintiff described making no retort to repeated insults, "having only taken some people of the company [other patrons in the tavern probably, as he made no mention of companions] as witnesses to the insult" (AN, Y10993b, 9 September 1751). In theory witnesses were paid the cost of the work they missed while making a deposition. In practice some refused the offer.

[18] Isambert, *Recueil général*, 18:382, ordonnance de 1670, defines the basic procedures for witnesses, in particular: "heard secretly and separately and will sign their depositions after it has been read [back to them]."

choice of a witness was often that of the plaintiff, we may be certain that they were not selected randomly from among tavern customers; however, only one-third were among the plaintiff's drinking companions. The police or guard also might solicit testimony if they came upon the scene of an incident. In either case the witnesses' testimony in the judicial records certainly depended on different motives and circumstances than the passions of the plaintiffs. On the other hand two-thirds of those who were merely mentioned in testimony were sitting with one or the other of the protagonists, more often with the accused. Clearly neither witnesses nor bystanders wholly escape a bias of some kind, yet overall nearly one-half of the noncontentious individuals in taverns actually drank separately and apart from the contenders. The independence of so many witnesses and bystanders from those involved in disputes is significant, for these people belong more obviously to the larger world of those who managed to use taverns peacefully day after day.

The noncontentious tavern customers in these records bore a striking similarity to the men directly involved in disputes. Taken as a group, they reflect essentially the same cross section of society as the contenders. The plaintiff evidently turned most often to his peers for support since, as a group, witnesses were very close to plaintiffs in social makeup. The composition of customers who were merely mentioned, on the other hand, is harder to identify because almost one-half of these bystanders were not identified by profession or social status. Of those who were identified, however, the social composition was similar to that of the men who were accused (see Table 3.1).[19]

---

[19] The 841 missing observations come largely from those in the "mentioned" category, where the testimony may only have noted that someone had been present without giving a profession. There is little reason to think that one social group or another was systematically excluded in that circumstance. The judicial roles of the 530 women were distributed in nearly the same pattern, although they were less often witnesses than merely mentioned.

TABLE 3.1
Judicial Roles of Male Tavern Customers

	Plaintiff	Accused	Plaintiff and Accused	Witness	Bystanders	Total
Noble	15	21	1	11	6	54
Bourgeois	79	63	6	76	44	268
Shopkeeper	61	59	8	76	49	253
Master artisan	139	160	20	145	107	571
Artisan[a]	74	139	10	114	92	429
Journeyman	91	190	13	105	140	539
Day laborer	71	162	11	97	68	409
Domestic	47	83	15	50	71	266
Soldier	42	140	3	40	123	348
TOTAL (N)	619	1017	87	714	700	3137
Status unknown	27	182	3	13	616	841

[a] The artisan without any indication of professional rank (identified by Daumard and Furet, *Structures et relations sociales*, as a "gen de métier au statut indéterminé").

It is clearly impossible to escape completely the violent origins of this evidence, even when considering bystanders, but the archives yield information from a very different perspective as well. The majority of tavern customers recorded in judicial archives were involved, not surprisingly, in some kind of tavern disorder. Yet it was not unusual for witnesses and testimony in other kinds of judicial cases to refer to individuals having visited taverns either before or after an unrelated incident. Without contributing much insight to the nature of violence in taverns, such information does shed added light on tavern sociability. Such cases add 876 individuals to the 3,632 men and women involved in tavern violence.[20] The customers in these cases usually enjoyed relative tranquillity in their visits, since the contentions they were reporting occurred elsewhere. They may be deemed, then, to be closer to the average customer in this respect.

[20] These judicial records augment the 932 incidents used to study tavern violence in Chapter One by a further 284 cases. Nearly three-quarters of the individuals from nontavern cases were witnesses or just mentioned.

When we consider all the plaintiffs, defendants, witnesses, and bystanders—whether involved in tavern disturbances or not—in the aggregate, the 4,508 tavern customers drawn from the records offer a tangible alternative to the common stereotype of the tavern customer as a wretched, even dangerous, figure. The male customers numbered 3,978, or 88 percent of the total, and a classification of this group by social standing reflects the overall social structure of the Parisian population fairly closely.[21] Over two-thirds (70 percent) labored with their

[21] A comparison with the social composition of Paris is extremely difficult, given the paucity of suitable records for Paris. The simplest approach is probably to compare the status of tavern customers with that of the men mentioned in the marriage contracts of 1749 recorded by Daumard and Furet, *Structures et relations sociales*, pp. 18-19. For the 2,165 men in Daumard and Furet and the 3,137 male tavern customers, the respective percentages are 22 and 10 percent for the elites, 26 and 26 percent for master artisans/shopkeepers, 14 and 14 percent for unspecified artisans, 21 and 30 percent for journeymen/day laborers, 16 and 8 percent for domestics, and 1 and 11 percent for soldiers. The elites would appear to be badly underrepresented and soldiers heavily overrepresented in taverns, yet Daumard and Furet recognize the bias in their source toward the upper end of the social scale. In contrast, using the taxe des pauvres, François Furet, "Structures sociales parisiennes au milieu du XVIIIᵉ siècle: l'apport d'une série fiscale," *Annales, économies, sociétés, civilizations* 16 (1961):945-958, reports only 14 percent in the top four tax brackets, which correspond to the same elite groups. Again, however, Furet notes that "an important part of the popular classes escaped" this tax and suggests that only half of the heads of household were actually counted. Another way to approach the problem involves estimating the number of men in Paris and comparing the number to figures for guild members, domestics, and so forth. Unfortunately, even the total population is disputed. Steven L. Kaplan, *Bread, Politics and Political Economy* (The Hague, 1976), 1:33, maintains that "most historians today prefer a figure between 6 and 700,000 around the mid-century," although he notes that other respected historians put it at less than 600,000. More recently Roche, *Le Peuple de Paris*, p. 33, settles for 500,000 in 1700 and roughly 650,000 at the Revolution. If 600,000 can be taken as a compromise figure for the population at mid-century, determining the composition of the population is still difficult. For male tavern customers should be compared with the male half of Paris (perhaps 300,000) and with the adult males—probably 55 to 60 percent, judging from figures in Peter Laslett, *The World We Have Lost* (New York, 1968), p. 108; Jean-Claude Perrot, *Genèse d'une ville moderne: Caen au XVIIIe siècle* (Paris, 1975), 1:138; Roger Mols, "Population in Europe 1500-1700," in Carlo M. Cipolla, ed., *The Fontana Economic History of Europe* (Glasgow, 1974), 2:51; and Kaplow, *The Names of Kings*, p. 81—of about 170,000. Thus 35,000 master artisans and shop-

TABLE 3.2
Social Standing of Male Tavern Customers by Year

	1691	1701	1711	1721	1731	1741	1751	1761	1771	Total
Noble	5	14	10	6	10	2	5	0	2	54
Bourgeois	28	32	25	35	26	25	53	20	24	268
Shopkeeper	22	43	15	29	15	27	50	26	26	253
Master artisan	59	117	67	44	44	68	108	35	29	571
Artisan[a]	63	63	29	26	16	40	86	61	45	429
Journeyman	53	44	36	37	51	27	130	96	65	539
Day laborer	33	23	18	30	46	38	110	59	52	409
Domestic	22	16	21	19	29	9	93	38	19	266
Soldier	43	33	32	23	39	35	72	22	49	348
TOTAL	328	385	253	249	276	271	707	357	311	3137
Status unknown	88	137	67	71	73	68	141	104	92	841

[a] See Table 3.1 for explanation and Chapter 3, note 19, for missing observations.

hands or worked at a trade, some as employers, but most (44 percent) as salaried workers (see Table 3.2). A further 9 percent served as domestics, and 11 percent more were soldiers. Only 10 percent claimed to be bourgeois or noble. The social composition of tavern customers suggests the importance of public drinking places in the society as a whole and argues strongly against the common depiction of taverns as haunts solely for the destitute.

Female tavern customers appeared far less often in the judi-

keepers, cited by Expilly, *Dictionnaire géographique*, 5:402-420, and commonly used by historians, would be 20 percent of the adult male population. The 18,878 male domestics also cited by Expilly would have been 11 percent of the adult males. Léon Cahen, using the taxe des pauvres in "La Population parisienne au milieu du XVIIIe siècle," *Revue de Paris* 16/17 (1 September 1919):146-170, estimated the number of nobles and bourgeois at 9,000 to 10,000, or 6 percent of the adult males. Estimates for the number of French and Swiss guards in Paris are roughly 7,000 to 8,000 toward the end of the century, plus more than 1,000 in the watch, guard, *maréchaussée*, and similar groups (Williams, *The Police of Paris*, pp. 68, 92), which would be 5 percent. Thus, the elites and master artisans may actually be overrepresented in taverns but the figures for Paris are clearly such rough estimates that there can be no definitive comparison. Only soldiers appear to be consistently overrepresented in taverns.

cial records, and indeed their place in the tavern was generally ambiguous. Women used the tavern differently from men and expressed certain hesitations about using it at all. The ambiguity of the woman's place lay less in the behavior of individual women, since some women used taverns no differently from men, than in the aggregate of women's experiences there. For this reason, anyone who looks randomly through the archives might well be struck by the integration of women into tavern life and by the similarity of their behavior with that of men.[22] Yet a more systematic study of these same documents reveals a striking disparity between men's and women's patterns of attendance, behavior, and treatment in the tavern. Women went to taverns significantly less often and did not use them in the same indiscriminate fashion that men did. The percentage of female customers in these records was as low as 7 percent throughout the first half of the eighteenth century and only rose to 14 percent in 1751. This surprisingly low figure does not appear to be due to any reluctance on the part of the police to take testimony from women, although some legal treatises cast aspersions on female witnesses.[23] In fact, women often gave witness to events in the neighborhood that they had observed from the windows and doors of their lodgings. The police actively solicited, up and down the street, the testimony of the women who seem to have been very aware of what went on in their neighborhoods. The conclusion must be that the tavern was not equally open to men and women and was predominantly male space.

[22] Farge, *Vivre*, p. 75, for example, claims that women were commonly found in cabarets.

[23] Ch. H. Fr. Dumont, *Nouveau style criminel* (Paris, 1778), p. 18, notes that "several authors claim that in criminal matters, women are not regarded as witnesses" but goes on to insist that their evidence be given equal weight as that of men. Nor does the number of women in taverns reflect their role in judicial cases of other kinds: Farge and Zysberg's study of violence throughout Paris, "Les Théâtres de la violence," found women were 24 percent of the plaintiffs and 7 percent of the accused.

Women did not use taverns as freely as did men and exhibited a reluctance even to enter. The husband would leave his seat and talk to his wife at the doorway, he without leaving the cabaret, she without entering.[24] A woman looking for her husband late one evening went to the cabaret "where he often passed the night gambling and lost much money." She herself did not enter but sent her son-in-law in to look for the man, and even he was prevented from searching by the "neighbors" who were playing cards in an upstairs room. Later that night she was attacked by the tavernkeeper as she passed his door.[25] To be sure, wives did not always wait outside, especially if the husband would not come out to join her, but once inside, the wife was confronted by the combined resentment of the other drinkers and of the owner. In some cases she was simply chased out. A woman looking for her husband was told by the owner that "she was certainly bold to come there, to which she responded that she would not come if it were not to look for her husband and that they would do her a favor not to receive him there any longer."[26] Few women went to cabarets unescorted, and most went with their husbands. Men acted as protectors and sponsors, providing women with an entree into a male world.

The treatment of women in taverns is a fleeting testimony, a clue at best, to the nature of their role in the tavern. In most cases women drank without incident. In many of the cases where the woman was the plaintiff, the violence done to them was of a decidedly sexual nature. One customer called out: "There is a little brunette here that I f——," to a woman in a tavern, though he did not know her.[27] Such abuse came generally from men, strangers to the women, and it suggests a desire

[24] AN, Y10837, 18 March 1720.

[25] AN, Y10732, 23 October 1701.

[26] AN, Y15133, 27 July 1701. See also Y10987, 5 December 1741; Y11218, 26 December 1731.

[27] AN, Y14671, 4 July 1751.

to reduce women to a subordinate, venal position; "letting her know he thought she was a whore," is how one complaint described it.[28] At the very least this treatment reflected a confusion over the woman's place in the tavern. How else can one explain the actions of a coachman who went up to a party of drinkers and said to one woman, completely unknown to him, "Look at this old procuress," while putting his hand on her posterior? The woman, however, was with her two sons and her husband who told the coachman that "he was wrong to say that and that this was his wife" and a fight ensued. The coachman, in his defense, insisted that she was a "whore."[29] If some of the insults were primarily the result of mistaken identities, they disclosed nonetheless a presumption that women in taverns were prostitutes.

The sixteen-year-old daughter of a bourgeois of Paris suffered similar violence when she was taken by a friend of her father's to a guinguette north of the city late one Sunday afternoon in July 1761. It is important to realize that by the end of Louis XV's reign, women could be found quite frequently in taverns, particularly in guinguettes on Sunday when everyone was dancing. She and her friend, a wine merchant, were looking for the girl's father and drank half a bottle of wine as they waited for him. A man from a table nearby had asked the girl to dance, "which she could not refuse for fear of drawing without doubt some unpleasant remark or some quarrel." The other men at the table nearby, all wearing swords, also insisted on dancing and on bringing the girl back to their table to share a drink, where the girl's escort joined them "so as not to abandon the girl." However, the men began to sing "infamous songs" and to speak indecently. When they would not let her leave, the escort went in search of the watch. By the time he returned the men had taken the girl to the house of a chevalier in their group

[28] AN, Y10139, 29 January 1751.
[29] AN, Y11238, 13 February 1751.

and raped her, the chevalier demanding his "droit de seigneur" to go first. The men, including the chevalier, an officer, and several merchant grocers, were subsequently caught and imprisoned. In their own defense, they argued that the girl was "very libertine" and that "certainly a girl who is in a cabaret at half past eleven in the evening, and who makes no difficulties offering herself to four men cannot be regarded as an abducted girl." In the end the girl's father withdrew his complaint, perhaps for fear of losing the case.[30]

The presence of women in public drinking places contributed, during the eighteenth century and since, to the tavern's infamy. The police occasionally accused taverns of harboring and organizing prostitution.[31] The accusation could even be heard in the mouths of tavern customers, as a verbal assault on a tavernkeeper who had offended them.[32] Yet the scale of the tavern's complicity in prostitution is difficult to gauge. When men spoke of prostitutes in their testimony, they had usually been stopped in the street and solicited; few looked for prostitutes in taverns. They might well then take the woman to a tavern for a drink, as part of the bargain. At the same time women in taverns generally alleged a degree of familiarity with their escorts and only rarely indicated that they did not know their partners. Most, indeed, claimed to be with husbands or friends. Thus it is nearly impossible to determine what percentage of women in taverns were prostitutes.

The woman's position in taverns is clarified somewhat by considering her age. Women in taverns tended not to be as old as male customers. On the basis of an admittedly small sample (only ninety-two individuals), the percentage of women be-

[30] AN, Y9663, 18 July 1761.

[31] See, for example, the sentence de police of 12 December 1732, in AN, Y9499; or Y9538, 22 September 1757.

[32] See, for example, the complaint of the café owner lodged against a customer who "has sought every occasion to insult the wife of the said Sieur plaintiff . . . proclaiming loudly that the home and shop are a brothel" (AN, Y14761, 10 April 1711).

TABLE 3.3
Age of Tavern Customers

Age	Men		Women	
	N	%	N	%
< 19 years	41	5	7	8
20–29	253	33	40	44
30–39	259	34	24	26
40–49	145	19	10	11
50–59	64	8	7	8
> 60	18	2	4	4
TOTAL	780		92	

tween the ages of thirty and forty-five was substantially lower than that of men in the same age group: 29 percent compared with 47 percent. If these were roughly the years of married and family life, then the records at least suggest that domestic life kept the woman away from taverns. They also suggest that wives went less often than maidens.

The male customer in these documents was, on the whole, slightly older than the women. Based on the small percentage of customers about whom details of age were given (20 percent), the average age of male customers was between thirty-three and thirty-four years; most were in their twenties or thirties. As the details of ages reveal, there were almost no teenagers (see Table 3.3).

The rarity of male customers in their teens (and there were scarcely any younger than that) is rather surprising. They may have had less disposable income, or simply other social spaces to frequent. By the time they turned nineteen or twenty years of age, however, they were becoming regulars at the tavern. Most of their drinking would be done in the two decades that followed. The man in his twenties was more likely to be unmarried than married.[33] These were the years in which he learned

33 Perrot, *Genèse d'une ville moderne*, 2:820, finds the average age at mar-

to frequent taverns, as a bachelor with his comrades. The habit died slowly; although a majority of the men who married did so by the time they were thirty, they continued to visit taverns, sometimes bringing their wives. Less than one-third of male and female tavern customers were over forty, indicating a precipitous decline in attendance. The percentage of customers in their forties was little over one-half the number in their thirties, and the amount in their fifties dropped by one-half again. Because the number of forty- and fifty-year-olds in the general population did not decrease so rapidly, it follows that the percentage of fifty-year-old men and women in the city who drank at taverns was smaller than among thirty-year-old men and women.[34] The tavern evidently became less attractive as a place to spend time as one became older.

At the same time, the tavern's male clientele was actually quite mature, despite the relative absence of customers in their fifties and sixties. A majority of the men identified here (62 percent) were thirty years or older. They were more likely to be married than not and had left behind that phase of life known as youth. The unmarried men of a city were traditionally riotous and unruly, often organized into youth groups that performed certain boisterous community rituals.[35] These youth groups were an important source of solidarity among young men and a form of civic expression for those who were not heads of households. These groups have been the subject of several excellent studies on early modern culture, but there is less

---

riage among male Caennais in the middle of the century to have been thirty; Maurice Garden, *Lyon et les lyonnais*, p. 56, reports the age to have been twenty-nine in Lyon.

[34] See Pierre Goubert, *Cent mille provinciaux au XVIIe siècle* (Paris, 1968), pp. 76-89, for a discussion of age structure in rural France at the end of the seventeenth century, and Mols, "Population in Europe," 2:49-51, for the age structure of urban Italy in the seventeenth century.

[35] See Davis, "The Reasons of Misrule," in *Society and Culture*, passim, for a discussion of youth groups.

known about the social groups or solidarities that succeeded youth groups. The age of tavern customers suggests that the tavern was an important source of company for those who were no longer youths. The tavern may perhaps have been a transitional institution for men in their twenties and thirties, weaning them from bachelorhood and the youth group and introducing them to role models of marriage, to the neighborhood or guild.

One final point about the age of customers raises questions about their social identity. Only 12 percent of the men under thirty years of age were master artisans or shopkeepers, whereas they made up 36 percent of those over thirty. Conversely, men identified as journeymen or simply artisans without specifying a rank comprised 47 percent of the customers under thirty but only 27 percent of those over thirty. It is not surprising to find that journeymen were younger on average than masters, who had to spend part of their youth serving as journeymen and apprentices. Yet the fact that journeymen under thirty were nearly twice as common as those over thirty years of age suggests that some of the young journeymen in taverns were acceding to masterships in their thirties and were thus more favored, whether by birth or wealth, than the majority of journeymen.

The general outline of tavern customers found in judicial archives points to a number of conclusions. The tavern, first of all, was primarily a popular institution. The overwhelming majority of customers belonged to the laboring classes and shared similar income, material culture, and mentalities. Thus the tavern served the needs of a definable range of people and became an integral part of their culture. The clientele was also predominantly, though not exclusively, male. Adult men are the subject of most of the rest of this study, for they imposed their comportment and their need for public space on the tavern. The need for space was an important requirement of the tavern's clientele. As men, they probably enjoyed a tenuous relation to domestic space; as working men, they could claim very little domestic space to begin with.[36] Most undoubtedly lived in a room or two, some had less. This need for space encouraged the constant reliance on the tavern in the daily lives of the laboring classes, as the patterns of attendance attest.

With only a modest sample to represent such a large part of daily life, it is difficult to assert more than the broadest outlines of the phenomenon of public drinking in the eighteenth century. Yet it is tempting to ask whether the changes in popular culture alluded to before, particularly in the nature of public drinking places and their use, were reflected in these documents. After all, these figures on customers are an aggregate of information from nine different decades, between the 1690s and the 1770s. They reveal gradual changes, some scarcely perceptible, in patterns of use and behavior. The percentage of customers who labored increased through the first half of the eighteenth century, as the professional and idle elite decreased. The increase, however, was among salaried laborers rather than employers. In the last years of Louis XIV's reign, one in every two laboring customers (including domestics) was a shopkeeper or master artisan; by the second half of the century, they represented one in four. Among the elites, those identified as noble had practically disappeared by the second half of the century. There does seem to have been a decline in the status of public drinking places, but on closer inspection the trends depend on which kind of drinking place is considered.

For, although speaking of taverns and their customers as a single entity is useful, it is also misleading. As the previous chapter explained, public drinking places (for which I am using the less cumbersome term "tavern") actually consisted of several distinct types of establishments with different clientele

---

[36] See Lucienne Roubin, "Male and Female Space Within the Provençal Community," trans. Patricia M. Ranum, in Orest Ranum and Robert Forster, eds., *Rural Society in France* (Baltimore, 1977), pp. 152-180, on the relation of men and women to domestic space. See also Roche, *Peuple de Paris*, pp. 113-125, on the amount of space available to salaried artisans.

and different atmospheres. Well over one-half (60 percent) of nearly four thousand male customers considered in this study were drinking in cabarets (that is, the wine shop in the city) in their testimony—a percentage roughly equal to the cabaret's proportional place among all public drinking places. A further 17 percent were identified as patrons of guinguettes, and 11 percent had drunk at cafés. Beer and brandy shops each served some 5 percent of the deponents. Without having exact figures for the number of these establishments in Paris, it is difficult to assess these patterns, yet some interesting discrepancies seem evident. Cabarets did not outnumber cafés by as much as five to one, as the numbers on attendance would suggest, so the clients of cafés are underrepresented in this sample. Considering the refinement of many cafés and their customers, this finding is not surprising. Guinguettes probably did not comprise as much as a third the number of cabarets, so they are slightly overrepresented. Yet their greater internal size certainly accommodated more customers per establishment, so the figures above may not be too far out of line.

This general picture conceals shifts in popular behavior that give some substance to the basic theses of elite commentators. The percentage of male tavern customers found specifically in cabarets did indeed decline gradually, from over two-thirds at the turn of the seventeenth century to one-half by the second half of the eighteenth century. At the same time, attendance at guinguettes increased substantially, from 8 to 25 percent, over the same period. Cafés enjoyed a more modest growth in popularity, from 8 to 12 percent, while beer and brandy sellers remained fairly stable (see Table 3.4). The cabaret's relative decline does not necessarily indicate a decrease in absolute numbers, but the shift in popular taste is evident. Still the numbers hardly justify tolling the death knell of the traditional cabaret, as historians have been tempted to do. Nor are there any grounds at all, given the particular social composition of

TABLE 3.4

Male Attendance in Different Types of Taverns by Year

	1691	1701	1711	1721	1731	1741	1751	1761	1771	Total
Urban cabarets	296	345	223	216	203	206	441	257	165	2352
Other cabarets[a]	19	20	6	19	3	12	13	6	11	109
Guinguettes	32	55	14	33	96	41	161	145	90	667
Cafés	20	51	36	35	28	43	131	31	46	421
Brandy shops	38	18	19	8	2	13	11	12	35	156
Beer shops	11	25	22	9	15	19	73	6	33	213
TOTAL	416	514	320	320	347	334	830	457	380	3918

[a] Taverns identified in records simply as "cabarets," without reference to their location inside or outside the city.

each kind of establishment, for dismissing the cabaret's clientele as representing the lowest levels of society.

One of the arguments in the preceding chapter points to the distinct social aspirations of different drinking institutions. Cafés, in particular, offered a unique ambience and did, in fact, attract a different clientele from that of the cabaret. Indeed, each level of society seemed to prefer a different kind of drinking place, though none did so exclusively (see Table 3.5). The cabaret's clientele was actually closest to the general outline of taverngoers just described (not surprisingly since it constituted 60 percent of the whole), although master artisans and shopkeepers were somewhat more likely than other social groups to patronize the neighborhood cabaret. At the same time they were less likely than most to drink at guinguettes or at brandy or beer shops. These were the haunts of a lower social level. Journeymen and workers went there proportionately more often, as did domestics and soldiers. Soldiers in particular were considerably more likely to drink at brandy shops than were other Parisians. In contrast, master artisans, shopkeepers, and elites used cafés three to four times more often than the rest of the population. In other words, these social groups consti-

TABLE 3.5
Social Standing of Male Customers of Different Types of Taverns

	Urban Cabarets		Other Cabarets[a]		Guin-guettes		Cafés		Brandy Shops		Beer Shops		Total
	N	%	N	%	N	%	N	%	N	%	N	%	N
Elite	173	9	15	17	19	4	92	28	7	6	11	6	317
Shopkeeper	164	9	7	8	28	6	32	10	6	5	13	7	250
Master artisan	426	23	15	17	41	8	57	17	9	8	13	7	561
Artisan	252	13	13	15	87	17	26	8	24	20	26	15	428
Journeyman	315	17	13	15	122	24	43	13	10	8	28	17	531
Day laborer	242	13	6	7	85	17	32	10	16	13	22	13	403
Domestic	142	8	4	5	60	12	22	7	11	9	23	13	262
Soldier	168	9	14	16	62	12	25	8	36	30	33	20	338
Total	1882		87		504		329		119		169		3090

[a] Taverns identified in records simply as "cabarets," without reference to their location inside or outside the city.

tuted 55 percent of the male customers found in cafés, whereas the same social groups constituted only 18 percent of guinguette patrons.

This is not to suggest that any drinking institution was reserved, as an institution, for any particular social group. Certain cafés—those known for a particularly literary clientele, for example—were unquestionably patronized by the middle and upper classes alone.[37] The master glazier, Ménétra, mentions very few cafés in his long itinerary of taverns, although he

[37] See Fosca, *Histoire des cafés*, passim, for a discussion of elite cafés. Robert Darnton, in "The High Enlightenment and the Low Life of Literature," in *The Literary Underground of the Old Regime* (Cambridge, Mass., 1982), pp. 23-24, argues that the café had been abandoned to the "lower species of littérateur." He too points to the social gradations among cafés and their clientele. Isherwood, *Farce and Fantasy*, pp. 240-249, lavishly describes the cafés in the Palais-Royal, to cite some of the most famous of them. I am not persuaded by his evidence, however, that "a genuine mixture of rank" occurred there, in part because so much of his evidence comes from the same kind of elite commentators who have so distorted our understanding of taverns.

claims to have gone with Rousseau to the café de la Régence.[38] The elites went occasionally to guinguettes; the courtier, Madame de Genlis, describes one such visit in her memoirs. The dancing, singing, and dining that she recounts made it "one of the gayest, most charming evenings" of her life. The telling point, however, is that she and her noble companions preferred to go disguised as common folk and were pleased (and relieved?) that "no one had the least suspicion" of their real identities.[39] Clearly she did not go often. Restif describes a trip to a guinguette, his first, as if he were visiting a primitive society. He hesitates about even going; "the place was not noble." Once there he finds it "full of fishwives, coachmen, lackeys, *coureurs*, soldiers, spies. . . . My appearance was as new to this honorable company as theirs was to me."[40] Ménétra also mentions an encounter with nobility in disguise at a tavern in the city. Evidently elites did not feel comfortable mixing openly with the populace in plebeian establishments, although their disguises evoke the role reversals of carnival when consorting with the lower classes was sanctioned.[41] This unease appears to have been growing through the century, as nobles and the middle classes shunned the popular cabaret in preference to the café. There was substantial mixing, then, in certain establishments—the cabaret more than the guinguette—but the fact remains that certain kinds of establishments were identified with one class more than another.

[38] In Ménétra, *Journal*, p. 375, Roche notes that Ménétra cites only one café, but there are a few other references scattered through the text.

[39] Félicité Ducrest de Saint-Aubin, Madame de Genlis, *Mémoires inédits sur le XVIIIe siècle et la révolution française* (Paris, 1825), 3:8-11. Alain Faure, *Paris carême-prenant* (Paris, 1983), p. 54, goes so far as to assert that "In the eighteenth century, nobles and courtiers liked . . . to frequent popular guinguettes," but appears to have little more than Mme. de Genlis as evidence.

[40] Restif de la Bretonne, *Les Contemporaines du commun*, cited in Marguerite Pitsch, *La Vie populaire à Paris au XVIIIe siècle* (Paris, 1949), 2:14.

[41] Ménétra, *Journal*, p. 166; Burke, *Popular Culture*, pp. 182-183, on carnival.

PATTERNS OF ATTENDANCE

The way that customers used taverns, their patterns of attendance, gives crucial evidence about the institution's role in Parisian society. The information recorded in judicial archives about when people went to taverns demonstrates the extent to which public drinking fit into daily life and leisure. In contrast to the common depiction of infrequent binge drinking, of drunken Sundays, Parisians appear to have used taverns regularly, throughout the day and the week. The pattern of customers' attendance during the week betrayed substantial disregard for the difference between days of work and rest. Men could be found in taverns every day, and not just on Sundays. Roughly one-quarter of all customers identified in the judicial archives drank on Sundays and holidays. Business then dropped to 17 percent on Mondays. From Monday to Saturday, attendance declined gradually from 17 to 9 percent. Thus a day of rest appears to have provoked only a modest increase in attendance, although it is not always clear which days saw a given customer working. The account books of several taverns lend support to this argument, showing fairly constant revenues through the different days of the week.[42] Some historians have argued that the "undisciplined" work force of a preindustrial society was accustomed to flaunting the work ethic by making a holiday of Mondays—"Saint Monday."[43] Patterns of drinking in taverns do not wholly support this thesis. Because attendance decreased so gradually from Monday to Saturday, Mondays do not appear to have been significantly "holier" than

[42] Arch. Seine, D5B⁶ 525 (1749-1753); and D5B⁶ 3881 (1723-1725), both reveal little discernible pattern of business by day of the week, whereas the wine merchant of D5B⁶ 3734 (1765), sold 17 percent of his wine (not the same thing as the number of customers obviously) on Sundays and again on Mondays. Business for him then decreased slowly to 12 percent on Fridays and 14 percent on Saturdays.

[43] E. P. Thompson, "Time, Work Discipline, and Industrial Capitalism," *Past and Present* 38 (1967):74-76.

any other day of the week. Instead, customers appear to have gone fairly regularly throughout the week, although this depended in part on their occupation. Half of the journeymen and "artisans" (those whose rank in the guild was not specified) were in taverns on Sundays (31 percent) and Mondays (21 percent) as opposed to 37 percent of other social groups. Thus master craftsmen and shopkeepers could drink more regularly through the week than their employees, but so could day laborers and servants, perhaps because of less regular employment. Clearly the demands of work impeded salaried laborers from enjoying quite as relaxed an attitude toward leisure as their employers.

The heaviest attendance in taverns came in the evening, after work, yet Parisians made use of drinking places throughout the day, even during the workweek. Customers could be found drinking at all hours, though only sporadically through the morning. Less than one-quarter came before noon, but the numbers increased to a peak around eight in the evening and diminished until midnight. Over one-half of the men found at public drinking places in the judicial documents were there between six in the morning and six in the evening, from Monday through Saturday—a time when most of the laboring population was theoretically at work. This pattern described the behavior of salaried workers almost as well as it applied to their employers. The laboring classes worked long hours, six days a week; a twelve-hour day was minimum.[44] Workers in the construction trades worked from six in the morning until six at night in the winter, and from five in the morning until seven at night in the summer.[45] Most trades kept men at work until six, seven, and even eight at night, after which time business in taverns picked up. Much of the attendance in taverns clearly oc-

[44] Emile Levasseur, *Histoire des classes ouvrières et de l'industrie avant 1789* (Paris, 1900-1901), 2:796.

[45] Micheline Baulant, "Les Salaires des ouvriers en bâtiment à Paris de 1400 à 1726," *Annales, économies, sociétés, civilizations* 26 (1971):465.

curred during the workday, however, when roughly half of the customers presumably went there around or during their work.

These figures cannot be easily interpreted, however. If testimony was fairly precise about the time of day and week when people were drinking, it gave much less information about their employment before and after their visit to the tavern. In most cases it is impossible to know whether a man drinking in the middle of the day was absenting himself from work or had not been able to find work. Workers generally experienced erratic employment opportunities. Even those who had work might be given the day off for one of the numerous holidays that evidently absolved them from many workdays.[46] Depositions do not always make it clear when the deponent was enjoying such a holiday. Still, there is ample evidence that much of the drinking was done in the midst of these people's work.

The testimony of tavern customers themselves suggests it was not unusual to have recourse to a tavern during their business. "Being at his work," a laborer explained, "he had left it for a moment" and had something to drink with two companions at a nearby café.[47] Others described meetings at taverns to discuss business, to seal a bargain with a drink, to ask a man to pay his debts. Their visit might be an extension of work but it might also be recreation. Two shopkeepers on a Tuesday morning "going about their business together" met an acquaintance while on the other side of town. The acquaintance, a barrelmaker, stopped them, saying, "Today is my feast day [*fête*], give me a bouquet." The two obliged him, but he then announced that, "We must water the bouquet and you must entertain me," and he took them out of town to a tavern in the northern faubourgs. They drank there and then moved to another tavern farther from the city where they dined. At about two in

---

[46] George Rudé, "Prices, Wages and Popular Movements during the French Revolution," in G. Rudé, ed., *Paris and London in the Eighteenth Century* (London, 1970), p. 167, uses 111 "unpaid Feast Days" to calculate incomes.

[47] AN, Y15449, 7 September 1751.

the afternoon, one of the shopkeepers got up and said, "I have business in Paris, let us leave." The other shopkeeper explained in his testimony that he was unable to leave, "since the barrel-maker and a companion obliged him to stay." They remained at the tavern the rest of the afternoon playing boulles.[48] The two shopkeepers did not hesitate to stop work in the middle of the day. One of them felt some obligation to return, but only after three or four hours. The other seems to have been persuaded by a combination of his friend's fête and his urging to forego the rest of the day.

In another incident, a group of buttonmakers, having gathered at one of their shops for business, turned from business to leisure without hesitation. They had visited a button peddlar's lodgings for more inventory, but had then decided—at three on a Wednesday afternoon—to "promenade." They did so, collecting a friend whom they met on the way, and proceeded to take the rest of the day off. They drank and danced at a guinguette in a northern suburb. They went to a village outside of Paris to visit their friend's child at the *nourrice*. They returned to the guinguette and stayed until half past nine that night.[49] Fortunately for them, these truants were independent tradesmen, answering to no master, and could afford to be flexible in their use of leisure time.

Even salaried workers at times betrayed a casual attitude toward their work. A journeyman leather currier who had left his shop at nine on a Friday morning to eat his supper was returning an hour later when he met a friend, "his compère," a snuff grinder, who offered to buy him a drink (*payer chopine*). The two went to a tavern near the journeyman's shop and stayed until one or two in the afternoon. They then moved around the block to another tavern where they stayed until dusk. Upon leaving, "they had been in the street and their intention was to

[48] AN, Y15228, 22 July 1721. Another case mentions giving someone a bouquet "because it was the day of his fête" (AN, Y14761, 5 October 1711).
[49] AN, Y10233, 14 June 1761.

buy something for their wives and children at the market."[50]
The journeyman seems never to have returned to work that
day. Domestics experienced very different demands on their
time from those of a worker, so it is less surprising to find a
coachman, "having left his master's house to run errands," still
drinking five hours later with a friend he had met.[51] But what
to make of two workers, left by their master to put a roof on a
building outside of Paris, who were found late that day in a cabaret, having done no work? The master roofer reprimanded
them, but they replied that they worked when they wanted to,
and they had wanted to drink.[52] Other evidence indicates that
such blatant absenteeism was not tolerated by employers.
Workers who took a day off to drink could be unceremoniously
fired.[53] Rather, the employees who appear to have stopped at
taverns throughout the day were more likely to have been there
briefly, fitting time for their leisure within their workday.

The rhythms of work in a preindustrial society have been described as being closer to the erratic pulses of rural life than to
the mechanical pace of modern industry. The sporadic nature
of much of the work, produced on demand for individual customers rather than made in assembly for an anonymous market,
meant that work hours could be more flexible. In many trades
men worked in spurts of intense activity, with periods of slack
in between.[54] Yet if this type of schedule might excuse the shopkeeper's absence from his store, the employee's leisure depended on a tug of war with his master.[55] The widow of a mas-

---

[50] AN, Y10226, 25 February 1761.

[51] AN, Y12337, 11 December 1711.

[52] AN, Y13911, 20 July 1731.

[53] AN, Y10233, 26 July 1761.

[54] Thompson, "Time, Work Discipline," pp. 74-76; Keith Thomas, "Work
and Leisure," *Past and Present* 29 (1964), passim; and Robert Darnton, *Business
of the Enlightenment* (Cambridge, Mass., 1980), pp. 203-245. In Ménétra,
Journal, pp. 370-372, Roche notes this pattern in Ménétra's account.

[55] Levasseur, *Histoire des classes ouvrières*, 2:704. See Michael Sonenscher,
"Work and Wages in Paris in the Eighteenth Century," in Maxine Berg, Pat

ter farrier complained that one of her journeymen had gone, on a Monday afternoon, "with his comrades to drink at a cabaret where they were for a very long time." Upon the journeyman's return, she reproached him for having been "out a long time," to which he replied "brusquely" that it had not been over three hours. At that she warned him that "he ought not to speak in that manner, or be away for three hours during work hours [*le temps de son travail*]." His response was to quit his job.[56] In a complaint sixty years later, the employees were fighting not for three hours but only a few minutes. A journeyman mason explained that nine in the morning was "the dinner hour of construction workers." He charged his supervisor with being abusive about the time that they returned to work. The supervisor had come storming into the cabaret "like a madman" when "the dinner hour had passed" and said "in an acid and sharp tone" that "the hour had passed and that they ought to be at work each according to his profession." The masons stayed to finish their bottle of wine, further infuriating the supervisor.[57]

The sharpness of the exchange between mason and supervisor may have been due, in part, to the size of the enterprise; it was a large construction project and the supervisor was concerned that such conduct might "make him despised" at other sites where he would work.[58] The relation between journeyman and master in smaller operations could perhaps be more relaxed. A master saddler complained that one of his workmen had left work in the morning and gone off to drink, either "to start a quarrel with the plaintiff or maybe in a spirit of intrigue." The journeyman had stayed out all day, but the master sent an apprentice out after him only toward the end of the day

Hudson, and Michael Sonenscher, eds., *Manufacture in Town and Country Before the Factory* (Cambridge, 1983), pp. 166-168, on the struggles between master and journeyman that concerned time.

[56] AN, Y14877, 8 August 1691.
[57] AN, Y11933, 14 September 1751.
[58] AN, Y15643, 13 September 1751.

"because he needed his work."[59] There are other similar complaints. An employee's behavior in a small enterprise was taken personally, as a sign of a quarrel, but his absence was not serious until the employer had something for which he needed him. There is a sense of leniency and flexibility underlying this complaint that partly accepts the absence, so long as the worker was not needed. An employee's ability to absent himself from work to drink at a tavern clearly depended on many things, but their patterns of attendance suggest that many of them found a way.

"Popular" theater, particularly the genre of poissard literature that used the jargon and behavior of the laboring classes as its subject, depicted the frequent, almost reflexive, recourse to the tavern among working people.[60] Writers like Vadé and Taconnet who produced much in this genre were themselves men of the people and often used taverns as the setting of their work.[61] Their writing demonstrates the intimate role of the cabaret in Parisians' lives. Vadé described workers down at the Seine who "every day, before the sun, go to the widow Rabavin to soak their hearts in eau-de-vie"—at least until their wives catch them.[62] In Taconnet's play, *Les Ecosseuses de la Halle*, the pea sellers have taken time off from their business at some point during the day to drink at a cabaret.[63] In both works the cabaret

[59] AN, Y15348, 19 February 1751.

[60] Alexander Parks Moore, *The Genre Poissard and the French Stage of the Eighteenth Century* (New York, 1935). Many of the plays in this genre were staged at the Foire St. Germain, which Robert Isherwood, "Entertainment in Parisian Fairs," *Journal of Modern History* 53 (1981):31-32, describes as appealing to an audience of both rich and poor alike and as selling tickets at a "low price" in order to encourage the populace to come. Michele Root-Bernstein has also discussed these plays, and the general absence of popular themes, in *Boulevard Theater and Revolution in Eighteenth-Century Paris* (Ann Arbor, Mich., 1984).

[61] Roche, *Le Peuple de Paris*, p. 45.

[62] Vadé, *La Pipe cassée*, p. 18.

[63] Toussaint Gaspard Taconnet, *Les Ecosseuses de la Halle*, in *Taconnet théâtre* (Paris, 1759), vol, 1, scene 2.

has been integrated into the workday. Two neighbors, in another play by Taconnet, meet by chance and repair to the nearest cabaret: "Let us have a drink at the closest place," they tell each other.[64] In each case the cabaret is close at hand, a regular aspect of life, and the drinking too forms part of the day's routine.

The last day in the life of a certain butcher's assistant named Robert Leger is an example of how short stops at a tavern could be integrated into a day. Admittedly, Leger was not typical in his behavior of that day: he was found dead by the end of it. Yet his actions before his demise surprised none of the dozen witnesses who recounted his tale. He went to four different cabarets in the ten hours between nine in the morning and seven at night on a Monday, ostensibly a workday. We find Leger first at nine in the morning eating at a tavern next door to his lodgings with his wife and several other people. One of his companions, a secretary of an *entrepreneur* of royal buildings, named Chardon, again ran into Leger and his wife at the place where she sold tripe, not far from where they lived, at half past one in the afternoon. Leger accompanied Chardon "to the place where he [the secretary] was going," presumably on business. From there Leger took Chardon to the shop of a locksmith, and the two of them went to drink with the locksmith's son until half past three. At five, a merchant butcher testifies to having been fetched from his stall by a tavern waiter to join Leger at a nearby tavern, where they drank a bottle of wine and "spoke about different business concerning them." Finally, at six, a master candlemaker reported having drunk a chopine (almost a pint) with Leger and another friend at a different tavern.[65]

Leger seems to have spent much of the day at taverns and little of it working, but there is no reason to judge his casual trips to the tavern as a sign that he had taken the whole day off. His

---

[64] Toussaint Gaspard Taconnet, *L'Impromptu de la foire*, in *Théâtres français* (Paris, 1732-1791), vol. 31.

[65] AN, Y14681, 20 February 1761.

various drinking companions were clearly going about their business that day. Their trips to the tavern were not an interruption of the day so much as an integral part of it. Some took their meals at a tavern. Leger and the merchant butcher discussed business at a tavern; people often preferred doing business at a tavern than at their shop. Leger and Chardon visited with a friend in a tavern, not in the shop of their friend's father. In every case the tavern was a place to meet people or to talk to them. No one seems to have drunk much—a bottle shared in one cabaret, a half bottle in another.

The vocabulary of leisure found in judicial testimony provides a further indication of perceptions of the distinctions between labor and leisure. The word itself, *loisir*, was of old extraction and meant, already in 1530, "time that one can dispose of freely outside of one's habitual occupations and the constraints that they impose."[66] Thus leisure had long been opposed to work, and contrasted a sense of freedom to the constraints of labor long before the eighteenth century. But the word does not appear in the testimony of the laboring classes. Rather than speak of time that was free, or not used for work, they spoke of the uses of the time. "*Se rafraichir*" and "*se divertir*," "*s'amuser*" and "*passer le temps*" are the phrases that described people's leisure in depositions but these carried different connotations.[67] In every case, and especially with the last three phrases, the words connoted a sense of time available, to be used at one's discretion. Above all, such phrases indicated the abundance of time, rather than time that was allowed, or for which permission was granted—concepts that are implicit in the term *loisir*. The vocabulary of the laboring classes, then, suggests a relation to time, and to work, that lacked the rigor of

[66] *Le Petit Robert*, s.v. "loisir." The root of *loisir* is the Latin *licere*, to allow.

[67] In the same vein, the seventeenth-century worker, Chavatte, described his time spent in taverns with the phrase, "Je me récréois avec mes camarades." See Lottin, *Chavatte*, p. 346.

constraints or compulsion. Leisure was not a hard-won respite, but time spent differently.

The simple dichotomy between work and leisure is inadequate, in many cases, to describe much of what people were doing with their days. It fails to account for much of the activity in taverns. One cannot help but be struck, for instance, by the amount of time people spent waiting there. Journeymen waited for work, especially at the taverns near their guild's hall, and at the taverns associated with certain trades.[68] Their employers also waited for work in taverns, waiting for their wife or shop-clerk to send for them when a customer came to the shop.

Similarly, people seem to have spent a great deal of time waiting for each other, to talk or conduct business. Witnesses spoke frequently of having looked for someone and of waiting for them in a nearby tavern.[69] The ties binding communities together depended on people seeing each other, whether for business or for fellowship. Furthermore, appointments came to have great importance, for any communication depended on people seeing each other. People spoke of agreeing to meet in terms of "giving one's word [*parole*]," thereby raising the importance of an appointment to the level of honor and reputation.[70]

The reciprocal of the importance of the appointment was the importance of the encounter. Witnesses spoke regularly of having met an acquaintance or friend in the street, and of then spending the rest of the morning, or even the day, with the person. When one's community depended on making and maintaining personal contacts, the chance encounter was not an interruption; it was an occasion to reinforce a relationship. As

---

[68] AN, Y15180, 6 July 1751, identifies a tavern near the bureau of the bakers' guild and an "auberge des garçons boulangers." See Kaplan, "Réflexions," pp. 65-68, for other examples.

[69] AN, Y14066, 14 October 1741.

[70] AN, Y15238, 31 July 1731. In this as in other cases, the witnesses who "gave their word" were of a generally higher social level than the normal witness and included, for example, a négociant and an officier chez le Roy.

work took people into the streets and around the city, they showed themselves willing to allow a trip to the tavern to interrupt the flow of the workday and also to use it to cement the bonds of their communities.

THE NEIGHBORHOOD TAVERN

Patterns of attendance make it clear that different kinds of taverns played very different social roles, indeed that certain public drinking places were developing distinct styles of recreation. Drinking establishments of various kinds distinguished themselves by the rhythms of their daily business, much as they had by their clientele. As these rhythms diverged, the institutions acquired distinct social roles, serving different communities and kinds of recreation. Although each tavern was undoubtedly individual, a consideration of two models of contrasting behavior may make the differences clearer. The traditional tavern, the cabaret, functioned much like a neighborhood tavern, serving a fairly limited community in a regular, daily fashion. Newer kinds of taverns, particularly the guinguette, served all indiscriminately, though less frequently; because of its location, the guinguette drew people away from their neighborhoods, as they sought more elaborate entertainment.

Daily rhythms of attendance give some idea of these differences. The brandy shop flourished before dawn, serving between midnight and six in the morning one-quarter of the men who testified in the judicial archives that they had drunk at brandy sellers. During the same period, other kinds of establishments saw less than 3 percent of their customers identified in these archives. Likewise, the marquis de Mirabeau claims to have seen "nothing open except some shops of brandy sellers," early one morning in the "popular and market parts" of Paris.[71]

[71] Mirabeau, in *L'Ami des hommes*, mentions having passed through "the pop-

TABLE 3.6

Male Attendance in Taverns During the Hours of the Day

	2400 −200	200 −400	400 −600	600 −800	800 −1000	1000 −1200	1200 −1400	1400 −1600	1600 −1800	1800 −2000	2000 −2200	2200 −2400	To
Urban cabarets	9	0	8	45	120	142	148	179	253	374	259	59	15
Other cabarets[a]	5	0	0	0	0	1	0	22	16	4	14	0	
Guinguettes	5	3	1	4	16	21	12	47	104	96	105	42	4
Cafés	10	15	13	7	10	9	9	23	8	53	67	77	3
Brandy shops	8	12	12	5	7	0	3	3	0	22	31	24	1
Beer shops	0	0	2	4	2	5	15	36	34	31	39	18	1
TOTAL	37	30	36	65	155	178	187	310	415	580	515	220	27

Note: Women followed very nearly the same pattern.

[a] Taverns identified in records simply as "cabarets," without reference to their location inside or outside the city.

For the middle of the day, cabarets commanded most business. Between eight in the morning and two in the afternoon, cabarets saw one-quarter of their customers while other drinking places served less than 10 percent. Everyone's business increased steadily throughout the daylight hours, to a peak between four and ten in the evening, when the cabaret and beer shop served 56 percent of their customers. During the same period the guinguette did two-thirds of its business, but most clients left cabarets and guinguettes soon after the closing time of ten. In the hours of the night, business switched back heavily to the cafés and brandy shops, which had nearly one-half of their customers come in between eight and midnight (see Table 3.6). Brandy seems to have begun and ended the day. Some police ordinances suggested that cafés tended regularly to stay open later than the curfew, a practice that they abhorred.[72]

ular and market part" of Paris one morning at six and "was astonished to see nothing open except some shops of eau-de-vie sellers" (cited in Levasseur, *Histoire des classes ouvrières*, 2:797).

[72] Arch.Préf.Pol., Fonds Lamoignon, ordonnance de police, 5 November 1677, and sentence de police, 12 March 1695.

Whatever the reason for this, cafés certainly figured more prominently after dark than during the day. In contrast to cafés and guinguettes, cabarets sustained a fairly even level of business throughout the day.

The men in these documents patronized the various kinds of establishments in very different rhythms through the week. Urban cabarets experienced the most continuous, stable use throughout the week. Attendance on Sunday reached just 55 percent above the average of the rest of the week. Guinguettes, in contrast, served four times more customers on Sundays than they did on the average for the rest of the week. There was also a higher percentage of customers at guinguettes on Mondays than at other establishments, though not substantially higher. Cafés and beer shops entertained clients in roughly the same pattern as the cabaret, and brandy shops experienced a surge on Sundays nearly as great as the guinguettes. Guinguettes diverged significantly from the behavior of urban cabarets, then, filling up on the days of rest when city dwellers could take the time for extended recreation. The patterns of attendance point to a dichotomy between an institution in constant use and one frequented primarily at the end of the week, a dichotomy that reveals an important evolution in popular culture. The one used constantly lay close at hand, a neighborhood tavern in many cases that formed an integral part of daily life and geography. The other appealed to its customers from beyond the city's barriers, offering them lavish entertainment and escape from the city and its cares.

The majority of tavern customers identified by judicial records as drinking in a city tavern came from its close vicinity, and often from the same street.[73] One-half of the tavern's clien-

---

[73] A little less than one-half of the people in this study (2,000) were identified by their address, but no addresses included street numbers until the end of the century. In many cases the address was specified by reference to a nearby intersecting street. In Paris many streets are quite short, but if the address is simply the rue St. Martin, or some other long street, the information is not especially helpful. Thus, this measurement is necessarily approximate. Those who did not

tele whose address was given lived less than 200 yards away from the tavern in which they were found. Nearly three-fifths of the customers came from less than one-quarter of a mile away—a short five-minute walk, and probably within the area that a Parisian would call his "quarter." In many cases the customers who were not from the close vicinity were in the company of friends or acquaintances who did come from the tavern's neighborhood; they were there as guests, so to speak, of the neighbor. Some people worked near the tavern they were found in. A few, such as coachmen, covered such broad areas of the city that they could be found anywhere, but they are an exception. The evidence shows that people tended strongly to drink at taverns near where they worked or lived, and that few people drank in taverns that were not in the neighborhood of at least one of their drinking companions. The close proximity of home and tavern for most patrons contributed to the intimate ties that bound taverns to people's daily lives and to neighborhood communities.

This familiarity is well illustrated by what was a comparatively rare phenomenon, the solitary drinker. In general, Parisians did not go to drink alone; they went to be with people. Few people in the judicial records—little more than 10 percent—were drinking in taverns by themselves. Those who did, however, came from a smaller radius than the average customer: over two-thirds from one-quarter of a mile. In some of the cases where the solitary drinker was not from the neighbor-

---

give depositions but appear in the testimony of others (that is, all those in the "mentioned" category and many of the accused) were not identified by address, sometimes because the person was a stranger, but usually because the deponent simply identified the person's name and occupation. The distance between customers' homes and the neighborhood tavern could be ascertained for only one-third of the men and women in this study (1,535). The distance for the rest of the customers is unknown, either because a location—of their housing or the tavern—was not given, or because they were not drinking in the city. Although there is certainly some tendency for these unknowns to have been strangers rather than neighbors, I would judge it to be minor.

hood, he was still a regular of the tavern.[74] The fact that people could go to a tavern by themselves, whether to be idle or to see others from the neighborhood, was an important aspect of neighborhood taverns. Their solitude points to the role of local taverns not just in sociability but in people's daily space. A middle-aged domestic in the parish of St. Sulpice testified that he happened "to go often to the cabaret to pass an hour of time and as a neighbor . . . [but] not having the intention of drinking."[75] Presumably the tavernkeeper put up with him sitting there because he was a "neighbor," for owners were known to eject people who were not buying drink.[76] The tavern may have been one of the few places where the laboring classes, so meanly housed, could feel at home.

The proximity of so much of the cabaret's clientele suggests that people went most often to the ten or twelve taverns in their neighborhood. There is little information about the behavior of individuals over time; the facts in the judicial archives deal essentially with given moments in time and rarely narrate more than a day's events. Parisians were probably regulars at certain taverns, usually taverns in their neighborhoods, but we have little evidence with which to identify them. The account books of certain cabarets indicate that customers drinking on credit went to the same tavern roughly twice a week, and sometimes more often.[77] Testimony before the police is more ambiguous.

---

[74] AN, Y10140, 19 February 1751.

[75] AN, Y10145, 19 August 1751.

[76] AN, Y11611, 16 August 1731.

[77] The average frequency of customers drinking on credit at a particular tavern is actually roughly once every four days, based on eighty-three customers in eight different taverns over periods of two to six months (Arch. Seine, D5B6 2704; D5B6 525; D5B6 5775; D5B6 248; D5B6 657; D5B6 4097; D5B6 2854; D5B6 2521). This figure understates the amount, of course, because such customers did not always drink on credit. Although there are many other account books of wine merchants from this period, interpreting the material is difficult, for wine merchants also sold wine to be taken out. In many cases the wine merchants dealt only with wholesale orders, for wine delivered to customers' houses. Even when the account books list retail sales—for example, for wine sold by the

Tavernkeepers rarely revealed any particular recognition of their customers, however regular their visits might have been. Customers, for their part, spoke occasionally of cabarets that they were "in the habit of frequenting" or where they went "very often." They spoke also of other customers whom they recognized as "coming habitually."[78]

Most of the people in the city taverns recorded in the archives came from a small area around it, giving it the character of a "neighborhood tavern."[79] Of course it may simply be that fights in taverns closer to home were more serious, because one knew the audience better, than those farther away and thus stood a better chance of being reported. Brandy shops in particular served the highest percentage of neighbors (77 percent within one-quarter of a mile), while the cabaret had 59 percent. Cafés contained the least neighbors (55 percent), partly because the elites tended to drink in their neighborhood least often (49 percent found within one-quarter of a mile). Artisans generally drank more often in the neighborhood (61 percent of them) as did domestics and day laborers. Perhaps the elites had weaker ties to their neighborhood or they were better able to afford the carriages that could open up the city to them. In the eighteenth century, much as today, the kinds of customers a tavern would serve depended on its physical location. Most of the taverns with strangers in them were on major arteries of the city or in

---

pinte—it is often impossible to tell whether the wine was being consumed in the tavern or taken home. In most of the above cases, telltale signs, such as food sold with the wine, or a note that the customer drank the wine with someone, or drank it "dans le jardin," clarify the issue. But many account books simply cannot be interpreted.

[78] AN, Y12025, 22 May 1731; Y11661, 4 December 1731; Y15238, 10 July 1731.

[79] A typology of modern taverns is suggested by Marshall Clinard, "The Public Drinking House and Society," in David S. Pittman and Charles R. Snyder, eds., *Society, Culture and Drinking Patterns* (Carbondale, Ill., 1962), p. 27. According to Clinard, the "neighborhood tavern . . . provides a meeting place to talk and relax from the monotony of work," and functions as a neighborhood social center.

the markets. Such cabarets, on the rues St. Denis, St. Honoré, St. Antoine, and Temple, lay on heavily traveled routes. There the circulation was busiest and the neighborhood was most open to the outside. The taverns on the boulevards, so richly described by Robert Isherwood, were also places where people came from all over the city to be entertained and jostled, much as they would travel to the guinguettes.[80] In most cases, though, taverns in the city were not so busy and served a more restricted clientele. They served the neighborhood, the small community that lived and worked within the vicinity. There was no other such social institution in the neighborhood, for lodgings offered little place for socializing.[81] The tavern was the obvious place for any community interaction, and was more flexible than either the house or the workshop in the kinds of intercourse and leisure it permitted.

The neighborhood tavern, particularly the cabaret and the beer and brandy shops, satisfied the basic need for public drinking and sociability for the majority of laboring Parisians. The emergence of the guinguette as a new kind of tavern at the end of the seventeenth century, however, and its increasing popularity during the eighteenth century suggest a shift in popular taste and behavior. To the extent that the guinguette was actually replacing the cabaret as a center of Parisian recreation—and this phenomenon should not be exaggerated—it was replacing a traditional sociability with something very different. For guinguettes contrasted with cabarets in their clientele and their patterns of business. As noted in Chapter Two, the guinguette distinguished itself from the urban cabaret by its distance from the city and the lower price of its wine. It was also larger and more colorful. Its distance from work and homes separated it from daily life and from the dense social relations of urban communities. It offered different recreation and dif-

---

[80] Isherwood, *Farce and Fantasy*, pp. 163-167.
[81] Farge, *Vivre*, pp. 35-39.

ferent attractions, no longer the casual drink at a shop down the street. The novelty of the guinguette should not obscure the enduring significance of the cabaret in popular culture, yet a comparison of the two reveals a subtle dynamic in popular culture.

GUINGUETTES

The guinguette exhibited a noticeably different pattern of use, and one that seems to prefigure a "modern" sense of leisure with its greater separation from daily routines and its more elaborate entertainment. One historian has recently distinguished between traditional "sociability," in which nonwork pursuits involved the individual with his community, and modern "leisure," which requires solitude and privacy.[82] Although the guinguette hardly offered solitude, it did take men out of their neighborhoods, away from wives and work, and away from the pursuits of daily life. The guinguette was principally a Sunday pastime and attendance during the rest of the week was much lower.[83] "On holidays and Sundays [guinguettes] are filled by an innumerable multitude of all kinds of people, above all artisans and laborers, who go to refresh themselves from the fatigues of the week."[84] The most obvious reason for this pattern is the greater distance and time involved in getting to the coun-

[82] See Marrus, *The Emergence of Leisure*, pp. 1-10 for a discussion of leisure. I am not entirely satisfied with his distinction between leisure and sociability: his one example of popular leisure, cardplaying, is in fact decidedly sociable by Marrus's own definition. However, his outline of increasing commercialization and dissociation of work from leisure is interesting. Burke, *Popular Culture*, p. 249, also speaks of a "gradual shift moving from the spontaneous and participatory forms of entertainment towards more formally organized and commercial spectator sports." Formality and commercialization seem to be the key.

[83] Over 40 percent of the guinguette customers mentioned in the judicial archives went on a Sunday or holiday. A further 19 percent went on Monday. In contrast, only 20 percent of the customers at urban taverns were drinking on Sundays and a further 17 percent on Mondays.

[84] Hurtaud and Magny, *Dictionnaire de Paris* (Paris, 1779), 3:198, quoted in Franklin, *Dictionnaire historique*, p. 377.

try tavern. From the center of the city it might take 2 or 3 miles to reach a guinguette, as opposed to the 200 or 300 yards that separated cabarets from most of their customers' homes. Yet distance was not the only reason for the less frequent use of guinguettes. The social density of the city fell off sharply outside of the city, which meant that men, who might easily stop at a cabaret while seeing a colleague or delivering something in the city had much less reason to venture into the country. Either one went to the country for leisure or one generally did not go.

The guinguette became the goal of elaborate excursions to the countryside. Men and women spent a day or an afternoon and evening promenading through the faubourgs and beyond, stopping at various guinguettes, and walking on. The extra time on Sundays meant that their walks were longer and farther afield; more friends could be visited, and the party of those out strolling became slightly larger. The space available in the suburbs meant that guinguettes could be much larger than cabarets.[85] Thus the guinguette had larger rooms and buildings, but more importantly they offered gardens and greens where customers could sit and drink, dance or play boulles. Pictures of guinguettes depict a large central room (much larger than that found in a neighborhood tavern) and spacious gardens. Those establishments inside the city that could seat their customers in a garden or give them room to dance had to contend with the problem of noise. Urban taverns risked the ire of their neighbors, living packed together on all sides, and there are occasional examples of such neighbors expressing dissatisfaction with rowdy behavior.[86] Guinguettes, in contrast, could spread out and provide the room and the occasion for dancing, games, and noise. Perhaps it was due to the size and the openness, or the distance from the constraints of the neighborhood, but for

[85] Dion, *Histoire de la vigne*, pp. 506-510.
[86] AN, Y9538, 8 July 1721.

whatever reasons guinguettes were used differently, and by different people, than urban taverns. Such differences of distance and density account in large measure for the different perceptions that were associated with cabarets and guinguettes, perceptions that in turn influenced behavior.

Contemporaries were certainly aware of the difference between the two institutions, and these distinctions were important enough to have figured in much of the literature on guinguettes. Popular literature portrayed the neighborhood cabaret as familiar and unremarkable, while the guinguette appeared exceptional and rather grand. Authors emphasized the entertainment, music and dancing at guinguettes, as well as an atmosphere that was very different from that found in the urban tavern. Thus they recognize different social roles for the two institutions. A trip to the guinguette was presented as an expedition, a Sunday outing. The men in Vadé's *La Pipe cassée*, who had been surprised by their wives while drinking at the local tavern of the widow Rabavin, are accompanied, in the next section of the poem, by these same spouses in a trip to a guinguette. They are all dressed up—"La Tulipe in a white shirt, Jean-Louis with an ornamented hat, Jerome's hair combed"—and exude a distinct holiday spirit. Once there they eat, drink, play cards, and get into the inevitable fight, before all ends happily with everyone dancing.[87] This was revelry, unlike the intermittent drinking that punctuated the working day. By juxtaposing one scene in a cabaret with the next in a guinguette, Vadé
' ' to contrast the sedateness and sexual segregation of the
he gaiety, bustle, and sexual interaction of the other.
btitled the "festivals of the guinguette" promised
inguette / all rejoice / the great, the small / are
/ they amuse themselves / they drink, they
e is nothing like these taverns / for making

p. 27.

178

merry at little cost."[88] As with Vadé's scene, the heroes are several laborers and their women out from the city. They seem to spend a great deal of time singing about the special attractions of the guinguette. "Come people of high style / Pass your moments of leisure / Instead of yawning in the city / Come enjoy real pleasure." Again there are fights and dancing and "everyone is content with his pittance."

A brief *ballet* by Taconnet takes place at Ramponeau's tavern, the famous guinguette of the Basse Courtille suburb.[89] A wedding party arrives, having come all the way from the middle of Paris. Again the trip has been something of an expedition. The groom's father tells Ramponeau that "we have come from quite far to see you," and one of the guests complains that "your Ramponeau is at the end of the world! May the devil strip me if I thought to get here in three days." The bride, meanwhile, asks why they bothered to come; "we have plenty [of taverns] in our quarter." The answer is that this tavern is not like the others. The groom sings the praises of the establishment, and each character praises the particular excellence of the wine, the customers, and the gaiety found at this tavern. The contrast with the attitude of the characters who drink at the "first place they come to" is striking. Guinguettes were exceptions to normal behavior and sociability.

Another play about a guinguette, Florent Carton Dancourt's *Le Moulin de Javelle*, although longer and more complicated, portrays the guinguette in much the same way.[90] The relationship of this tavern, in the country, to Paris is a major theme. It is close enough to be accessible, especially for the bourgeois characters of this play who come by carriage, but at the same

[88] André Charles Cailleau, *Le Waux hall populaire*, in *Three Centuries of French Drama* (Louisville, Ky., microfiche edn., 1969).

[89] Toussaint Gaspard Taconnet, *La Mariée de la Courtille*, in *Ballets, pantomimes, tableaux, etc.* (Paris, n.d.), vol. 5.

[90] Florent Carton Dancourt, *Le Moulin de Javelle*, in *Les Oeuvres de M. d'Ancourt* (Paris, 1711), col. 2.

time is far enough away to ensure privacy from one's community. This guinguette was a lovers' rendezvous, and its distance from Paris recommended it for surreptitious meetings. As the coachman remarks, "No one lodges here but that doesn't stop them from sleeping here." Much of the humor is concerned with just how private the guinguette really was not. Wives attended by lovers are surprised by husbands in drinking parties. The wives complain to the owner, "You ought not to receive husbands here," and the husbands agree that "sensible husbands never should go where they might meet their wives."

There are important similarities in the way these plays portrayed guinguettes. People did not go frequently. Some went on weekends, others went only on the occasion of a wedding. One of the wives in *Le Moulin de Javelle* is so impressed at having visited a guinguette two days in a row that she remarks she might as well live there. In contrast the porters in Vadé's *La Pipe cassée* make no such statement about their local cabaret, though they went frequently, because in fact they did live there. The drinking place of the widow Rabavin was simply an extension of their homes, and congregating there was as much a part of their lives as sleeping in their lodgings. The role of women in this literature further distinguishes cabarets from guinguettes. In several plays, women are depicted as intruders in urban taverns, as they discover their husbands away from work and chastise them. At guinguettes, however, they willingly join the drinking party, perhaps because guinguettes were for Sundays and threatened worktime less. Whatever the reasons, guinguettes were associated with women in a way that cabarets were not. As a picture of Ramponeau's establishment advised, "officers and financiers / abbés and students / all go to la Courtille / to look for a nice girl."

The iconography of guinguettes (most of them pictures of Ramponeau's tavern, the Tambour Royal) makes the same points about their unusual size and gaiety (see Figures 3.1 and 3.2). There are several scenes of this guinguette: the main room, shown from various angles, and the garden, each with a caption extolling the merits of Ramponeau and his establishment. Whether or not they are accurate representations, the scenes are consistent in their images. The vast size is the most obvious characteristic: rooms are immense and packed full of people. There are references scattered throughout the pictures to the crowds of customers. People stand at the door asking, "Is there any room?" and above one window is the caption, "All full." Another image that predominates is the near-chaos of the scene. "What a crowd, what noise," says one caption, and another, "Everyone is laughing, everything sparkles." People are dancing, drinking, singing, vomiting, sleeping, wandering around. Above them is the exhortation: "Drink, smoke, sleep, it is a pleasure for us." One picture advertises, "The Parisian spirit and frivolity / bring an abundance here / here you will find extravagance."

The pictures are, in fact, extravagant, in the commotion, the revelry, the numbers. This is what Ramponeau's establishment was advertising: its lack of restraint, its excess and freedom. It was a place of revelry rather than relaxation. At the bottom of one picture the caption reads "the guinguette is a place one goes to be free, to devote oneself without witnesses to the development of sweet affection. . . . It is the freedom of the countryside." Again there was the image of the guinguette as free from the restraints of the city.

The role of the tavernkeeper in these plays illustrates another interesting difference between urban and suburban taverns. The importance of the tavernkeeper in the plot of these plays suggests his relation to his customers and his tavern and provides a measure of the public nature of the cabaret. The cabaret owner is mentioned only to identify the cabaret, or he is there to serve and take orders. The wine merchant of the guinguette, le Moulin de Javelle, in contrast, is a central character. He and his wife are shrewd, venal, and manage everything that goes on at the guinguette with great skill. Similarly, Ramponeau ap-

FIGURE 3.1
The Guinguette. (Phot. Bibl. nat. Paris)

pears in *La Mariée de la Courtille* while making his rounds, shouting directions to his servants about where to put customers and greeting people as they come in. It is Ramponeau, moreover, who stops the fights that break out. When the beer seller tries to intervene in *L'Impromptu de la foire*, everyone turns on him. The owner of the local cabaret, both in *L'Impromptu* and the *Les Ecosseuses de la halle* is a cipher, servile and completely in the background. In *La Pipe cassée* the cabaret owner is not even present.

The differences could be a matter of style, but they suggest a basic difference between the neighborhood cabaret and the suburban guinguette. The guinguette was glamorous and entertaining and essentially an exception to the daily routine. Customers there are merely guests, and the owner retains complete control of the guinguette's space. The owner's dominance over the guinguette underlines the lack of an owner's authority in the neighborhood cabaret. The customers in plays have taken over the local cabaret; it has become their space. At the very least they challenge the owner's authority over the cabaret and his right to control its use, in much the same way as did people found in the judicial records. In contrast to guinguettes, the urban cabaret might appear small and unexciting, yet it was an integral part of people's lives.

If Parisians believed what they were hearing in plays and seeing in pictures, they would have formed an image of their neighborhood taverns as dull, small, and mediocre, in contrast to the guinguette. The cabaret also had a problem of being too close to wife and workshop, and wives could be expected to arrive at the cabaret to remind their husbands of their responsibilities. The guinguette, in contrast, offered gaiety and freedom from responsibilities, as well as harmony and perhaps even flirtation between the sexes. There was no attempt to suggest that a customer would find the ambience of a neighborhood tavern at a lower price. No, everything was different, and the guinguette was proud of it. These taverns outside of the city

FIGURE 3.2

Invitation du Sieur Ramponneau. (Phot. Bibl. nat. Paris)

were free, secondly, from the constraints of space, of decorum, of social status, even of work.[91] Wine, finally, was an important attraction, but the lower cost was mentioned only rarely. Rather it was the quality of Ramponeau's wine in particular, or (in a play about another guinguette) the magic properties of the wine that cured all ills, that the playwright calls to our attention.[92]

The guinguette has its own attractions for historians who expect that popular culture was rowdy and extravagant.[93] The guinguette could be Rabelaisian and was, in fact, proud to portray itself in those terms. More particularly, the guinguette appeals to those historians who have accepted a certain syllogism: the poor preferred to drink as much as possible on their inadequate incomes, wine at the guinguette was cheaper, therefore they preferred guinguettes. Of the cheapness of wine there can be no doubt, but the major premise is questionable, and reduces popular culture to a desperate search for a drunken escape and misses more important behavior.

The contemporary portrayal of guinguettes reviewed here should give us pause. It was not the price of wine that was being emphasized, nor was it the possibility of drunkenness. If the guinguette provided an escape, it was an escape from the neighborhood with its promiscuous intimacy and dense social relations.[94] The countryside offered an escape from the decorum of the city, not to mention the heat and smells. In short, the guinguette offered a different kind of sociability and a different kind of leisure. The guinguette heralded a more modern leisure, separated from work, domesticity, and neighborhood.

[91] Several of the pictures depicting Ramponeau's tavern allude to the freedom from work. A caption at the bottom of one claims that "l'on voit aujourd'hui courir nos Badaux / sans les achever quitter leurs travaux / Pourquoi? C'est qu'ils vont chez M. Ramponneau." An interior scene of Ramponeau's tavern shows a wall drawing entitled, "Je quitte mes travaux pour boire chez Ramponneau."

[92] Alain René LeSage, *Les Désespérées*, in *Three Centuries of French Drama* (Louisville, Ky., microfiche edn., 1969).

[93] Faure, *Paris carême-prenant*, pp. 12-36.

[94] Farge, *Vivre*, pp. 15-40.

Yet if the guinguette's popularity and business were increasing, it should be clear that the cabaret's demise has been much exaggerated. Parisians from the laboring classes continued to have recourse to cabarets on a regular and constant basis. Many may have made the trip beyond the barriers on Sundays, but cabarets too were busy on that day. And if cabarets often lacked some of the carnival atmosphere of the guinguette, they offered a place to meet, to wait, to fight, to find work, or to supplement one's lodgings. They were embedded in the daily experiences of the laboring classes, an extension of the shop, a foyer to the home, and yet distinct from either professional or domestic space.

Quite possibly the elites used cabarets less than before the advent of the café. On looking back, they saw only the brutality and debauchery of the populace as it assembled in its neighborhood taverns and they refused to return. From their growing isolation they failed to see that the traditional sociability of cabarets, intimately connected as it was to work and neighborhood life, continued to be important to the culture and to the very social existence of the laboring classes.

Four. Drinking and Drunkenness

Public drinking brought men together for leisure, recreation, business, or idleness and contributed to the formation of their social bonds. But public drinking also caused alarm, as the elites became apprehensive about the excesses of drink, and this attitude has characterized studies of popular culture in the old regime since then. Drink often serves as a barometer of the health of an individual, class, or society. Widespread drunkenness tends to be seen as an indication of a deeper social malaise that is causing alcoholic excess. Thus historians speak of alcohol as a drug, of drunkenness as solace or oblivion from problems that lie deep in the society.[1] This equation of drink with something sinister is an old one. At least as early as the sixteenth century, French writers identified drunkenness as a scourge that troubled the state. Historians and writers since then have pointed to drunkenness as a sign of the dissolution of public morals, particularly those of the poor. Yet their emphasis on drunkenness obscures the importance of alcohol in people's diet and in their culture. The consumption of alcohol, particularly social drinking in taverns, provided the structure of popular sociability and a ritual form to public and communal comportment. If we are to assess the health of old-regime society accurately, we must recognize the social and cultural role of drinking and taverns.

The traditional portrait of alcohol consumption, especially consumption in taverns, has been one of excess. The poor supposedly got drunk at every occasion, especially on Sundays when they would leave Paris to drink in the suburbs. "In Paris,

---

[1] According to Marrus, "Social Drinking," p. 116 "scholars commonly associate drink and social distress in describing a society." To support this point, Marrus gives several examples of historians of the eighteenth and nineteenth centuries.

regiments of drunks return to town from the suburbs every night, staggering, beating the walls. . . . The drunkenness of the Parisian people is abominable and horrifying."[2] This contemporary description is still echoed by historians today. "Too often workers passed their evenings at the cabaret; drunkenness was considered a social scourge by the government."[3] The taverns both inside and outside the city bore the reputation of "Bacchic stews" where the populace went to get drunk.[4] Nineteenth-century historians, reflecting their society's horror of alcoholism and of a drunken proletariat, maintained this depiction of the eighteenth-century cabaret.[5] Few modern historians of Paris have gone much beyond this caricature of the drunken and disorderly patrons of the Parisian tavern.[6] If we wish to understand the implications of drink in the old regime, we must do more than rely on Mercier, as so many have done. The impact of alcohol depended on how much was actually drunk, how often, and how it functioned in popular culture. The answers to these questions reveal that the tavern was far more than a place to get drunk; alcohol was more than a drug or an escape; and drunkenness was still far from an epidemic. Alcohol served, rather, as a symbol of community and an idiom of social exchange. If its consumption resulted at times in drunkenness, the central aim of public drinking was sociability.

[2] Mercier, *Tableau de Paris*, 12:275-276.

[3] Saint-Germain, *La Vie quotidienne*, p. 17.

[4] Braudel, *Capitalism and Material Life*, p. 166. He is quoting a verse from the eighteenth century.

[5] Attitudes in the nineteenth century are well analyzed in Barrows, *Distorting Mirrors*, pp. 43-73. Surprisingly, Chevalier, *Laboring Classes*, has little to say about the question, but some of the "historians" of the cabaret writing in the nineteenth century, such as Michel and Fournier, and Colombey, illustrate the point adequately.

[6] Taverns and drunkenness are treated briefly—and in most cases synonymously—by Braudel, *Capitalism and Material Life*, pp. 165-166; Mandrou, *Introduction*, pp. 302-303; Kaplow, *The Names of Kings*, pp. 78-79; Farge, *Vivre*, pp. 70-78; and Saint-Germain, *La Vie quotidienne*, p. 17. A notable exception to this view is provided by Daniel Roche in his two books on Parisian culture, *Le Peuple de Paris* and *Journal de ma vie*.

The ideal place to begin a discussion of drinking would be with an extensive set of fiscal records that could document how much Parisians consumed. The tax on alcohol entering the city was a major source of income both to the crown and to the tax farms, and a sizable bureaucracy existed simply to keep track of the Parisian wine trade. Yet the records of this tax that survive are fragmentary and isolated and offer little encouragement toward making a comprehensive assessment about the amount of alcohol sold or consumed in Paris. One fact that emerges most clearly is that alcohol in Paris meant wine, above all else. Reports from 1711, 1712, and 1714 indicate that the average importation of wine into the city ran at more than 600,000 hectoliters a year, whereas imports of spirits were less than 3 percent of that amount. Lavoisier's calculations of consumption in Paris at the end of the century showed no change in this ratio of wine to spirits.[7]

Given a population of roughly half a million Parisians at the beginning of the eighteenth century, the average annual consumption of wine was about 120 liters per person per year. Figures from eighty years before, in 1637, were higher—as much as 155 liters per person. The amount of wine calculated from taxes for the years 1744 to 1757 was practically identical to the figures earlier in the century, but the population had undoubtedly grown. The wine merchants' guild claimed that provisions of wine for Paris in the years around 1761 were generally be-

[7] Figures for 1711 and 1712 are 555,000 and 670,000 hectoliters; see Saint-Germain, *La Vie quotidienne*, p. 17. The figures for 1714 are 128,834 muids for the period 1 October 1713 to 1 May 1714, or roughly 345,000 hectoliters, according to AN, G⁷, 1182-1215. Averaging 18,400 muids per month, the annual rate was probably in the neighborhood of 221,000 muids or 592,000 hectoliters a year. A muid de Paris is 268 liters. The average amount of eau-de-vie and liqueur imported for the three years 1711, 1712, and 1714 was 15,000 hectoliters. Antoine Lavoisier, *Résultats extraits d'un ouvrage intitulé De la richesse territoriale du royaume de France*, in *Oeuvres de Lavoisier* (Paris, 1893), 6:429-431, cites 250,000 muids (670,000 hectoliters) of average annual wine consumption in Paris before the Revolution, and 8,000 muids (21,440 hectoliters) of eau-de-vie.

tween 640,000 and 670,000 hectoliters. Arthur Young cited roughly the same amount for the last decades of the old regime, but this was only 11 percent above figures for the beginning of the century (not including the 17 percent that he added for fraud, which had probably remained fairly constant over the century), while the population had increased by some 30 to 40 percent. Thus per capita consumption would seem to have been declining, toward 110 liters per year at mid-century and even 95 liters by the end.[8] Figures for Lyon suggest a similar decrease in consumption, from 201 liters per year at the beginning of the century to 150 liters at the end.[9]

The decline in Parisian consumption may perhaps be explained by considering that wine sold at guinguettes was not included in these tax figures. Ramponeau's guinguette alone sold several hundred muids a year, and the rest of the guinguettes in his parish brought the figures up to 22,000 hectoliters sold in 1766 and 31,000 hectoliters sold by the end of the old regime.[10] Consumption figures indicate that the amount of wine

[8] Orest Ranum, *Paris in the Age of Absolutism* (New York, 1968), pp. 176-178, gives the figure of 240,000 muids for 1637. Lachiver, *Vin, vigne et vignerons*, p. 275, lists 227,888 muids per year between 1744 and 1757, or 610,000 hectoliters a year. When divided by 600,000 Parisians, the average is 102 liters per capita. *Pièces diverses*, Pt. 2, p. 77, gives 240,000 to 250,000 muids "commonly" entering Paris around 1761. Arthur Young, *Travels in France during the Years 1787-1789*, ed. Jeffry Kaplow (Garden City, N.Y., 1969), p. 374, gives 245,000 muids per year, equal to 657,000 hectoliters. To this Young added a sixth part again, for the amount of wine that the tax farm estimated escaped taxation each year. His computations resulted in per capita daily consumption of one-third of a quart. To these figures should be added Lavoisier's estimate of beer consumption in the 1780s—53,000 hectoliters a year, or 8.2 liters of beer per capita; see Lavoisier, *Résultats*, 6:431. Frank Jellinek, "Cultural Differences in the Meaning of Alcoholism," in Pittman and Snyder, eds., *Society, Culture and Drinking Patterns*, pp. 384-385, points out that average daily consumption of pure alcohol by modern French men is 130 cc, or roughly 1.3 liters of wine. He also argues that even 3 liters taken over the course of a day would "not cause visible symptoms."

[9] Durand, *Vin, vigne et vignerons*, p. 48.

[10] Lachiver, *Vin, vigne et vignerons*, p. 267, using figures from Ch. Mathis,

sold in the city, at cabarets, remained fairly constant, while business increased rapidly beyond the barriers, much as the attendance figures in the previous chapter suggested. Clearly per capita consumption of wine was not decreasing overall. In all probability it stayed at least as high as the figure for 1637 (155 liters), before guinguettes became so popular. Even then the figure does not include wine sold fraudulently. The wine taxes provoked a massive fraud in wine entering Paris itself. Tax collectors were suborned, walls were secretly pierced by pipelines, and a hundred different schemes kept the tax farm waging a ceaseless and unsuccessful war to control the traffic in wine.[11] A more realistic figure for per capita consumption could easily be over 155 liters of wine a year, but that is an average of the whole Parisian population. To discover the amount of wine consumed by adults, this figure should be nearly doubled. Thus adults probably consumed more than 250 liters a year, or roughly three-quarters of a liter a day. But how often did they drink, and how much at a time?

The price and the frequency of consumption are essential elements in a proper understanding of the amount of wine consumed. The price of a pinte (slightly less than a liter) rose slowly from 8 to 12 sous over the course of the eighteenth century, though it fluctuated frequently. With wages at about 30 sous per day or less for many workers, three-quarters of a liter of wine each day would have meant roughly 25 to 30 percent of a worker's pay spent on wine. A contemporary estimate, by Lavoisier, gave a figure of 15 percent as the average amount of income spent on wine by a craftsman, which would have allowed him one-half a liter each day.[12] A medical treatise from

---

"Belleville et Menilmontant au XVIIIe siècle" (mémoire de maîtrise, Paris 1974), lists 8,105 muids in 1766, 11,045 in 1776, and 11,570 in 1788.

[11] Marcel Lachiver, "Fraude du vin et fraudeurs en l'Ile de France, XVIIIe siècle," *Revue d'histoire moderne et contemporaine* 21 (1974):420.

[12] Wages of course varied considerably. Kaplow, *The Names of Kings*, p. 54, concludes that the "great majority of the laboring poor had to make do with about 1 livre and 10 sous a day or less." Rudé, in "Prices, Wages and Popular Move-

the end of the century offered one-tenth to one-half liter as the range of normal and healthy consumption.[13] The skilled artisan, or master craftsman, making two or three times the wages of a laborer, was obviously in a better position to add wine to his diet. Indeed, judicial records indicate that he drank in taverns comparatively more often.

Most people, then, could drink only a modest amount of wine on a regular basis. Alternatively they could have done all of their drinking on Sundays, filling themselves with cheap wine in the country and making do with hangovers for the rest of the week. A variety of contemporary authors, including Vadé, Cailleau, and the inevitable Mercier, have stressed the latter syndrome, and historians have tended to accept them.[14] Some Parisians clearly spent their Sundays drinking in the suburbs, and the number making the trip appears to have increased through the eighteenth century. The distance to the country made the outing inconvenient, however, and the records of Parisians filing complaints with the police suggest that most drinking was done in the city, where cabarets were patronized steadily throughout the week. As argued in the previous chapter, the Sunday binge was more common at guinguettes than in the city, but in general a considerable majority of customers drank during the rest of the week. In addition, account books

ments," p. 169, citing Lavoisier, agrees that "few wage earners could afford to buy even the comparatively modest quantity of one litre per day." But see Sonenscher, "Work and Wages in Paris," passim, for a reconsideration of income.

[13] Jean Baptiste Pressavin, *L'Art de prolonger la vie et de conserver la santé: ou trait d'hygiène* (Lyon and Paris, 1786), cited in Durand, *Vin, vigne et vignerons*, p. 44.

[14] Vadé, *La Pipe cassée*; Cailleau, *Le Waux hall populaire*. Thierry Fillaut, *L'Alcoolisme dans l'ouest de la France pendant la seconde moitié du XIXe siècle* (Paris, 1983) offers a model of different types of drinking behavior that range from the infrequent binges of peasants to the regular (and much greater overall) consumption of the middle class. Drinking patterns of urban workers fall between these two types. Fillaut points out that the middle classes were shocked by the peasants' binge drinking and ignored the contrast between the peasants' general sobriety and their own regular and much higher levels of alcohol consumption.

of individual customers buying wine on credit every day give a rough idea of individual attendance. Two or three times a week seems to have been common, and of course that figure is a minimum, for men patronized more than one establishment regularly and did not always drink on credit. People appear to have gone often, if not to the same cabaret, then to some cabaret.[15] Drinking in the tavern in the city, the neighborhood cabaret, seems to have been both regular and moderate.

There is little more that we can know about the amount of wine consumed or the frequency of trips to taverns. The questions of drunkenness—its prevalence and its implications—must be addressed indirectly, then, through sources and records that do not lend themselves to quantification but still offer rich insight into the significance of alcohol consumption. Various sources, as well as common sense, suggest that people did become intoxicated. Yet there are discrepancies in these sources, differences of interpretation and definition, that reveal how complex the problem of analyzing drunkenness really is. Government and church, the elites and the common people, all yield different and sometimes contrasting perspectives on the question. The study of these various perceptions of drunkenness, as well as the light each perception sheds on the realities of the problem, gives us the opportunity to reconstruct the meaning and experience of drinking and drunkenness in the eighteenth century.

DRUNKENNESS

Drunkenness, we are told, did not appear as a problem until the seventeenth century in France. "One does not perceive in France, before the end of the sixteenth century, any trace of the profound and general anxiety that the word alcoholism [*alcoolisme*] causes in us today."[16] This statement from the historian of

[15] See note 77 in Chapter Three.
[16] Dion, *Histoire de la vigne*, p. 488.

wine and vines, Roger Dion, is not easily dismissed, nor is his conclusion that drunkenness (*ivrognerie*) increased rapidly after the sixteenth century. Dion's principle evidence in reaching this conclusion was provided by Bernard de Laffemas, who published several works at the end of the sixteenth century describing the problems besetting the country. Laffemas pointed particularly to "the intoxications [les yvrogneries] that very often ruin households and families" and blamed the recent extension of the problem on the number and indiscipline of taverns.[17]

The terms used by Laffemas, however, illustrates the difficulty of our understanding early modern drunkenness. The most common word for drunkenness in the old regime, ivrognerie, covered a wide range of physical conditions. Ivrognerie referred to everything from intoxication to alcoholism, and its more precise definition, "habit, or practice, of getting drunk [*habitude de s'enivrer*]," does little to clarify its meaning.[18] Few in the old regime spoke of ivrognerie as a medical problem, although one jurist just before the Revolution defined ivrognerie as an "inveterate passion for drink." When the term alcoolisme was introduced in the mid-nineteenth century, a doctor declared, "There may be a good many drunkards [ivrognes] in France, but happily there are no alcoholics."[19] Most contemporaries referred to ivrognerie as a "vice," emphasizing its moral dimension. Furthermore, the word denoted nothing about the specific scale of the problem. The vagueness of the vocabulary reflected the ambiguity of contemporary perceptions. Thus, before concluding that alcoholism, or even drunk-

---

[17] Bernard de Laffemas, *Source de plusieurs abus et monopoles qui se sont glissez et coulez sur le peuple de France depuis trente ans ou environs* (n.p., 1596), p. 16, cited in Dion, *Histoire de la vigne*, p. 488.

[18] *Petit Robert*, 1972 ed., s.v. "ivrognerie."

[19] Muyart de Vouglans, *Les Loix criminelles*, 1:14. The *Petit Robert* gives 1859 as the first known use of the word, s.v. "alcoolisme." Barrows, *Distorting Mirrors*, p. 61, finds the word used first by a Swedish doctor in 1852. The French doctor is quoted in Barrows, "After the Commune," p. 206.

enness, was increasing, it is essential to examine what the sources were talking about.

The work of Laffemas had been preceded only a few years before by an essay on drunkenness that described the problem in very different terms. Michel de Montaigne considered drunkenness (yvrognerie) a "gross and brutish vice," but one that "costs our conscience less than the others."[20] For Montaigne, drunkenness was considered in terms of the individual rather than economy, though he noted that drunkenness was "less malicious and harmful than the other [vices], which almost all clash more directly with society in general." Nor did he perceive drunkenness as a widespread problem among his compatriots. He described the "French style of drinking" as "at two meals [a day] and moderately, for fear of your health," and even argued that "we should make our daily drinking habits more expansive and vigorous."[21] Between the mercantilist Laffemas and the skeptic Montaigne, there was little agreement; they do not appear to have used the same terms in the same way. The "yvrogneries" of Laffemas arguably refer to habitual drinking on the scale of alcoholism. "Yvrognerie" for the tolerant Montaigne seems closer to a moral failing, a weakness of minor and occasional proportions, with no sense of permanent degeneracy. The books of Laffemas may well reflect a new awareness of mercantilist principles rather than a discovery of changed conditions in society.[22]

The vocabulary of drunkenness gained little precision in the following two centuries, nor did social commentators refine their understanding of the problem. The mercantilist perception of drinking echoed in the writing of Colbert, who condemned wine for being a "great obstacle to work" and taverns

[20] Michel de Montaigne, *The Complete Essays*, trans. Donald M. Frame (Stanford, 1958), p. 247.

[21] Ibid.

[22] Charles W. Cole, *Colbert and a Century of French Mercantilism* (Hamden, Conn., 1964), 1:28-39.

for "having no principle other than idleness and debauchery."[23] The work of eighteenth-century magistrates, such as Nicolas Delamare's *Traité de la Police*, sounded a note of implacable hostility. "The disorders caused by an excess of wine have long made cabarets odious . . . because very often what happens there degenerates into debauchery and drunkenness [*yvresse*]; in any case, it is very certainly an imminent chance of falling into this vice, and into all its dangerous, fatal . . . consequences, without counting how many men of honor lose their reputation, and others ruin their health and their families."[24] The *Code de la Police* of Duchesne identified drinking as a cause of indigence: "In those places where there is a superabundance of wine that is not exported . . . the low price of wine means that the common people are drawn into the cabarets . . . leave their work, their business, and become miserable." The *Dictionnaire économique* also blamed the poverty of "peasants and artisans" on their drinking in taverns.[25] The volumes on jurisprudence in the *Encyclopédie méthodique* at the end of the old regime addressed the subject of "l'ivrognerie, above all in cabarets and other public places" as the responsibility of the police of morals. "This vice is one of the most hateful and most common among the populace [*peuple*]. . . . [It is] equally a vice that the police ought to prevent since it renders subjects incapable of fulfilling their duties to society."[26] Colbert and later magistrates essentially reiterated the principles of social utility already formulated by Laffemas.

The definition of yvrognerie in the *Encyclopédie*, however, appearing at about the same time in the eighteenth century as the work by Duchesne, was virtually copied from Montaigne's essay. Thus, the parallel traditions of utilitarian disapproval

[23] Ernest Lavisse, *Louis XIV* (Paris, 1905-1906; rpr., 1978), 1:217.

[24] Delamare, *Traité de la police*, 3:719.

[25] Duchesne, *Code de la police*, titre XII, I: Police des pauvres; and *Dictionnaire économique*, cited in Durand, *Vin, vigne et vignerons*, p. 44.

[26] *Encyclopédie méthodique: jurisprudence*, 10:538.

and classical tolerance existed still, and were little closer to each other in their judgments. Elsewhere in the *Encyclopédie* the authors described the ill effects of an excess of wine on the balance of solids and liquids in the body and the "impotence in venereal exercise of men lost to drunkenness."[27] Yet the philosophes were little more willing to condemn drunkenness than was Montaigne.

The *Encyclopédie* did go beyond Montaigne in one important aspect. What for Montaigne had been a vice was for the philosophes an offense against reason. "One should conclude that drunkenness . . . is not always a fault, against which it is necessary to be on one's guard; it is a breach that one makes in natural law, which orders us to preserve our reason." The abuse of wine produced "irrationality [*la déraison*] . . . let one stiffen his reason as much as he will, the least dose of an intoxicating liquor suffices to destroy it."[28] Although such objections did not seriously alter the generally tolerant tone of the *Encyclopédie*'s definition, the identification of intoxication with irrationality reveals an important theme in early modern perceptions of drunkenness. "Drunkenness [yvresse] . . . is a brief madness," Delamare had asserted in his treatise on the police at the beginning of the eighteenth century, "all the worse . . . for being voluntary."[29] Still, drunkenness as "irrationality" had little in common with the mercantilist objections of Laffemas or Duchesne. For Duchesne drunkenness separated a man from society; for the philosophes it separated a man from humanity.

The *Encyclopédie*'s tolerant attitude toward drunkenness did not extend to taverns, however. The author of the essay on thrift (*épargne*) attacked "cabarets so multiplied, so detrimental among us, that they are for the populace the most common cause of its misery and its disorders. Cabarets . . . are a perpetual occasion of excess and waste [*pertes*]. . . . It would be

[27] *Encyclopédie*, s.v. "eau," and "vin."
[28] Ibid., s.v. "ivrognerie."
[29] Delamare, *Traité de la police*, 1:612.

. . . important to forbid them during working days to all people established and known in each parish."³⁰ The tavern bore the brunt of opprobrium, rather than drink, and its chief sin was against "thrift." Indeed the tavern's responsibility for social disruption figured prominently, and sometimes quite independently of any attack on drunkenness, in many commentaries.

The church used a vocabulary of drunkenness that was similar to that of the philosophes but expressed a censure that equaled the mercantilists. The Doctors in Theology of the Faculty of Paris, in instructions to confessors in 1721, assured them that yvrognerie was a mortal sin.³¹ They went on to describe various manifestations of the sin, distinguishing between those who drank to the point of "losing the light of reason," and those who drank "beyond need and even beyond propriety," and those who "heat their head" and are unable to "fulfill the duties of their profession." Thus the single term yvrognerie referred to anything within a wide range of incidental to uncontrollable intoxication. Yet their methods for dealing with the problem of drink suggest that the Doctors were aiming particularly at those suffering from a physical reliance on alcohol.

Drunkards, especially those with a head "so weak that a small quantity of wine is capable of intoxicating them," should be told not to drink at all. No drunkenness was to be tolerated, and "frivolous excuses," such as the "invitation of a friend to drink" or the "conclusion of a business deal," should not be accepted. However, those who were "so accustomed to drink, that they fall into a swoon when they are deprived of it" were to be allowed to drink moderately if they had shown a desire to avoid drunkenness and a "firm resolution to work effectively to conquer little by little the unfortunate necessity in which they are put by their drunkenness [yvrognerie]." Although this advice

³⁰ *Encyclopédie*, s.v. "épargne."
³¹ "Cas de conscience sur l'yvrognerie et sur les danses, décidés par MM. les Docteurs en Théologie de la Faculté de Paris," *Journal des savantes* (14 April 1721).

sounds a humane note, the church was unambiguously hostile to taverns, particularly as they threatened their parishioners' willingness to fulfill their Sunday duties.[32]

The government had long since expressed its official condemnation of drunkenness. An ordinance on the punishment of drunkards (yvrognes) in 1536 declared that "whoever shall be found drunk [yvre]" was to be put in prison with bread and water for a first offense and whipped for recurrences.[33] Such severity sought to avoid the excesses of the drunkard, the "idleness, blasphemy, homicides, and other damage and harm that comes from drunkenness [*ébriété*]." Thus the drunkard, for the government, was a potential troublemaker, but it is not clear whether the ordinance refers to alcoholics or to anyone found drunk.[34] The ordinance further stated that "if by drunkenness or the heat of wine drunkards commit any bad action, they are not to be pardoned, but punished for the crime and in addition for the drunkenness at the judge's discretion." Drunkenness, then, was seen as an aggravating circumstance, not unconnected to other crimes.

The ordinance against drunkenness was enforced only fitfully. Commissaires occasionally noted in their reports that a suspect was inebriated and might even weigh that fact in their judgments, though not always consistently. In a fight between two people who blamed each other for the initial aggression, it was the person who "besides appeared pris de vin" that was sent

[32] See letters from curés to Joly de Fleury, BN, Ms. fr. na. 2414; Philip T. Hoffman, *Church and Community in the Diocese of Lyon, 1500-1789* (New Haven, 1984), pp. 99-100, describes increasing clerical hostility to taverns in the eighteenth century.

[33] Edit sur la punition des ivrognes . . . , Valence, August 1536, in Isambert, *Recueil général*, 12:527.

[34] The *Petit Robert* defines ivrogne as "qui a l'habitude de s'enivrer," whereas ébriété refers to simple ivresse. A police report (AN, Y10993b, 17 May 1751) described an officer arresting four "yvrognes" who had gotten into a fight. Apparently anyone found drunk could be an yvrogne. Muyart de Vouglans, *Les Loix criminelles*, 1:343, identified yvrognes d'habitudes as the real problem, thus suggesting that there were yvrognes who were not habitual.

to prison.³⁵ A commissaire locked up a woman found sleeping on the street since "her behavior seemed suspicious (being still drunk)."³⁶ In contrast, the watch brought in a master brewer who had started a fight, but "because he was extremely drunk and out of his senses [*il n'a aucune raison*]," he was sent home.³⁷ Yet such incidents were infrequent, and the police inspecting taverns at night made little effort to arrest those who were found drunk.³⁸ Someone found drunk on the street at night—particularly a woman—might be incarcerated but more, it seems, for being out at night than for drunkenness. Thus an inspector who had come across a person "sleeping on the street dead drunk [*mort yvre*]" at midnight arrested not only the drunk, but two friends who were trying to get him home.³⁹

Unlike ordinances on closing hours for cabarets and cafés, or edicts against taverns serving alcohol during Mass, the ordinance against drunkenness, was not incorporated into the litany of ordinances dealing with cabarets, and morals in general, that was repeated and repromulgated regularly throughout the old regime. There was no reissuing of the edict against drunkenness in the eighteenth century and probably none in the seventeenth.⁴⁰ If drunkenness was truly a "scourge" after the sixteenth century, the government did not consider it serious enough to necessitate renewing the law.

Elite perceptions of drunkenness ranged from broad toler-

³⁵ AN, Y10139, 29 January 1751.

³⁶ AN, Y13166, 19 April 1751.

³⁷ AN, Y12900, 29 October 1771.

³⁸ In fact, relatively few of the reports of these night patrols make any mention of drunkenness in taverns: exceptions include the report of 21 November 1751, which found "many yvrognes, soldiers . . . and other suspicious people" but did not arrest any of them (BA, Arch.Bastille, Ms. 10139).

³⁹ AN, Y13166, 12 May 1751.

⁴⁰ The various eighteenth-century treatises on law—those by Duchesne and Delamare, for example—find nothing more recent than the 1536 edict to which to refer. Such treatises were careful to cite not only the oldest examples, as precedent, but generally gave the most recent reeditions. Dion, *Histoire de la vigne*, p. 488, also comments on this lacuna.

ance to alarmed condemnation. There would seem to have been no common ground for understanding the meaning or implications of the term. By and large, however, those who harshly condemned drunkenness were talking about the populace, the lower classes; those who expressed toleration were speaking more generally of humanity. The theme unifying these disparate texts and attitudes may simply be that when drunkenness was a problem, it was a lower-class problem. As an historian has recently remarked, "this official literature [on drunkenness] . . . reveals the secret of a rage among the upper classes at seeing a social distinction diminish in a consumption from which they hoped the poor would remain excluded as a sign of inferior condition."[41] From the traditional preserve of the elites, wine had become an item of common consumption. Its value to commoners lay perhaps in its power as a symbol of status, the very reason that so provoked elite commentators. Such an attitude could help explain the obsession of the government and writers at the time with the quality of wine produced and consumed in France. As farmers responded to growing demand for wine in the cities in the seventeenth and eighteenth centuries by replacing the traditional vinestock with new varieties that produced wine in much greater quantities but lower quality, the government looked for ways to outlaw the innovations. Wine merchants profited from the growing demand by adulterating their stocks and dyeing the cheap white wine from the Parisian area red to command Burgundy prices.[42] Laments about the miserable, even unhealthy, quality of wine drunk by most Parisians appears as one of the most consistent features in descriptions from the period. "To get drunk with good wine, as they do in some countries, is pardonable to a certain point," Mercier concedes. "The drinker ends up with a light headache and goes to bed; but the Parisian gets drunk with bitter, hard,

---

[41] Durand, *Vin, vigne et vignerons*, p. 45. See also Daniel Roche, "Le Temps de l'eau rare," *Annales, économies, sociétés, civilizations* 29 (1984):395.

[42] Dion, *Histoire de la vigne*, pp. 532-605.

detestable wine at great cost . . . which is hardly conceivable."[43] His disgust represents the attitude of many others. If this statement is an expression of sincere concern for public health, it is also an appeal to snobbishness. The canaille might be drinking wine, but it only emphasized their inferiority. Invested with such significance, wine was clearly both a potent element of popular consumption and aspirations and an acrimonious symbol in elite discourse about society.

The languages of work and of rationality seem to have provided the basic vocabularies with which people of all ranks comprehended drinking and drunkenness, though work figured more prominently. Certainly many of the authors of this period spoke of drunkenness in terms of social utility and work, and nearly all perceived taverns that way. Yet while those like Duchesne in his *Code de la police* continued to see drunkenness as an offense against a work ethic, both the church and the philosophes condemned drunkenness for destroying the "light of reason" and for producing "irrationality." The conjunction of these two languages may perhaps be explained by the "new sensibility to poverty, . . . to the economic problems of unemployment and idleness, a new ethic of work," as it has been outlined by Michel Foucault. This is also, Foucault argues, a sensibility that "included madmen in the proscription of idleness."[44] He describes the fall of madness from its privileged position in medieval culture because of the growing repression of all social deviance during the seventeenth and eighteenth centuries. Foucault has pointed to the conflation in early modern culture of what he calls "unreason" and true insanity. The realm of "unreason" was populated by "the debauched, spendthrift fathers, prodigal sons, blasphemers, men who seek to undo themselves, libertines"—in short, by those who resisted

[43] Ibid., pp. 595-605; Mercier, *Tableau de Paris*, 12:276.

[44] Michel Foucault, *Madness and Civilization*, trans. Richard Howard (New York, 1965), pp. 46, 57; see also pp. 38-84. Foucault mentions drunkenness only briefly.

the ethic of labor and social utility. Within this general paradigm of social utility, there was a "special modulation which concerned madness proper . . . those called, without exact semantic distinction, insane, alienated, deranged. . . ."[45] Thus eighteenth-century perceptions of drunkenness reflected the contemporary connection between social utility and insanity.

If drunkenness was not identified as a widespread problem before the seventeenth century, as Dion argues, it may be that drunkenness, like poverty, perhaps even like madness, was seen hitherto with more charity. Drunkenness in Rabelais, for example, is relatively benign, almost divine, in its access to truth and was similar in that regard to contemporary perceptions of madness.[46] By the seventeenth and eighteenth centuries, however, drunkenness was condemned and the drunkard might be confined. Mercantilists and some Parisian depositions spoke of drunkenness in terms that were identifiably a part of the language of social utility. The "debauchery of wine," the "derangement" and "libertinage," all indicate an underlying coherence to the perception of drunkenness: drunkenness, whether perceived as idleness or as madness, had been placed outside of the "community of labor."[47] Therein lies the logic of the antithesis between cabaret and work. Drunkenness shared the moral opprobrium that was attached to poverty and unemployment as early as the middle of the seventeenth century. In

[45] Ibid., pp. 65-66.
[46] Mikhail Bakhtin, *Rabelais and His World*, trans. Helene Iswolsky (Cambridge, Mass., 1968), pp. 295-296. Voltaire went so far as to call Rabelais a "drunken philosopher, who only wrote when he was drunk [dans le temps de son ivresse]." Voltaire, *Letters on England*, trans. Leonard Tancock (Harmondsworth, 1980), Letter 22.
[47] Foucault, *Madness and Civilization*, p. 58. Foucault has been challenged by several historians, among them H. C. Erik Midelfort, "Madness and Civilization in Early Modern Europe: A Reappraisal of Michel Foucault," in Barbara C. Malament, ed., *After the Reformation. Essays in Honor of J. H. Hexter* (Philadelphia, 1980), pp. 247-267. While I am not attempting to defend Foucault here, in pointing to parallels I am accepting some of his basic arguments about the eighteenth century.

the nineteenth century, when the "disease of drink" is baptized "alcoholism," drunkenness, like madness, becomes a medical problem, though unlike madness, it never sheds the indictment of moral debauchery.[48]

Given the changing, sometimes contradictory perceptions of drinking and drunkenness, it is difficult to ascertain how much drunkenness there actually was. An English visitor in 1776 claimed that "this vice is almost unknown in France."[49] Other contemporary evidence seems to confirm the Englishman. An historian who has recently surveyed seventeenth-century authors concludes that excessive drinking was uncommon in France and notes, as evidence, that the French customarily drank their wine mixed with water. He contrasts the East Europeans' reputation for drunkenness with French moderation and suggests that the French drank wine with meals while Germans drank it as a "social rite of complex signification."[50] Such a description is not adequate for the eighteenth century, however accurate it may be for earlier periods. The testimony of common Parisians in the eighteenth century gives no hint of adding water to wine, except as part of the cure for venereal disease. When one Parisian, who described his drinking in detail, was forced to follow this regime, it was sufficiently unusual, at least for him, that his companions immediately divined his malady.[51] And if Parisians drank at meals, it is certain that they also drank without eating at taverns, where drink clearly functioned as a social rite. Still, there are good reasons for describ-

---

[48] Barrows, *Distorting Mirrors*, p. 61.

[49] *Observations in a Journey to Paris* (1777), 1:50, cited in Albert Babeau, *Les Artisans et les domestiques d'autrefois* (Paris, 1886), p. 208. Babeau, pp. 207-208, states that: "The French artisan, more polite than the English worker, is also more sober than he, . . . a sobriety animated in part by sentiments of economy."

[50] Jean-Louis Flandrin, "La Diversité des goûts et des pratiques alimentaires en Europe du xvie au xviiie siècle," *Revue d'histoire moderne et contemporaine* 30 (1983):70-73.

[51] Ménétra, *Journal*, p. 215.

ing seventeenth- and eighteenth-century Frenchmen as relatively abstemious.

Parisians drank far less liquor than East European societies appear to have consumed, and they drank far more wine than stronger alcohols.[52] Recent studies suggest that liquor is socially disruptive as much because of its novelty as because of its potency.[53] If it is sold and consumed in nontraditional settings, without ritual forms to structure its use, then liquor has no social meaning beyond its intoxicating effects. This situation seems largely to have been avoided in Paris. The relatively small amount of liquor that was consumed in Paris was sold in establishments quite similar to taverns, and seems not to have provoked the excess caused by gin in England.[54]

POPULAR ATTITUDES

The attitudes of the laboring classes of Paris toward drunkenness are more difficult to assess than are official attitudes. The testimony of men in taverns had almost nothing to say about drunkenness, a remarkable fact in itself but not easily interpreted. The records that addressed drink and drunkenness explicitly derived most often from the extreme cases of alcoholic excess and abuse. They offer rich evidence but must be used

[52] Mercier, *Tableau de Paris*, 12:225-227. In 1714 the importation of eau-de-vie and liqueur into Paris was about one-fortieth that of wine (AN G⁷ 1182-1215). Unfortunately there is no way to know how much of the wine brought into Paris was distilled by the master distillers of Paris, although the increasing attendance at places selling brandy noted in Chapter Three suggests brandy consumption too was rising.

[53] Medick, "Plebeian Culture," pp. 104-106; Taylor, *Drinking, Homicide and Rebellion*, pp. 36-45.

[54] On the "gin lane" problem, see T. G. Coffey, "Beer Street, Gin Lane: Some Views of Eighteenth-Century Drinking," *Quarterly Journal of Studies on Alcohol* 27 (1966):669-683; and M. Dorothy George, *London Life in the Eighteenth Century* (London, 1951), pp. 27-42. The gin lane problem has been, in some ways, a paradigm of modern perceptions of drunkenness and the poor in early modern Europe.

with caution for they represent exceptions to accepted behavior. Such records in the police archives include complaints brought by Parisians against members of their family for drunkenness, for libertinage and debauchery. Some depositions sought protection from violence, others demanded imprisonment of the culprit, still others requested the legal separation of a married couple's communal property.[55] Such complaints linked drunkenness to a variety of other concerns such as taverns, idleness, and filial disobedience that were often more central to people's indignation. These plaintiffs perceived drinking as an escape, as an abdication of responsibility, and complained for reasons that were economic as well as moral.

A few who complained of libertinage addressed the problem of drunkenness in terms of madness much as the church had done, particularly when speaking about women. A clockmaker denounced his wife for having "deranged herself" with constant drink.[56] He described her drinking as "a wicked inclination" and "this habit." The clockmaker's vocabulary was unusually blunt. His wife was "continually drunk [yvre]" and "*saoule*." Both of these terms seem to have been reserved for instances of serious drinking problems, as well as for serious disapproval. The complaint of a journeyman mason described an equally grave situation. His wife was "given to an excess of wine and brandy" but, more tellingly, was "in a despair so frightful that she wishes to destroy herself." The husband suggested that she had a "spirit alienated . . . by debauchery of wine."[57] The mason seems to have been moved by concern for

[55] These records actually consist of two distinct legal documents: the séparations des biens and the plainte of libertinage, which could lead to the police imprisoning someone for immorality. See also Arlette Farge and Michel Foucault, *Le Désordre des familles* (Paris, 1982), passim, for an extensive analysis of requests for lettres de cachet that are quite similar to the requests for separations.

[56] AN, Y10993b, 20 November 1751. Examples in Farge and Foucault, *Le Désordre des familles*, pp. 95, 112-113, speak of folie and "deranged spirit."

[57] AN, Y12952, 22 November 1751. See also Y12548, 27 February 1701, for a husband describing the "alienation of her [his wife's] spirit."

his wife, who had already tried to kill herself and was still seriously wounded on the head from falling down while drunk.
Thus he asked that she be confined in order to "keep his wife in
a place of security." The mason's vocabulary indicates that he
had identified his wife's drinking in terms of madness.

Drunkenness was clearly contrary to plaintiffs' notions of
honorable behavior. The way a "respectable woman" ought to
act, according to a domestic, was "in staying home attentive to
her household." Instead, his wife "abandoned her household
and her child," and "gave herself to a continual debauch of
wine."[58] A barrister thought his wife should apply herself to
"maintaining peace and the union with her husband," but she
was "given to drunkenness [yvrognerie]."[59] Drunkenness
caused problems by keeping men and women away from home.
Thus a plaintiff styling himself a "merchant-bourgeois" complained about his son-in-law "throwing himself into all sorts of
debauchery, coming home late every day drunk [saoul et pris
de vin]."[60] But drunkenness was also linked to violence. The
wife of a juré in the guild of basketmakers accused him of "almost always coming home late, drunk, and in this state, he
beats the plaintiff. . . ." The woman was particularly concerned about a different aspect of her problem, however, accusing her husband of "neglecting his profession, consuming
everything he can earn in debauches without working, even
what they had amassed through the diligence, work, and thrift
[ménage] of the plaintiff." She had protested "gently" that he
"ought to satisfy himself with his work and not consume, as he

[58] AN, Y14527, 6 October 1731.

[59] AN, Y15219, 29 December 1712.

[60] AN, Y13926, 20 March 1741; Y14877, 18 April 1691. Farge and Foucault's reading, in Le Désordre des familles, pp. 34, 161-165, of similar documents is that the dérangement so frequently referred to in the complaints means
primarily "spatial conduct," that is, absence from the home or comings and
goings at odd hours that disrupt the household. The witnesses whom I have used
generally interpreted absence as a sign of professional and economic irresponsibility.

does, not only what they have amassed but even the plaintiff's wealth," but he became furious and attacked her.[61] A dissolute husband threatened a woman's income, even her dowry, as much as her person.

Most depositions objected less to drunkenness than to drinking, because of the time and money spent at taverns and the consequent absence from work. The most frequent descriptions accused the spouse of "spending days and even entire nights in the taverns," or of "going daily to taverns" without really mentioning that he was drunk.[62] "Instead of working and occupying himself with something, he [a merchant] leaves in the morning and does not return until evening, sometimes very late . . . and passes his time drinking in taverns." This same merchant, "instead of devoting himself to work, does nothing but go for walks, with cane in hand, and debauches himself."[63] Although drunkenness was perhaps implied, the primary complaint was that the husband spent a great deal of money and time away from his job. Thus one "abandons his business to pass the day in the tavern," and another "often quits his shop to go play boulles and to go to the tavern."[64] The Sieur Harcourt gave himself to "drink, gambling and to all pleasures, which causes on the one hand the neglect of his commerce and on the other a great deal of useless expenses."[65] The time spent at the tavern

[61] AN, Y10732, 30 December 1701.

[62] AN, Y14174, 3 August 1731; Y11228, 12 October 1741. In a study of lettres de cachet in eighteenth-century Paris, Farge and Foucault, Le Désordre des familles, p. 28, report that two-thirds of the requests for action against a spouse complained "as much about the personal misconduct of a spouse . . . as about his economic conduct." The other one-third focused on personal misbehavior, which often involved drunkenness and abuse. Alain Lottin, "Vie et mort de couple; difficultés conjugales et divorce," Dix-septième siècle 102-103 (1974):70, argues the importance of both "frequenting cabarets and the abusive consumption of alcohol" in divorce cases.

[63] AN, Y13005, 11 January 1781.

[64] AN, Y14537, 30 December 1741; Y14877, 21 November 1691; Y11228, 12 October 1741.

[65] AN, Y12177, 23 January 1771.

was evidence of time not spent working and could indicate as well that the husband was "no longer willing to work."[66] In general, then "tavern" represented everything that was antithetical to "work"; one was either in one's shop or in the tavern.[67]

The tavern was presented in these complaints as a refuge from responsibility and authority. Such complaints of libertinage were, in fact, as much complaints against a family member escaping the family's authority (usually embodied in the father) as they were complaints of misbehavior.[68] Thus a fruit seller complained that his fifteen-year-old daughter had run away five times and "retires with many libertines to drink in the guinguettes."[69] Similarly, a master heelmaker accused his son of "refusing to work at his profession and passing the time roaming and in the different quarters and cabarets of Paris where he makes acquaintances whose example can only be dangerous."[70] A wigmaker, whose wife had left him "to have greater liberty to live as she likes [*à sa fantasie*]," complained that she would not apply herself to "keep house as an honest woman" and instead was "given to debauchery."[71] Plaintiffs clearly considered escaping from work and responsibilities to be signs of debauchery. These complaints were directed as much against the cabaret as an escape as against drinking.

Wives took this tone even when they were not making official complaints. They appeared in popular plays scolding their husbands for drinking instead of working: ". . . and drinking is your only employment." Their complaints have a familiar

---

[66] AN, Y14527, 25 October 1731.

[67] As one witness, a wine merchant, put it, the husband was "at the cabaret as often as at his work" (AN, Y14877, 5 December 1691).

[68] Perrot, *Genèse d'une ville moderne*, 2:836-838, notes that in the lettres de cachet that he examined, conflict was most often between generations, particularly between a widow and her children.

[69] AN, Y11178, 9 September 1761.

[70] AN, Y11947, 6 February 1761.

[71] AN, Y15219, 21 November 1712.

ring. "At the cabaret you pass each instant . . . you eat all my money."[72] Wives, as they were portrayed in literature, objected not so much to the drinking—indeed they joined their husbands readily enough on Sundays—as to drinking on a workday. "Have the holidays come so soon?" is how one wife taunts her husband.[73] But her concern is unmistakable. "You are reducing us to the poorhouse." This kind of drinking is not necessarily even drunkenness but it is idleness and an escape from work.

But wives were not alone in expressing these sentiments. It was predominantly men, after all, who bore witness against husbands in requests for separations. Their testimony generally confirmed not only the faults, but the censure of such faults as well. Men spoke of husbands as "lazy and debauched, he is a drunkard." One was an "eyewitness of the misbehavior of [a master draper] . . . he has seen him almost daily returning late full of wine."[74] A master tailor was accused of "frequenting cabarets where he spends whole nights causing him to neglect his business."[75] Men were generally expected to pay for themselves, and those who paid too often for others were considered merely profligate. "When he is drunk he pays for those who are with him," said a bourgeois about a husband, "and he has the same readiness with all those he meets." A witness had been with him at a tavern where "he was in such disorder from excess of wine that he paid for everyone there."[76] Another man "frequented cabarets with many of his friends for whom he often pays large expenses."[77] One witness accused a husband of spending "days and nights in taverns where he runs up very considerable expenses, paying often for those who will keep

[72] Taconnet, *Impromptu de la foire*, 31:10.
[73] Vadé, *La Pipe cassée*, p. 22.
[74] AN, Y14334, 16 March 1771; Y11218, 17 August 1731.
[75] AN, Y13334, 22 February 1701.
[76] AN, Y12115, 24 December 1711.
[77] AN, Y13468, 21 April 1711.

him company in his debauches."⁷⁸ Witnesses spoke too of several men like the one who "in his debauch pledges himself easily for his friends."⁷⁹ Above all, men were passing judgment on each other's professional behavior. "He only frequents cabarets where he drinks . . . it is very rare to see him in his shop in charge of his business [*à la tête de ses ouvrages*]." Witnesses condemned a man who "prefers his diversion and pleasures to his business and even though he was sometimes quite busy he would voluntarily quit to go to the tavern with the least person."⁸⁰ The merchant dyer, Bonin, was "given to his pleasures and diversions, daily frequenting cabarets, giving no order to his business or his commerce, which he neglects entirely for his diversions."⁸¹ Witnesses in these suits, like the defendants, came from every social level, though more often from among shopkeepers and master artisans. They clearly condemned those whose "pleasure" interfered with their profession and expressed contempt for "drunkards."

The attitude of laboring men to drunkenness and taverns displays considerable ambivalence, however. Employers complained, on the one hand, about their workers drinking when it interfered with work, although again the real issue lay in the question of time more than inebriation. On the other hand, as noted in Chapter Three, employers and employees alike could be found in taverns throughout the day. The same men who condemned their neighbor for "passing his days at the tavern" probably were regular patrons themselves. They were not condemning the tavern itself, as elite authors were wont to do; rather, they objected to men who used taverns too often or at the wrong time. Of course, the appropriate time for such recrea-

---

⁷⁸ AN, Y14527, 25 October 1731.

⁷⁹ AN, Y14611, 12 January 1691, (s'engage); 27 November 1691, (s'oblige). In another document (Y13334, 2 December 1701), a bourgeois is accused of being too willing to "endorse notes."

⁸⁰ AN, Y13334, 26 February 1701; Y11788, 14 February 1771.

⁸¹ AN, Y10762, 28 April 1691.

tion could be a matter of some dispute. The jurés of one guild threatened to send journeymen "who drank and caroused [*ribotoient*]" to jail. This stung the journeymen into defending themselves publicly with a song: "All the journeymen silversmiths / are good carousers /. . . [the jurés] say they must be imprisoned, / and put into Bicêtre [prison] / We laugh at that /. . . [the jurés] will learn that the jolly chaps / are not scoundrels."[82] But while workers defended their right to carouse—meaning their right to leisure and conspicuous consumption—they employed the harsh language of time and utility against employers who idled in taverns. Journeymen arrested at the behest of their jurés for caballing at a tavern, accused the jurés in turn of being "those who have no work, who are more often in taverns than in their shops, and employ journeymen not to work but only to guard their shops."[83] The artisan Ménétra captures this same dichotomy in his memoirs. He flatly condemns fathers, his own and others, who "by their drunkenness [yvrogneries] are responsible for the downfall of their children." Yet he expresses evident pleasure in recounting his own "carousing [*ribotes*]."[84] Drinking is a frequent theme in Ménétra's story, but he insists that however much he "sacrificed to Bacchus," he "never sacrificed except in company"—that is, in social drinking.[85] Nor does he ever identify himself as intoxicated. There was an ideal of sociable behavior that was being implicitly contrasted with excess, but no clear line separated them.

The real issue, identified by most wives and neighbors, lay in the time spent in taverns. Drinking problems existed on the periphery of many of these cases but they did not draw the full fire of condemnation. Thus it is impossible to use the com-

[82] Quoted in Sonenscher, "Les Sans-culottes de l'an II," p. 1097.

[83] Ibid., p. 1099.

[84] Ménétra, *Journal*, p. 192, identifies his drinking as "carousing" only on a few specific occasions; see, for example, p. 185.

[85] Ibid., p. 259.

plaints of libertinage to prove that serious drinking problems were widespread in the old regime, although they clearly offended public opinion when they occurred. In any case, such documents focus our attention on the exceptional cases of extreme behavior. The bulk of judicial testimony, vastly more numerous than demands for separation, dealt with more mundane problems and contentions in people's lives. This depiction of tavern comportment contains little indication of widespread drunkenness and almost no overt reference to it. If drinking to the point of intoxication was as prevalent as some authors have suggested, it is curiously hidden in the depositions before the police. This testimony suggests that drunkenness was not a problem of epidemic proportions.

The daily complaints of insults and injuries in taverns brought before the commissaires dealt not with habitual drunkenness but with daily social relations and conflicts that often involved the defense of honor and reputation. Such complaints tell us about simple intoxication, to the extent that it marked conflicts in taverns and streets, yet accusations of drunkenness are surprisingly rare in the complaints brought by Parisians before the commissaires. Barely 3 percent of the individuals in this study were identified as drunk, although the percentage was increasing (from 1.7 to 4.4 percent) between the last three decades of Louis XIV's reign and the last three decades of Louis XV's. Much of the increase came from people volunteering the information about themselves and from the police mentioning it, where neither had had much to say at the beginning of the century. The men so identified resembled the general profile of tavern customers discussed earlier; although journeymen and day laborers were proportionately more prominent and shopkeepers less, drunkenness was not a problem of the lowest social levels alone. The amount of reported drunkenness at cabarets was proportionately lower than the percentage of customers there would have indicated: cabarets served 60 percent of all tavern customers but had to deal with only 45 percent of those

identified as drunk. The amount of drunkenness at places selling brandy and beer was proportionately greater, particularly
at cafés where 20 percent of all cases of drunkenness occurred
although the café served only 11 percent of all tavern customers. Evidently the police were correct in describing "those
sorts of liqueurs of which the excess is incomparably more dangerous than that of wine."[86] The increasingly frequent reports
of drunkenness, and the greater openness of individuals about
their own intoxication would seem to point to changing attitudes and behavior, but in the end the number of cases of reported drunkenness is so small that they remain terribly impressionistic.

Some of this reticence was certainly due to the legal tenet that
inebriation [yvresse], particularly if unexpected and extreme,
could diminish the gravity of a crime.[87] Thus plaintiffs would
not have been anxious to speak of factors mitigating an assailant's fault. Yet roughly one-fifth of those identified were reported by a plaintiff. Furthermore, testimony comes from accused, who could be expected to excuse themselves with their
drunkenness if they could. Indeed a master candlemaker
claimed that he "was drunk [yvre] and without reason when he
was arrested and not knowing what he was doing, which ren-
dered him absolutely excusable."[88] But practically all deponents—plaintiffs, witnesses, accused, even the police—were silent. In most of the cases where the commissaire or nightwatch
noted that someone arrested was drunk, they were the only ones
to mention it, and they generally treated it as an exacerbating
factor.[89] The very infrequency of any mention of drunkenness,

[86] Arch.Préf.Pol., Fonds Lamoignon, ordonnance de police, 5 November
1677.

[87] ". . . drunkenness [yvresse] being potentially the effect of surprise, can
also serve, when it is extreme, to render crimes less punishable," according to
Muyart de Vouglans, *Les Loix criminelles*, 1:14.

[88] AN, Y9668, 28 December 1761. There is no indication what the judge
thought of this plea.

[89] The commissaire sent two men who had been creating a disturbance to

in a source where drunken brawls could not have been so uncommon, is a striking comment on the attitude toward, if not the extent of, drunkenness.

The very silence of judicial testimony on the subject of drunkenness gives voice to popular ambivalence. Thousands of men and women appeared before the commissaires to report violent or criminal behavior taking place in taverns, and only a handful spoke of drunkenness. The depositions for separations and complaints of libertinage indicate that habitual drunkenness was not unknown, even among the bourgeoisie. Furthermore, they attest to some degree of hostility, even among working men, to serious drunkenness and show a willingness to express condemnation. Why then were men so silent about drunkenness in complaints of tavern brawls? Little of the opprobrium directed at habitual drinking and idleness that was expressed in depositions of libertinage appears in other complaints. Perhaps popular attitudes, so harsh when condemning men "giving themselves to the debauchery of drink," accepted incidental inebriation, indeed did not even think it worth mentioning.

In the few cases that depositions did mention someone being drunk, it was more as an afterthought, or to explain otherwise bizarre behavior. A plaster beater claimed he had become involved in a fight because of a head "heated by wine" and spoke in "terms customary to a man who has drunk and who lacks education."[90] Similarly, a wine merchant having a fight with a customer accused her of having "drunk a glass too many, that it was the wine that made her talk."[91] In both cases the drink was responsible rather than the drinker. Intoxication excused sexual misbehavior, or so implied several plaintiffs who ex-

---

prison "because of their behavior, . . . their insolence and drunkenness" (AN, Y9657, 7 January 1761). See also note 38.

[90] AN, Y10233, 2 August 1761. This reference to education is also quite unusual.

[91] AN, Y11238, 23 July 1751.

plained that they had been with prostitutes only because they, the plaintiffs, had been drunk. One had "had the weakness to accept the prostitute's propositions, being a bit *remply de vin*"; another conceded that he was "giddy [*étourdie*] from drink."[92] It was the drink that made them weak or giddy and to some extent absolved them.

The popular literature of the period also presented drunkenness as often accidental. The drunkard was generally a comic figure, harmless, impertinent, victimized perhaps by his wife. There was a good deal of sympathy for him, even when the other characters, generally the wives or girlfriends, disapproved. The dramatic tension of a play (this was not sophisticated drama) might center on the hapless hero becoming drunk, unintentionally or through someone's malice, and then having to face a woman's reproach. In the *Impromptu des harangères* of Farin de Hautemar, a rival gets the hero drunk in order to discredit him in the eyes of the girl for whom they are vying. The girl is horrified, but the hero's true intentions become clear and they are reconciled.[93] Ménétra gets women drunk to take advantage of them and makes a brother-in-law drunk out of spite: "it gave me pleasure . . . to see him sprawling the length of the road."[94] Literature like this often portrayed drunkenness as a disadvantage or a mishap, comic perhaps, but rarely as a desirable condition.

The vocabulary of drunkenness found in depositions and complaints illustrates this point. There were many ways to describe the condition: *yvre*, *plein de boisson*, *pris de vin*, *remply de vin*, *gris*. One-half of those so described were called pris or plein de boisson or vin—most often pris de vin. One-third were described as saoul, or mort yvre, or most often yvre. The rest were gris, trop bu, or étourdie. Yvre and saoul appear to

[92] AN, Y15931, 8 August 1731; Y10837, 5 April 1720.
[93] Farin de Hautemar, *Impromptu des harangères* (1754) in *Three Centuries of French Drama* (Louisville, Ky., microfiche edn., 1969).
[94] Ménétra, *Journal*, pp. 177, 191.

have been less euphemistic terms than the rest: they were preferred by plaintiffs speaking of others, whereas individuals were far likelier to speak of themselves as pris de vin. Depositions often said only that the person "seemed" or "appeared to be" drunk. Yvre may have implied too much of a clear demarcation between drunk and sober. Instead most people spoke in terms of the drink, that someone was either full of or taken by drink. The vocabulary, then, reflected the tendency to blame the drink for the drunkenness. The implication was that the drink had gotten the better of the drinker, that the drinker had not intended to get drunk.

Evidently popular culture was also engaged in a discourse about drink. Unlike elite discourse, however, which pilloried drinking and drunkenness in terms of unreason and social utility, popular discourse preferred not to speak of drunkenness and cloaked it in terms of sociability. As Roland Barthes said ironically of the "myths" of the twentieth century, "in France, drunkenness is a consequence, never an intention. A drink is felt as the spinning out of a pleasure, not as the necessary cause of an effect which is sought: wine is . . . the leisurely act of drinking."[95] There are clear parallels with the popular myths of the eighteenth century. The realities behind these myths, the existence and nature of popular drunkenness, remain elusive. Yet the myths themselves are revealing. The elites managed to evoke a world in which the lower orders apparently rejected the values of thrift and hard work. As an external problem, drunkenness conveniently explained the failure of capitalist virtues among the poor without challenging their internal logic. Popular myths about drink may get us no closer to the truth, yet anthropologists point to the ability of cultures to impose meaning on, and mold the sensation of, their drinking.[96] If the la-

---

[95] Roland Barthes, *Mythologies*, trans. Annette Lavers (New York, 1972), pp. 58-60. I am indebted to David Price for bringing this quote to my attention.

[96] MacAndrew and Edgerton, *Drunken Comportment*, pp. 88-89, 165-172. Karp, "Beer Drinking," pp. 105-113, discusses several models of drunken com-

boring classes had already created a myth of drinking as conviviality and of drunkenness as accident rather than intention,
as seems to be the case, there is reason to believe that this model
could in fact shape the experienced nature of drinking just as
surely as any biological absolutes of metabolism and alcohol.

The evidence suggests that the line that separated simple intoxication from alcoholism was not clearly understood in the
old regime; that the very notion of alcohol abuse, in fact, was
only half formed; and that those who would look for the rise of
such excess in the old regime must remember that perceptions
of drunkenness were evolving and reflecting changes in social
values as much as changes in social behavior. In addition, judicial testimony indicates that the line separating drinking and
drunkenness was unclear. It is difficult to imagine that people
could not tell when someone was drunk, yet there is a certain
reticence about the fact on the part of witnesses, plaintiffs, suspects, and police. Their silence on the subject expresses the primacy of drinking over drunkenness, the centrality of drinking
in sociability as opposed to the unpremeditated quality of
drunkenness. The people of Paris claimed not to drink to get
drunk and viewed drunkenness as a side effect. Drinking, even
to excess, was an essential instrument of tavern fellowship and
social relations; as a result, drunkenness was tolerated, but not
sought, by those who valued such sociability.

DRINK

If the motives of most people's drinking remain so elusive, and
if there is little evidence, in fact, of widespread drunkenness,
then drinking must be approached in a different manner. Only
by integrating drinking with other activities in the tavern and
with other motivations for going to a tavern can it be under-

portment and says of the Iteso that he studies that, "Inebriation is not drunkenness so long as the person remains in control of himself or herself." I wish to
thank Hans Medick for bringing this article to my attention.

stood as the laboring classes experienced it. The quick drink with a chance acquaintance as well as the slower, more leisurely drinking with friends were part of the sociability of the tavern and contributed to the tavern's function as a public and communal space. Only in conjunction with the other activities in the tavern, to which drinking might be subordinated, does drinking become understandable.

Drink, it should be remembered, was the price of admission to taverns. The records speak only fleetingly of this issue, but they remind us occasionally that the wine merchant made his living from the wine he sold. If a neighbor or friend of the tavernkeeper might be found sometimes enjoying the space without paying for drink, other cases reveal the owners irritation with those who "did not drink enough and were more attached to their play [skittles in this case] than their drink."[97] As one customer explained about a visit, "following the laudable custom of wine merchants which is to sell their drink and in order to induce the Sieur plaintiff and his friends to guzzle [*godailler*]," the wine merchant had brought their dinner to them half an hour later than they requested.[98] The story hints at a desire to resist the tavernkeeper's efforts, a sort of contest where the customer tried to avoid expense and drunkenness.

Wine was a source of refreshment and nourishment and thus a legitimate end in itself. The drink as symbol, as something shared, a sign of friendship, a token of esteem, or a bond, was more important. It was common to seal bargains by drinking over them. One drank at the end of a business transaction "to conclude the deal."[99] The church was aware of this practice and warned confessors to discourage it.[100] There is evidence, in fact, that contracts included the price of a concluding bottle at

[97] AN, Y12308, 7 September 1701.
[98] AN, Y11788, 8 September 1771.
[99] AN, Y10233, 31 October 1760.
[100] "Cas de conscience sur l'yvrognerie."

a cabaret, paid for by the buyer.[101] Even prostitutes, on establishing a liaison, suggested that they begin with a drink at the nearest tavern. Thus the drink was something of a handshake, a courtesy, and a sign of good faith. Wine was offered as a recognition of a favor done, or in thanks for a service. A worker for instance bought a drink for a man who had just agreed to employ him.[102] The sharing of wine initiated relationships and established a bond between those who partook.

Men met and invited each other to public fellowship in taverns with phrases like "buy someone a drink," "offer someone a drink," "or pay for a pitcher." They often spoke of drink as a gift in these circumstances but apparently understood it as a purely symbolic exchange in which sharing was more important than owing. A person's explicit offer to "pay for a pint of wine," when among friends, was usually translated into each paying for himself. His friends would accept and consume his pitcher, and perhaps some more wine, but the bill was paid by all on leaving the tavern. In practice there seems to have been a general unwillingness to create unequal obligations of any duration through these exchanges. Each man knew how much he had drunk and paid for his share. An equitable alternative sometimes took the more complicated form of friends paying for alternate rounds or bottles at different taverns—people spoke of "paying their turn"—yet they seem to have paid attention to what each owed regardless of the method.[103] This is not to suggest that everyone always agreed about the division of the bill; there are occasional complaints against drinking companions who would not "give their part of the expense."[104] A master shoemaker complained that, having paid for a round of

---

[101] *Encyclopédie méthodique: jurisprudence*, 8:239, refers to a "vin de marché" that is exchanged at the moment of a contract.

[102] AN, Y12661, 21 September 1761.

[103] See, for example, AN, Y11626, 22 August 1691.

[104] AN, Y11238, 26 January 1751; or see Y13376, 21 May 1751, for reference to a man attacked because he "refused to pay his part."

wine with a friend he had met at a cabaret, the friend refused his "turn to pay for a chopine" and they got into a fight. The friend claimed, however, that the shoemaker "had spoken in *languedocienne* and called him a swindler" and continued to do so despite being told that "we have known each other for a year and can find each other and I will buy you a drink, I will not be a swindler."[105] The shoemaker was less interested in a future debt than in an immediate reciprocation. So, evidently, was a master jeweler who had invited a colleague for a cup of coffee despite being told that his companion had no money with him. The jeweler could not resist seizing a gold brooch from the man's hat when the time came to pay, although he insisted later that it was "only as a joke and not to make him pay."[106] The protocol of paying for drinks reveals a disinclination to elaborate obligations, despite the language of generosity. Indeed, extravagance in treating others to drink could elicit criticism from other men, as in the testimony, found in the *séparations des biens*, against husbands who paid for their companions. The social exchange in drinking existed less in creating monetary obligations through gifts than in the honor done another by joining him for a drink or by inviting him to join.

Between strangers, in contrast, there was no presumption that the cost would be shared. Invitations to drink were taken at face value, and several plaintiffs claimed that they had drunk only "at the solicitation and request of the person . . . who had promised to pay the expense."[107] There is indirect evidence as well that men often paid for other men's alcohol. It was an occasional trick of people who did not know each other but were drinking together to leave without paying, leaving the last of the party to be held responsible for all of the bill. Tavernkeepers must have been aware that this was sometimes the case, yet they were quite ready to hold any single member of a party of

[105] AN, Y15238, 19 February 1731.
[106] AN, Y10732, 28 January 1701.
[107] AN, Y14661, 25 October 1741; Y14661, 20 January 1741.

drinkers responsible for the whole bill.[108] When we do find a person buying someone a drink, it often emphasizes the inequality between them. Usually this was an economic inequality, as between one person who was working for another. Thus people bought wine for their carriage drivers. A master cabinetmaker, finding his journeymen drinking in a tavern, paid for their drinks "in order to oblige them to push ahead with urgent work."[109] One woman even claimed that "when men are present they ought to pay," though the woman's escort had expected her to pay because she had invited him.[110] The drink a master shoemaker offered to buy his colleagues when he attempted to solicit their votes for a guild election was clearly seen as an obligation by his companions, for a number of them testified pointedly that they had refused and "each had paid his part."[111] Conversely, some of the jurés of the cauldroners' guild attempted to bully one of the masters into paying for their drink, saying he ought always to pay for the jurés when he was with them.[112] Obligations of this kind tend to emphasize the inequalities rather than the social bonds between men, which may explain the general reluctance to create such debts. More important was the power of the shared drink to symbolize respect and equality.

Basic courtesy demanded that men seated, sharing wine, present a newcomer with a drink, even when he was not an intimate and would not join the group for any length of time. The presentation of a drink could be merely a salutation. An artisan explained that when an acquaintance presented him with a drink, he had "responded to his honnêteté and drunk to his

[108] AN, Y11238, 26 January 1751.
[109] AN, Y10732, 23 May 1701.
[110] AN, Y10993b, 21 August 1751.
[111] AN, Y10732, 20 September 1701.
[112] AN, Y12337, 31 July 1711. The master was complaining because he feared their retribution for his refusing to pay would take the form of a formal visit to his shop to cause him trouble.

health," and then retired to another table.[113] A party of artisans and a notary's clerk in a tavern "invited a coachmen of their acquaintance and others [domestics] with him to have a drink [*boire un coup*] with them, and this [was done] from politeness though they did not know the others, which they accepted without sitting down."[114] An offer like that, to someone who briefly joined a drinking group but did not stay long, was clearly a gift, not presuming an immediate return or sharing of a bill. This was so obvious to a bourgeois of Paris who had just been "presented" with a "coup de vin" that when the wine merchant tried to hold him equally responsible for the bill, he presumed it was an insult.[115] The offer of wine, whether as a salutation or as an invitation to join, was described in depositions as a matter of "civility" or "politeness," of "honnêteté" and "honor." "He was doing him a real honor to drink with him," a master mason assured his colleague, who answered that "he was as respectable [honnête] a man as [the other] in the profession."[116] The drink constituted a symbolic or social exchange, which mediated the equality, friendship, or respect among men, as well as "strengthening the bonds of kinship, neighborhood, or friendship" that knit a community together.[117] It acted as an investment in the web of reciprocity that bound men together and signified their social relations.

The wine acted as a way of integrating others into a group, and of defining those who belonged and excluding those who

[113] AN, Y12308, 19 December 1701.

[114] AN, Y9668, 23 November 1761.

[115] AN, Y14611, 6 February 1691.

[116] AN, Y13197, 23 November 1711. See AN, Y13037, 26 November 1691, and Y12337, 29 December 1711, for the phrases.

[117] Medick, "Plebeian Culture," p. 92, also discusses "social exchange" as an alternative to capitalist values of thrift and saving. This topic has been considered by Marianna Adler, "From Symbolic Exchange to Commodity Consumption: The Historical Evolution of Drinking as a Symbolic Practice," paper presented to the conference on "The Social History of Alcohol," Berkeley, 1984.

did not. Witnesses spoke of being given a glass of wine upon joining a group of drinkers, as a formal act of inclusion. Thus a laborer met a group of soldiers in his local tavern who "offered him a drink [coup] of wine, which he accepted and began to drink with them."[118] If two groups were already drinking separately in a tavern, they might be brought together with the offer of a drink or by joining the contents of their pitchers. Two bourgeois prevailed upon some friends to move from a separate table to the bourgeois' table by taking the bottle and glasses from their friends' table and carrying them back to their own, "to admit them to their [the bourgeois'] table where they drank all together."[119] Those who had been sent for by a group of drinkers to join their company were formally presented with a glass of wine upon their arrival.[120] Thus a group of drinkers was more than individuals gathered together; they were united by the drinking, and drinking made the group, briefly, a community. Witnesses often referred to a group of people drinking together as a "company," and occasionally as a "society." The sense of community was strengthened by the fact that wine was generally served in a single pitcher or bottle. There was, then, a joint possession of wine as each filled his glass from the pitcher.

Men in taverns seem to have used the wine consciously as a token of their immediate community. Their refusal to offer wine made this point just as clearly. When a master pastry-maker sat down, unbidden, at a table with others of his guild, they protested that he had not been asked. "Because they did not offer him a drink," he had ordered a glass from a waiter, at which effrontery the whole group attacked him.[121] Or a group at a table, described in a popular poem, vent their irritation at one of their members simply by inviting each other to drink

[118] AN, Y10086, 5 October 1741.
[119] AN, Y10141, 6 April 1751.
[120] AN, Y14499, 26 April 1691.
[121] AN, Y12952, 6 October 1751.

another round without inviting him. "What, you forbid me to drink?" he asks, recognizing his exclusion.[122] In another case, witnesses remarked that two bakers who had met in a tavern to argue a dispute did not drink together, as a sign of their hostility.[123] Ménétra haughtily tells an enemy he meets in a tavern that he is "unworthy to drink with me."[124] Wine, offered or withheld, signified the relationship between individuals.

The bond-reinforcing nature of a shared drink was sufficiently strong that it was used to reestablish ties that had been disrupted. A number of cases involve people drinking together after feuding, as a reconciliation or, as a plaintiff said, "to forget everything that had passed between them."[125] Thus a falling-out between two professional associates, both master locksmiths, was patched up at the urging of other guild members, with a drink at a nearby cabaret, "with the design of reconciling them."[126] Two water carriers, both women, met with their families, having fought the previous day at the fountain. The two families treated each other to drinks at several cabarets, to pacify the two women, and the families left the last cabaret treating each other as friends. Here the wine was recognizably a catalyst as well as a symbol. Its role was recognized even in jurisprudence: drinking with someone who had offered an injury was seen as a "tacit . . . mark of reconciliation."[127]

The power of the symbol is seen as clearly when the offer was refused. One witness explained that he had refused the offer of a drink by an accused "because of the suspicion attached to the

[122] Cailleau, *Le Waux hall populaire*, pp. 110-111.

[123] AN, Y14066, 22 December 1741.

[124] Ménétra, *Journal*, p. 226.

[125] AN, Y10726, 19 May 1691.

[126] AN, Y15643, 14 May 1751. Steven G. Reinhardt, "The Selective Prosecution of Crime in Ancien Régime France: Theft in the Sénéchaussée of Sarlat," *European History Quarterly* 16 (1986):18, notes the frequency of a drink at a tavern "to seal the agreement" when antagonists settled out of court. See also N. Castan, *Justice et repression*, p. 48.

[127] Muyart de Vouglans, *Les Loix criminelles*, 2:313.

man and because of the debauched company he was keeping at his table."[128] The drink would have associated the witness too obviously with a potential murderer. A master glazier seems to have been motivated by no such apprehension when he refused a drink offered by another master glazier and explained that he was looking for someone else.[129] Yet by declining the proffered glass the glazier was denying a gesture of equality and interdependence and violating an "ethic of generosity."[130] In response the repulsed glazier insulted the first and beat him up. A master shoemaker declined a glass of wine from a journeyman coppersmith, saying only that "he had not wished to accept." He does not seem to have known the journeyman well, and the journeyman was drunk (though it was the police and not the shoemaker who mentioned this); however, his refusal may have stemmed from the social distance between a master and a journeyman. Whatever the reason, the journeyman waylaid the shoemaker later that evening and broke his leg.[131] Even in accepting a drink, a pastrymaker managed deliberately to insult his colleague who had offered it, telling him that "he received it less from him than from all the others" at the table.[132] The glass of wine, then, allowed men to demonstrate their distance as well as their intimacy, their hostility as well as their amity.

Public drinking in taverns was central to popular culture. It gave substance to the rituals of friendship and social interac-

---

[128] AN, Y13942, 12 October 1751. A journeyman refused the offer of a drink from a soldier "because of the persons in his [the soldier's] company." The soldier was so "shocked" by the refusal that he attacked the journeyman. See Y12100, 10 April 1691.

[129] AN, Y13908, 13 January 1728. For reference to similar fights between day laborers, see Y15366, 23 October 1761, and Y15496, 7 October 1751. Numerous cases illustrate the anger provoked by refusal of a drink; see, for example, Y13018, 14 March 1751.

[130] Karp, "Beer Drinking," p. 97, borrows the notion of "ethic of generosity" from Meyer Fortes, *Kinship and Social Order* (Chicago, 1969). Also see Y. Castan, *Honnêteté*, p. 31.

[131] AN, Y11178, 14 August 1761.

[132] AN, Y14990, 4 October 1771.

tion; it was the common denominator of all customers and all activities. A glass of wine, the drink, was an idiom of social exchange. As a gift, or as a communion, it bound people together in ties of respect and equality, of friendship and solidarity. Social drinking used the signs and rituals of gift-giving to cement personal ties and articulate social relations. Such sociability—dense, constant, and embedded in the neighborhood or professional community—is central to the significance of taverns and of drink. Drunkenness and taverns, on the other hand, were the metaphors of a consistent and recurring critique of popular culture by the elites. Drunkenness summarized the waste of money and time, the idleness and immorality of those in the popular classes who refused to respond to a new ethic of work and self-discipline. Taverns became a symbol of their unrepentant reliance on sociability and public consumption in daily life. Whether it was seen as social drinking or as drunkenness, then, public drinking constituted a battlefield of conflicting cultures.

Five. The Ties of Sociability

In the fall of 1771 a woman named Brisset appeared before the commissaire of police in her quarter of Paris to demand a separation from her husband, a café owner.[1] Her husband, it seems, was debauched and a libertine. He ran after women and wasted his time in taverns and his wealth in card games with his friends. The woman was filing the complaint to protect her share of their wealth, the part that she had brought as a dowry, from the rapacity and waste of her husband's activities. Thus she requested a séparation des biens, a separation of wealth, that would legally shield her dowry portion from the inevitable effects of her husband's misconduct.[2]

This was a familiar tale. The commissaire had similar complaints in his files and there were more in the files of his predecessors. Through them all ran the recurring theme of a husband's profligacy. "Instead of applying himself to his commerce and business he is always abandoned to debauchery," another complaint read, "frequenting taverns with the first person who comes along which has put their commerce to rout. . . ."[3] And like most of the complaints considered in Chapter Four, Brisset's complaint made no mention of drunkenness. Rather she accused him of spending too much time and money at taverns, particularly in gambling. Her complaint illustrates the fact that drunkenness was not the only, or even the central, issue in objections to men using taverns. Although some wives associated taverns with their husbands' drunken-

[1] AN, Y12990, 19 September 1771.
[2] More precisely, the woman had returned to her control her *propres*, or immovables and land that she brought to the marriage as dowry or acquired subsequently as inheritance; see Paul Ourliac and J. de Malafosse, *Histoire du droit privé* (Paris, 1968), pp. 225, 267.
[3] AN, Y14511, 14 April 1711.

ness and brutality, to many women the tavern meant gambling and expenses: he "frequents cabarets and other places of diversion where he consumes much wealth to the great prejudice of his wife."[4] Like Brisset's wife, they denounced the tavern for debauching their husbands, for seducing them away from work and industry. Her suit also raises the larger question of how men spent their time in taverns and why they went. Although it may seem paradoxical to address their behavior in taverns through the very records that condemned it, these records focus our attention both on the time men spent in taverns and on the discordant evaluations of this behavior.

The commissaire dealt with Brisset's wife as he had handled other women with similar complaints of dissipation, debauchery, or abuse, by taking her deposition and the testimony from the witnesses she had brought to support her case. The first witness reported that he had seen Brisset in a tavern with another woman. Another added that a tavernkeeper had told him that Brisset "came often in the evenings to the tavern where there was a gambling society." The tavernkeeper (a woman) testified that Brisset came often to drink with a "society" of wood merchants and others, sometimes eight days in a row and sometimes not at all. She did not know if they played, she said; they used an upstairs room and she did not go up. True she had given them a dominoes game, but she could not know who played. A final witness was less reticent. Brisset, he said, "passed for a general libertine and a gambler." The reports differed little from those that the commissaire had heard about other men, but they were sufficient to damn Brisset. They proved financial irresponsibility, which threatened the wife's portion. Further they indicted the man's character. Gambling was outlawed by church and state; frequenting taverns was censured by both. Case closed.

The case was not closed, however, for the husband re-

4 AN, Y15904, 29 March 1691.

sponded by coming to the commissaire a week later to complain in his turn.[5] He too brought witnesses, who would defend his character and attest to his probity. A grain merchant assured the commissaire that "Brisset did not pass in the quarter for a man of ill conduct; to the contrary he is polite to everyone and is very honorable." A master wigmaker agreed that Brisset was a man of good conduct and good quality. He had never seen Brisset do any wrong to his wife. Finally a wood merchant came forward. He had "known Brisset for ten years, he said, and he had been at his second marriage with the demoiselle now his spouse. He had seen that the said lady, his spouse, had no other ambition than that her husband gain a position in the King's household. . . . Brisset conducted himself very wisely and very honorably. He had never seen Brisset play at cards to lose money and if he lost it was only 8 or 10 sous, amounting to an amusement expense, as when one went to a café and one played to see who would pay for the two cups of coffee, or when one went to drink a half bottle to see who would pay for that." The wood merchant had also heard that Brisset's wife drank, which did not surprise him since he had seen her drunk the day after her wedding. Some of the other witnesses agreed. She was known to be drunk, for drinking "le petit coup" frequently.

The husband's stout defense suggests that there was disagreement in people's assessment of taverns and gambling. We are presented with radically contrasting evaluations of a man's character, based on an underlying divergence of opinion about his behavior and his use of taverns. This case defines certain popular values and illustrates disagreement over these values. The man's activities were profligate and libertine in the eyes of his wife, and of those who gave testimony against him. Yet to others he was polite, respectable, wise, and honest. How are we

[5] AN, Y12990, 25 September 1771. Such a step was theoretically available to any husband, but I have found no other example of it in the commissaires' archives.

to understand this divergence and to what extent can it help us to understand Parisian society as a whole?

The woman's case was a powerful one because it reflected concerns that were profoundly troubling to others in the society. Wives, employers, and the police all denounced taverns at various times and complained about men who spent their time in taverns. The testimony against Brisset evoked themes that were common to separations and to police courts: it presented his character and behavior in recognizably threatening patterns and language.

The convergence of the woman's complaint with the preoccupations of police rhetoric was no mere coincidence, of course. Plaintiffs clearly used judicial vocabulary and concerns to strengthen their cases. But at the same time, such issues were a matter of very real concern to women. Gambling and taverns seemed to strike at the basis of the household economy.[6] They threatened to subvert a husband's income, not simply because the tavern kept him idle but particularly because gambling could ruin him. A woman's livelihood and family were jeopardized by her husband's misbehavior. Thus witnesses spoke frequently in their depositions about husbands who gambled in taverns, or ran up "considerable expenses, liking to gamble." One of them spent "a great part of his time in places of pleasure and diversion where he plays and often loses his money"; another "very much liked to gamble and often loses considerably, which is causing his entire ruin."[7] A master buttonmaker faced charges of "dissipating the [wife's] dowry in gambling, in taverns and cafés with prostitutes."[8] Such complaints focused on time and money; the two were associated and both were wasted

[6] For an excellent discussion of the household economy and competition over consumption, see Hans Medick, "The Proto-industrial Family Economy," in Peter Kriedte, Hans Medick, and Jürgen Schlumbohm, *Industrialization before Industrialization*, trans. Beate Schempp (Cambridge, 1981), pp. 64-73.

[7] AN, Y13468, 20 February 1711; Y12107, 10 November 1701; Y13468, 21 April 1711.

[8] AN, Y13092, 10 October 1741.

in taverns. Taverns and work became functional opposites in the vocabulary of some wives, symbolizing the vice of debauchery and the virtue of industry. This dichotomy echoes in the verses of boulevard theater, and in complaints by employers.[9] Even the journal of an artisan of the period reflects this tension. "Our wives grumbled at us," writes Ménétra, about an afternoon spent at a tavern, "and scolded us for leaving our shops, for going out with our slippers and smocks on."[10] Yet he laughs at his wife and shows her how productive his leisure could be by producing a winning lottery ticket acquired during the day. He accepts her underlying concern for income yet challenges her values of application and industry with the windfalls of fortune.

Brisset and his friends attempted to articulate a different perception of taverns and gaming. His witnesses constructed his defense out of references to popular attitudes and norms, in much the same way as his wife. But whereas his wife had access to an explicit corpus of legal language and judgments to describe her husband's activities, the popular culture of consumption and tavern sociability was not expressed except implicitly in people's behavior. Yet their behavior is eloquent testimony to the central importance of tavern sociability in men's lives. The general patterns of men's attendance demonstrates their judgment of the tavern and their reliance on its social mediation. The attitude of others who shared this perception can be identified only indirectly, through their behavior. Men drank and gambled, despite the objections of wives and police, but few defended their activities as explicitly as Brisset had done. The records they left show little more than their comportment yet it is through men's use of the tavern that we will understand their, and Brisset's, perception of it.

Brisset's use of taverns must be set against the background of

[9] Kaplan, "Réflexions," pp. 64-70.
[10] Ménétra, *Journal*, p. 230.

Parisians' use of taverns, so that we can detect general patterns of more significance. For Brisset's case is only one among hundreds that came before the police and there is nothing unique about the tale that his wife told. However, the clash between husband and wife illuminates larger issues that touched everyone's life in this century: issues of work and leisure, thrift and generosity, sociability and solidarity. These issues emerged whenever taverns touched off quarrels between husband and wife, between employer and employee, between police and the people. To understand Brisset's case, and to understand the behavior of tens of thousands of his contemporaries, we must consider why he was in taverns and what he was doing there.

The fact that Brisset spent time in taverns was not an indication of deviant behavior. As discussed in Chapter Three, men of every social level drank at taverns, and shopkeepers like Brisset were generally more likely to choose the urban cabaret than any other kind of drinking establishment. His evening visits were equally typical of a majority of tavern customers, although his choice of a cabaret outside of his neighborhood was not. Brisset's contemporary, Ménétra, also appears to have spent a great deal of time in taverns. They formed the locus of much of his social and public existence. Whether as carefree journeyman or married shopkeeper, he recounts love stories, confrontations, trysts, and friendly diversions in taverns all over Paris. Ménétra abandoned his work to go drinking, though perhaps less often after becoming master of his own shop.[11] Ménétra too came before police commissaires occasionally, both as plaintiff and as accused. He too found marriage stormy, although not to the point of legal separation. Like Brisset, Ménétra gambled. He saw fortune as a way of getting ahead, but it is also an assertion of his independence. Ménétra relates this behavior with evident pride and treats the tavern as the obvious location for those activities that did not require a

[11] Ibid., p. 361.

workshop or a bed. Likewise Brisset's neighbors praised his probity not in spite of his going to taverns but probably because of it. Taverns were an important medium for the demonstration of one's honnêteté, through willingness to spend and consume, to socialize and associate.

Thus Brisset was scarcely different from other customers of taverns. But it was not just his presence in taverns that seems to have bothered his wife. Rather she accused him of "frequenting taverns," of "abandoning his shop" for taverns. Indeed this is generally the case in family quarrels that revolved around the tavern. Women used time spent at taverns as evidence of neglect of business and male witnesses echoed their condemnation of men who spent too much of their time drinking. About Brisset's drinking habits there is little evidence, only that he often went in the evenings. The profile of several thousand Parisians' use of taverns, however, points clearly to the frequent and casual patronage of drinking establishment and to the intimacy of this institution in their daily lives.

SOCIABILITY

Although Brisset's appearance in taverns does not make him unusual, his use of them was certainly distinctive. He seems to have gone almost every evening to join a party of wood merchants and others in the upstairs room of a tavern at some distance from his neighborhood. There are several ways in which this behavior differs from the patterns exhibited by the thousands of tavern customers considered in this study. Brisset's group was certainly larger than the three to four companions in an average drinking group. His nightly visits to a tavern suggest a regularity of attendance beyond that of most Parisians. The continuity of his drinking companions was also exceptional. Most drinking groups were less organized and more spontaneous. Men would enter after work, with friends they had met on the street or in their shop. The tavern became an extension of their encounters, their business, and their leisure during the day. The pattern of most Parisians' sociability gathered in the whole of one's social network over the course of time, providing a link to friends, relatives, colleagues, and acquaintances in endless permutations. The majority of such drinking groups met in their neighborhood taverns, usually in downstairs rooms. All of these differences point to the greater organization of Brisset's group, a greater sense of identity as a group. This sense is reinforced by the way witnesses spoke of them—as a *société*.[12] The title société distinguished Brisset's group, and others like it, from the ordinary tavern crowd. A société of butchers, for instance, met in one tavern every Friday for at least eight years.[13] A tavernkeeper steadfastly reserved an upstairs room in his tavern for another société that met every day at a certain hour.[14] The police records yield several examples of such tavern sociétés, the regularity of whose meeting times and places bestowed an identity that transcended the fellowship of individual encounters.

Some testimony reveals friendships and tavern associations that approached the self-conscious identity of a société. While not always as regular in attendance as Brisset's group, some drinking companions evidently met often enough to have a routine and a sense of habit. A merchant goldsmith described a Sunday outing to the suburbs beyond the St. Martin gate, just north of where he lived. He met some friends at a cabaret

---

[12] According to Sewell, *Work and Revolution*, pp. 143-144, "The terms 'social' and 'society' implied a conscious, voluntary act of association by independent individuals. . . . [Society] might signify a number of things: social intercourse, . . . or what we might call a 'voluntary association.' " It should be noted that the société was perilously similar to the "assemblies and associations" that the police still actively prohibited in taverns in the eighteenth century; see for example, BN, Coll. Delamare, Ms. fr. 21710, sentence de police, 18 June 1745.

[13] AN, Y11218, 28 September 1731.

[14] AN, Y14671, 27 April 1751. A baker mentioned in a complaint that he had been the "Monday before at the Porcherons at the cabaret de la Hotte Fleury where several bakers gather [se trouvent] and form a société in the evenings [sur les neuf heures du soir]"; see BA, Arch.Bastille, Ms. 10060, 26 June 1761.

where they were accustomed "to go ordinarily to pass some hours there." The wife of the wine merchant running the cabaret testified that she "knew the customer, who had been coming to her cabaret for a long time." They stayed some two or three hours, consuming a bottle of wine each and a pound of bread. On their way home, they stopped at another cabaret "where they were in the habit of going" and stayed to drink another half bottle.[15]

This group resembled Brisset's société. The members of the party, most of whom lived less than two hundred yards south of the St. Denis and St. Martin gates, seem to have had a number of cabarets at which they were regulars. They made a "habit" of frequenting these taverns, though how often that might be we cannot say. In one cabaret they were recognized. In the other, the "master of the cabaret" on the rue St. Denis claimed that he did not know the men, except one whom he knew only by sight. Tavernkeepers were not always the best sources of information about their customers, though they may have been purposefully vague.[16] The protagonists came from a variety of disparate ranks and economic levels (including a merchant, a clerk in the tax farm, and a guard), but shared similar ages and physical proximity. And they appear to have shared their leisure together at taverns.

A société much like Brisset's was raided by the police in the same year as his separation. The guard had heard that a café provided cards for gaming and went to investigate late in February. In a room on the second floor they found nine people "who appeared to be bourgeois and young men" seated around two tables. The lack of refreshments on the tables struck the guards as suspicious so they searched the men and found a pack of cards on one of them, a secretary of the intendant of Paris.

[15] AN, Y10141, 6 April 1751.
[16] Customers, in turn, were not always familiar with the tavern owner. AN, Y10233, 26 July 1761, records that a postillion drinking at a cabaret down the street from where he lived could not remember the owner's name.

The corporal of the guard pointed out that it was illegal to allow cardplaying and have "secret places" where one could drink at night. The café owner denied that they had been playing and explained that they were a "société of friends who amused themselves together and invited ladies sometimes, who would not wish to appear in a shop room [and so prefer the more private upstairs room]."[17] Groups like this one, or like Brisset's, generally availed themselves of the greater privacy offered by an upstairs room, further distinguishing themselves from the average tavern customer sitting in the main rooms downstairs.

Other drinking groups, less regularly constituted than Brisset's yet not spontaneous, met in taverns. Several judicial cases reveal master artisans or senior members of a guild meeting semi-officially for a repast.[18] The practice was common enough for the police to remind them that guild meetings were not supposed to be held outside of the guild's hall.[19] Journeymen also met as a group together in taverns, for their journeymen's confraternities, and for other professional activities.[20] This too worried the police, who forbade meetings in taverns of more than four journeymen at a time.[21] The injunction was mentioned still at the end of the century by the *Encyclopédie methodique*, but journeymen ignored it so regularly that it could not have been seriously enforced.[22] A splendid example of such meetings appears in the "typographical anecdotes" of the eighteenth-century printer, Contat, which detail the ritual feast or-

[17] AN, Y9474a, 8 February 1771.
[18] See, for example, AN, Y12115, 23 March 1711, and Y15449, 14 October 1751.
[19] AN, Y14527, 15 February 1731.
[20] See Garrioch and Sonenscher, "*Compagnonnages*, Confraternities and Associations of Journeymen," passim, for a discussion of these confraternities.
[21] See Kaplan, "Réflexions," p. 67.
[22] *Encyclopédie méthodique: jurisprudence*, 9:576. The *Méthodique* agreed that the prohibition was impractical and rarely executed, however, Kaplan, "Réflexions," p. 68, cites several examples of taverns fined for serving journeymen without their "certificats."

ganized by the journeymen of his shop to mark an apprentice becoming a journeyman or "taking his smock." The feast took place in their "chapel," one of the "accredited cabarets" on the rue de la Huchette. There, in the "most beautiful room on the second floor," the senior members tasted the wine and checked that all the wine brought up to them was as good; then all stood, glass in hand, to witness the ceremony and drink to the recipient's health. Then they feasted and poured "frequent bumpers of wine, which are all drunk to the health of the recipient." The author congratulates them in the end on the sagacity of their conversation, on the amount of food eaten, and remains characteristically silent on the state of their sobriety.[23] Tavern sociability like this was both more and less formal than Brisset's. The journeymen's ceremony clearly drew on precise traditions that prescribed everything from the buying of food in preparation to the tip offered the tavern waiters at the end. Yet this kind of ceremony occurred irregularly. Nor did the sociability of the journeymen's ritual or the guild meetings transcend the limits of a uniform corporate composition or of corporate business in the manner of Brisset's société. His group distinguished itself rather completely from Contat's more traditional sociability.

The sociability of Brisset and his friends, unusual as it was among tavern patrons in Paris, has quite a bit in common with the patterns of bourgeois sociability as Maurice Agulhon has described them in eighteenth-century Provence.[24] Brisset's société occupies an intermediate position between the informal sociability of most tavern customers and the organized associations of confraternities or Masonic lodges of Provence. The confraternity played a major role in the social and religious life of towns in southern France and operated on a substantially larger and more elaborate scale than Brisset's gatherings. Yet

[23] Contat, *Anecdotes typographiques*, pp. 37-41.
[24] Agulhon, *Pénitents*, esp. pp. 165-230.

their primary purpose was essentially the same desire for organized fellowship as Brisset's. The regularity of meetings and participants and the fixed locus of activities gave both tavern societies and confraternities an important source of identity and continuity.

Of the various forms of sociable organization found in Provence, Brisset's group probably resembled most the informal manifestations of popular sociability known in Provence during the eighteenth and nineteenth centuries as *chambrées*. Small groups of men from the lower levels of society met in taverns chiefly for the purpose of playing cards, but increasingly developed into organized associations. Yet men of Brisset's social level in Provence, what Agulhon calls an "intermediary world," would probably have disdained using taverns to congregate. Men from this level would have gathered in *cercles*, at private homes or clubs, for the pleasure of associating, without the trappings of organized confraternities. They too spent their leisure at cards and games, and provided a model, according to Agulhon, for the chambrée of the lower classes.[25] Brisset's group would thus have combined much of spirit and design of the bourgeois cercle and the lower-class chambrée.

Tavern societies in Paris and Provençal cercles alike differed from confraternities in their lack of social mixing. In contrast to the open, socially heterogeneous composition of confraternities, Brisset's companions nearly all possessed the same social status. Those who are identified were merchants or shopkeepers and several were from the same guild, as were, of course, all of those in the butchers' group. The witnesses who spoke up for Brisset illustrate the same tendency to associate with social peers, being all merchants or master artisans and coming from the same neighborhood as Brisset.

This pattern actually recurred in many Parisian drinking

[25] Ibid., pp. 212-230, on the cercle; p. 235, for the "intermediary world"; and pp. 235-250, for the chambrée.

TABLE 5.1
Percentage of Customers Drinking with Socioprofessional Peers

	1691–1731		1741–1771		Total	
	%	N	%	N	%	N
Elite	77	143	58	80	69	223
Shopkeeper	62	90	43	87	54	177
Master artisan	78	268	58	168	69	436
Unspecified artisan	49	141	62	174	55	315
Journeyman	74	187	72	249	73	436
Day laborer	76	119	73	177	75	296
Domestic	70	76	67	128	69	204
Soldier	79	130	72	130	76	260

groups, however informal. Most tavern customers found in the judicial archives were drinking with men from their own social level, often from their own guild, and often from their neighborhood. Over three-quarters of the journeymen and shopboys found in taverns were with men from the same social level. Two-thirds of the domestics were drinking with other domestics. At the same time there was relatively little associating between different social or professional levels. Employers and professionals were somewhat less discriminating, yet over two-thirds of masters and merchants also drank with their peers (see Tables 5.1). This pattern appears to have shaped tavern sociability of all kinds: not just among artisans or tavern sociétés but among all tavern customers. In contrast to the sociability of confraternities, Parisians may have resorted to more limiting group identities and institutions in an urban society that was significantly larger and probably more anonymous than the towns of southern France.

The patterns of drinking companions—of public sociability in taverns—offer a unique insight into the nature of social identities and relations. Tavern customers described a network of friends and colleagues through their associations, and the solidarities maintained by frequent congregation at taverns were important ones.[26] Such networks constitute a significant "social environment" according to sociologists, and some historians describe the same concept by the term sociability.[27] Philippe Ariès, for example, argues that sociability provided people with allegiances and support systems that complemented and competed with the family.[28] Robert Muchembled argues that such associations were often stronger than the marriage bond as an affective tie.[29] Both men are referring not simply to the constituted youth or penitential organizations but to the more ephemeral congregations created by leisure activities.

Fellowship in taverns may have been ephemeral yet it expressed deliberate choices about men's comrades and encouraged the continuity of such ties of comradeship. Drinking companions were clearly chosen with some care. Drinking groups were generally formed before going to a tavern, and there is relatively little evidence of drinking groups mixing together inside the tavern. The drinking companions around a table behaved as a distinct unit, with an identity that was reinforced by the shared cost of a pitcher. Men drank together for various reasons: business, pleasure, rivalry. They reveal not only their friends and "comrades" but their colleagues, their acquaintances, their enemies. Although it is impossible to measure the intensity of the relationships and ties between drinking companions two hundred years ago, determining the frequency

[26] References to taverns as an important source of solidarity are gradually becoming common in social history monographs, although the mechanics of tavern sociability have yet to be examined. See, for example, Samuel Kline Cohn, *The Laboring Classes of Renaissance Florence* (New York, 1980), p. 89 and passim; and Hanagan, *The Logic of Solidarity*, pp. 102-105, passim.

[27] The classic study of social networks by Elizabeth Bott, *Family and Social Networks* (New York, 1957; rpt., 1971), p. 99, argues that "the immediate social environment of urban families is best considered . . . as the network of actual social relationships they maintain." Weissman, *Ritual Brotherhood*, uses a similar theoretical approach in his work on social structure and confraternities.

[28] Ariès, *Centuries of Childhood*, pp. 390-402.

[29] Muchembled, *Culture populaire*, pp. 47-55.

with which certain social interactions occurred is feasible. These networks, then, map the contours of Parisian communities and social relations.

The strong tendency to associate with one's peers suggests the degree to which society was stratified, rather like the tendency to endogamy that was widespread at the time.[30] A substantial portion of drinking companions not only came from the same social stratum but shared a corporate identity as well. In the associations between master artisans, for instance, two-thirds of the men were likely to have belonged to the same guild. The figure is roughly the same for shopkeepers and even higher for journeymen. Corporate solidarity, then, comprised an important factor in the social homogeneity of drinking groups. It had a weaker, though still noticeable, impact on relations between different social levels. Among men outside of the corporate world, day laborers for instance, the drinking group revealed even narrower affinities, such as those between water carriers or among the domestics of one household. Men's primary solidarities, as they manifested themselves in tavern sociability, were delineated both by their social level and by their corporate or occupational bonds.

At the same time, men from different social levels did congregate together in taverns, and their selection of drinking companions clarifies social identity as well as larger social structures. A drinking group sitting at the same tavern table was most likely to contain men from the same social levels, but different social levels were sometimes represented. Table 5.2 expresses in percentages the frequency with which all of the drinking groups containing one or more members of a particular social level (y) also contained members of a different social level (x); certain general patterns emerge. As we might expect, the associations along the diagonal enjoy the highest percent-

[30] Roland Mousnier, *La Stratification sociale à Paris aux XVIIe et XVIIIe siècles* (Paris, 1976), pp. 25-40; Daumard and Furet, *Structures et relations sociales*, pp. 74-75.

TABLE 5.2
Relative Frequency of Association by Drinking Group, 1691-1771

	Elite	Shop-keeper	Master artisan	Unspecified artisan	Journeyman	Day laborer	Domestic	Soldier	Total N
Elite	47	18	21	17	—	—	14	13	124
Shopkeeper	20	30	33	15	17	—	—	—	117
Master artisan	10	17	43	26	21	—	—	—	216
Unspecified artisan	—	—	29	34	30	12	—	—	197
Journeyman	—	—	20	27	52	15	—	—	218
Day laborer	—	—	—	17	21	53	—	—	158
Domestic	17	—	12	—	—	—	48	—	112
Soldier	11	—	—	—	—	—	—	54	132

Note: Table shows the number of groups in which members of categories along the y-axis associated with members of categories along the x-axis, presented as a percentage of the total number of groups in which members of the categories along the y-axis were found. Dashes indicate associations of less than 10 percent. Note that the sum of either the rows or the columns may equal more than 100, because each drinking group can include members of more than one social group simultaneously.

ages. These measure the frequency of drinking groups that brought together more than one man from a given social group. The prominence of such socially homogeneous ties in the choice of companionship demonstrates again the degree of solidarity within social groups, although this measurement overemphasizes the impact of the minority who did not associate with their own social peers.

Table 5.2 gives some idea of the intensity of affinities between different social groups. In most cases the frequency of association between different social levels was less than one-half what it was within a social level. This pattern is particularly true for groups at the lower end of the table—groups that seem to be more socially isolated than those in the middle. Thus soldiers and day laborers tended to stick together and were found only with someone of relatively similar status. Domestics also describe a fairly closed world, a fact attested to by a number of studies of servants.[31] What contacts they did have were more often with men of the possessing or leisured level than with other wage earners. In contrast, the men listed in the middle of Table 5.2 displayed a wider sociability, though they too congregated most often with their social peers. Their frequency of association was greatest with men in levels just above or below their own status, as we might expect, yet there was substantial interaction among all groups belonging to the artisanal world.[32] This pattern suggests the importance of corporate ties and perhaps even the existence of some general artisanal identity. It is difficult to call it a guild mentality since the master artisan's experience of the guild was so different from the journeyman's, yet these patterns of sociability are reminiscent of the easy familiarity that a journeyman glazier like Ménétra displayed to anyone working as a glazier, regardless of his status.[33] Certainly the guild was extremely important to associations. The vast majority of associations within social groups, between peers, was also between men of the same craft or trade.

The nature of the source limits our knowledge of these people to little more than their stated profession, domicile, and age. These last two factors were also potential sources of solidarity. The existence of age groups among drinking compan-

[31] See Olwen Hufton, *The Poor in Eighteenth-Century France* (Oxford, 1974); Roche, *Peuple de Paris*, passim; Sarah C. Maza, *Servants and Masters in Eighteenth-Century France* (Princeton, 1983), pp. 139-153 (although Maza argues that servants did not enjoy solidarity among themselves either).

[32] The relatively low homogeneity and broad sociability of the group identified as unspecified artisans—that is, without the title of maître or compagnon but merely with the profession—are anomalous for several reasons. Other studies, such as Daumard and Furet, *Structures et relations sociales*, pp. 29-30, have already pointed to this group as an intermediary between masters and journeymen, judging by their marriage unions and their wealth. Without either indicator available to let me fix their actual rank, I am aware that some in this category may well be men who were improperly identified in testimony. Thus, some in that group were actually masters and journeymen, and their behavior is pulling the associations of unspecified artisans in both directions.

[33] Ménétra, *Journal*, passim; see also Roche, *Le Peuple de Paris*, p. 72.

ions might signal the vestiges of the *jeunesse*, and the neighborhood has been identified by other studies of Paris as an important bond.[34] Age turns out to have had relatively little influence on companionship in taverns, but neighborhood played a major role indeed.

Parisians spoke of three physical areas in their testimony: the neighborhood, the quarter, and the parish. People identified their addresses by street and parish but otherwise seldom referred to the parish. They used the term *quartier* more commonly. An "homme de quartier" often referred to individuals who were known by sight but not by name or acquaintance. Thus, witnesses spoke of someone "known only by sight, being from the quartier."[35] The term was not used to indicate a degree of affinity with the other person, yet it marked off an intermediary step between the neighborhood and the outside world. Someone from the quarter was not necessarily a good companion, but at least he was familiar.

In contrast the neighborhood carried with it a wealth of meaning. The neighbor was not only one's peer, with whom one lived and perhaps felt affection, he was also a judge and keeper of one's reputation. Testimony portrays "companie[s] of neighbors" dining out together; plaintiffs objected to insults "in the presence of neighbors" much as they would mention colleagues or friends.[36] "Friend" and "neighbor" were not synonymous but parallel; they belonged to the same mental category, although they did not have equal weight.

Patterns of association in taverns demonstrate the importance of neighborhood to people's solidarity. Nearly one-half of these tavern customers drank with someone who lived less than two or three streets away from them (within roughly 100 yards).

[34] Richard Cobb, *Death in Paris: The Records of the Basse Geôle de la Seine* (Oxford, 1978), p. 62.

[35] See, for example, AN, Y9668, 17 November 1761.

[36] AN, Y14088, 8 December 1761; Y14527, 17 October 1731; Y14877, 23 June 1691.

Over three-quarters of drinking companions lived within one-third of a mile from each other. On a purely numerical basis, then, physical proximity rivaled social identity as a source of community. Depending on what the size of the neighborhood is taken to be, the neighborhood drew almost as many men together as the guild, although the two probably coincided in many cases. The affinities of neighborhood were actually somewhat less important for the upper social levels in taverns (master artisans and those of higher status) than for those of lower social status. The average distance separating these men from their drinking companions was greater than among wage laborers. Several factors may account for the greater dispersion of employers. Men from the wage-earning levels of society were less often natives of Paris than were their employers.[37] The recent immigrant's unfamiliarity with the city may well have kept him closer to home when he sought friends and companions. The weaker sense of neighborhood among shopkeepers and master artisans could point also to a lower density of such men throughout the city. But the differences between employer and employee should not obscure the fundamental attachment of both to their neighborhoods.

The overall patterns of social solidarity and relations are testimony to the enduring importance of professional identity and neighborhood in people's communities. At the same time it is possible to detect gradual changes in these patterns that may indicate wider changes in society. Neighborhood, on the one hand, remained fairly constant as a source of companionship. On the other hand, the frequency of association between and within certain social groups changed perceptibly over the nine decades of this study. Essentially, men from certain groups seem to have turned outward toward a wider sociability. This evolution is more noticeable among the upper levels of society than the lower. The social homogeneity of companionship, as

[37] Daumard and Furet, *Structures et relations sociales*, pp. 59-65.

TABLE 5.3
Relative Frequency of Association by Drinking Group, 1691-1731

	Elite	Shop-keeper	Master artisan	Unspeci-fied artisan	Journey-man	Day laborer	Domestic	Soldier	Total N
Elite	55	14	15	14	—	—	10	15	73
Shopkeeper	19	39	33	12	16	—	12	—	56
Master artisan	10	14	51	21	18	—	—	—	118
Unspecified artisan	12	—	29	29	31	10	—	12	85
Journeyman	—	—	24	29	53	13	—	—	90
Day laborer	—	—	—	16	17	55	—	13	64
Domestic	17	14	14	—	—	—	47	—	44
Soldier	15	—	—	16	—	13	—	56	64

Note: See note to Table 5.2.

measured by individuals rather than drinking groups, declined for these upper levels by roughly 25 percent (Table 5.1). The lower social levels remained relatively unchanged.

The evolution in social interaction stands out even more clearly when the associations between social groups are considered. Domestics, for example, continued more or less to keep to themselves, as did soldiers and, to an extent, day laborers. The upper levels of elite, and the shopkeepers and master artisans, on the other hand, drank less often with their immediate social peers and more often with men of a different social level, particularly with those at the upper end of the social scale. This pattern can be illustrated by two tables that break the nine decades of this study into two halves (Tables 5.3 and 5.4). The frequency of association between different social levels rises in most of the data in the upper left hand corner of the tables. It might be easier to imagine a block surrounding those percentages with some arbitrary minimum number, say 20 percent. In the early decades of the century (Table 5.3), this block would include most of the interactions of artisans with each other,

TABLE 5.4
Relative Frequency of Association by Drinking Group, 1741-1771

	Elite	Shop-keeper	Master artisan	Unspeci-fied artisan	Journey-man	Day laborer	Domestic	Soldier	Total N
Elite	38	22	29	21	12	—	19	10	51
Shopkeeper	22	21	32	16	20	21	—	—	61
Master artisan	16	21	33	33	24	—	—	—	98
Unspecified artisan	—	11	28	41	28	15	—	—	112
Journeyman	—	—	16	25	50	17	—	—	128
Day laborer	—	18	—	19	25	50	—	—	94
Domestic	16	—	10	—	—	—	48	—	68
Soldier	—	—	—	—	20	—	—	52	68

Note: See note to Table 5.2.

from master down to journeyman. This block gradually expanded by the second half of the century (Table 5.4) to where it includes elites and shopkeepers.

At one end of the social spectrum, then, the narrow limits of social identity and sociability seem to have been breaking down and swelling to encompass a wider network of affinities. Even where a certain homogeneity still existed in their associations, that is when shopkeepers or master artisans drank with their peers, they looked less and less to members of their own guild. The percentage of associations between social peers who were also from the same guild declined from roughly four-fifths at the beginning of the century to less than one-half by the 1760s and 1770s. This decline is far more pronounced among master artisans than among journeymen or shopkeepers, but there is evidence of a decline for both. For some reason, the guild was no longer the primary link in tavern sociability.

The explanations for this evolution are diverse. The composition of the "elite" category, for example, changed through the century as its social ties were changing. By the second half of the century the elites in public drinking places apparently included far fewer nobles, and as a result the increasing links of the elites with other social levels actually spanned shorter social distances. Other social groups maintained a steadier composition, with the exception of "unspecified artisans" whose identity is necessarily vague and may have changed as well. The rest, then, particularly the artisans and tradesmen of all levels, manifested a diminution in corporate solidarity and a growing inclination to interact with a larger social world.

Drinking groups reveal communities based on narrowly defined similarities of social level, profession, and location. Such affinities portray a closed, compartmentalized, predominantly homogeneous sociability, as narrow as the endogamy then current. Yet there were signs of change. The corporate world seems to have been giving way to solidarities of a more general nature, among men with similar economic power and position. This trend, particularly clear for men at the upper levels of the guilds and from the professional and leisured middle classes, foreshadows a similar alliance during the Revolution, when these same social groups would collaborate as the leaders of the sans-culottes.[38]

GAMING

The case against Brisset rested on a double indictment: not only was he frequenting taverns, he was gambling with his friends there. Gambling was illegal, and the regularity with which the police reiterated laws against gambling demonstrates how much it offended them. The police saw gambling as a threat to the very fabric of society. Gaming resulted in "considerable losses, which are the occasion of quarrels, which trouble the repose and union of families, and are no less contrary to a person's interest than prejudicial to public order."[39] Gambling was

---

[38] Andrews, "Social Structures," pp. 71-112.
[39] AN, Y9498, 18 December 1699.

"very harmful to the tranquillity of families and to the conser-
vation of the fidelity of young persons."[40] It corrupted their
morals, diverted them from the path of sober industry and
thrift. The police routinely linked the problem of gambling to
their even greater concern with the disorder of taverns and accused tavernkeepers of complicity in their patrons' gaming.
Practically every ordinance directed at gambling closed with an
injunction against taverns that allowed cards or gambling—to
no avail.[41] Police inspectors gave repeated evidence of taverns
breaking these laws, and plaintiffs even admitted casually to
their own cardplaying. The problem seems to have been widespread. Thus Brisset's wife had prepared a good case. To accuse
her husband of gambling and frequenting taverns was to con-
vey just the right sense of waste, dissipation, irregular passions,
and disorderly morals.

Drinking and gambling have been for so long the symbols
of the moral lapses of the laboring classes, a consequence of
either their misery or their debauchery, that it is difficult to
achieve a different perspective on this kind of behavior, a different assessment of its meaning. Brisset's testimony suggests
that there is an alternative view. Like Ménétra, Brisset challenged his wife's judgment of his leisure. His witnesses insisted that his gambling was purely sociable and that his behavior was honorable. They formulated an alternative approach to
our understanding of tavern culture. He and his friends do not
deny that they gamble, or that they meet regularly in taverns as
a society. But they argue that their meetings are perfectly respectable and that their gambling is only an adjunct to the basic
aim of sociability. They only played for the price of a round of

[40] BN, Coll. Delamare, Ms. fr. 21710, sentence, 3 June 1725.

[41] A general regulation on the "repression of the most frequent contraventions" included, no. 20, "very express prohibitions to all wine merchants, traiteurs, cabaretiers . . . to provide or suffer cardplaying. . . ." See ordonnances
de police 24 September 1720, 28 February 1761, 8 November 1780, 21 May
1784. Isambert, *Recueil général*, 25:72, ordonnance de police, 27 July 1777.

drinks, the wood merchant explains, or for coffee—the tokens whose shared consumption helped define their group. There was little skill in their gambling, and luck could be expected to hand each of them the bill at some point. Gambling functioned as a distributive mechanism, a way of randomly sharing the costs of their leisure. The wood merchant was careful to distinguish first between what they were accused of and what they were actually doing. The gambling was on a small scale, he asserted, and this assertion was meant to placate and not to challenge the moral objections of wife and police. Yet on another level Brisset's friends were insisting that cards formed an integral part of tavern sociability, a sociability that emphasized consumption as social integration, a sociability that they were defending.

The police would not have been terribly impressed by Brisset's defense. Their ordinances prohibited gambling, "even when they do not gamble for money, under the pretext of paying the expenses at the cabaret."[42] In theory the police were concerned only with games "where one risks money in order to gain it."[43] At the root of their condemnation lay a concern for the moral effects of gaming, for the indolence occasioned by easy gains, and the disruption caused by large losses. Yet they perceived at every hand those "not content to play for the expense that they have incurred [who] play for money." The police feared that "with the pretext of playing simply for coffee, license is pushed to the point of playing for very considerable sums."[44] Thus they rejected, throughout the eighteenth century, any claim of playing for the expense as a "pretense" or "pretext." Their severity seems to have been based on the assumption that cardplayers could not control their "license" and

[42] Ibid.

[43] Augustin Gazier, ed., "La Police de Paris en 1770 par Jean Charles Le Maire," *Société de l'histoire de Paris et de l'Ile de France* 5 (1878):93.

[44] AN, Y9498, 18 December 1699. Arch.Préf.Pol., Fonds Lamoignon, ordonnance de police, 30 January 1737.

that gambling without money was an impossibility. They insisted that all gaming, "even when they pretend not to play for money," was illegal.[45]

Brisset was not unusual in his gambling. Agulhon points out that "this diversion is very often the occasion or aim of the formation of groups and the establishment of cercles" in the south of France, and he sees the popularity of gambling among the lower classes as an unconscious claim to a "right to idleness" in imitation of the elites.[46] Others identify gambling squarely in the traditions of popular culture. Gaming offered drinking companions something to do when they had not met for any specific business or discussion, or when they met often enough to have exhausted the topics of conversation.[47] Certainly the commissaires of Paris recorded many examples of gaming and wagering among tavern customers, but usually on a modest scale. Plaintiffs and witnesses reported their gambling with disarming candor, invariably describing it as petty wagers.[48] Suits often referred to a "*jeu à manger*": four master artisans sat down to "consume the loss," a fried chicken that the loser had to pay for, and later played boulles to see who would pay for the drink.[49] Another group "played for the supper [*jouer à souper*]," and the phrase "play [for] a pint [*jouer chopine*]" was not

[45] BN, Coll. Delamare, Ms. fr. 21710, 24 July 1720; Arch.Préf.Pol., Fonds Lamoignon, 18 February 1718.

[46] Agulhon, *Pénitents*, p. 237.

[47] Yves Castan and Nicole Castan, "Les Figures du jeu dans la société languedocienne au XVIIIe siècle," in Philippe Ariès and Jean-Claude Margolin, eds., *Les Jeux à la renaissance: actes du XXIIIe colloque internationale d'études humanistes* (Paris, 1982), pp. 235-236, develop this theme; see also Robert Muchembled, "Les Jeunes, les jeux, la violence en Artois," in Ariès and Margolin, eds., *Les Jeux à la renaissance*, p. 566.

[48] According to Castan and Castan, "Les Figures du jeu," p. 237, "To see the calm with which players and witnesses evoked the scenes of the most forbidden gambling, in their testimony of insults and fights, it is clear that no scruples surrounded these challenges to very ancient laws."

[49] AN, Y13037, 10 October 1691.

uncommon.[50] The stakes of a game were seldom more than the price of a pitcher of wine or the whole bill. And when a journeyman playing *petit palet* with someone found he had won "three times more than the expense that they had made together, he settled for the expense alone."[51] Playing for expenses seems to have been far more common in laboring-class taverns than serious gambling for money.[52] Gambling like this was another way of sharing the costs of drink, like buying rounds. The personal fortune or misfortune of the individuals contributed to the enjoyment of the group as a whole. Wagering on games functioned in this way to reinforce the fellowship of a group and to distinguish it from others.

Thus tavern customers echoed the police's distinction between playing for money (that is, to gain money from other players) and playing for expenses. The players themselves objected when the money was pocketed rather than going "to pay for the expense."[53] A group of master artisans complained of a player who had joined their game and had kept his winnings, to the "scandal" of his companions. The game had been played with the understanding, they said, that each would "leave his gains for the bill . . . to use what had been lost for drink." In their disgust they asked him to "leave them alone" and told him that "he was not capable of being with respectable people."[54] Playing for the expenses of a drinking group benefited the

[50] AN, Y10145, 8 August 1751, for the jouer à souper; and for jouer chopine, among others: Y14643, 30 July 1721; Y9668, 22 December 1761; Y15643, 25 May 1761.

[51] AN, Y12308, 10 September 1701.

[52] Jean-Michel Mehl, "Les Jeux de dés au XVe siècle d'après les lettres de rémission," in Ariès and Margolin, eds., *Les Jeux à la renaissance*, p. 629, working with evidence of gaming in taverns for a much earlier period, also finds that the stakes "consisted most of the time of small change used to pay the bill. Larger stakes were . . . very rare."

[53] AN, Y14877, 10 December 1691.

[54] AN, Y15170, 22 January 1741.

group as a whole, regardless of the winner.[55] Gambling for personal gain, on the other hand, was an egotistical activity benefiting no one but the winner. Playing for gain did not necessarily result in considerable losses, but it did flout the common interest of the group. The distinction made by the plaintiffs, then, was not between money and expenses but between group and individual.

Games were generally played for money, then, but the players would "use what was lost for drink." This practice probably limited the scale of the wager in most cases, yet it does seem that individuals occasionally played for wine not consumed on the spot but added instead to the complex web of debt that already bound men together. The expenses involved were still not large but would exceed normal consumption. Two master bakers drinking one April evening with several colleagues fell to fighting over 10 sous worth of coffee that one had lost to the other at *pair et non* a week earlier. When one tried to settle the debt by taking coins belonging to the other that were on the table, he was attacked with a knife.[56] A locksmith who had lost a quart of wine in a wager invoked an old debt to cancel his loss and pointed out that the winner ought to buy the bottle to pay back the remainder of the sum. The winner rejected this kind of bookkeeping, as did others in similar circumstances, preferring to treat the two debts separately.[57] For whatever reason, this tendency suggests how important the distinction between gaming for money and for expenses could really be. The latter created debts in kind, which were not necessarily consumed at once. Even if the sums were trivial, they were debts of honor and were canceled only with the appropriately symbolic exchange of shared consumption.

---

[55] Agulhon, *Pénitents*, p. 221, gives an example in the south of France of a cercle that used the winnings from its card playing to pay the rent of the café room it used.

[56] AN, Y14499, 26 April 1691.

[57] AN, Y15055, 31 March 1751.

Consumption and expenditure were the root of Brisset's problem. Public consumption, whether in drinking or gambling, served an important function in popular culture, yet impinged so immediately on the family and the household economy that expenses precipitated the tensions inherent in these two aspects of a man's life.[58] The wife of another café owner bringing action against her husband for his "penchant for gaming and dissipation" found herself locked in a struggle with him over control of the daily receipts from their shop. She attempted to guard the money to "be able to meet their engagements": to pay the rent and to repay her own mother for the money advanced to furnish the boutique. When her husband took it anyway and asked her why she was meddling, she insisted that "this was an attention that she was permitted to have for the well-being of their house."[59] The woman was defending the household, the shop, and her mother's interests. The husband had exceeded, evidently, the limits on public expenditures and thus jeopardized his domestic interests.

It is important to recognize the possibility, however, that his expenditures, presumably among his peers and at taverns, were as crucial to his honor and interest. The bonds of social networks were forged through such associations and social exchange in taverns. "Ready coin realised its worth . . . ," argues an historian of popular culture, "primarily in the transformation of economic goods into those symbolic and communicative acts, i.e., into socio-cultural actions and manifestations, which first and foremost gave meaning to the plebeian existence."[60]

[58] Medick, "The Proto-industrial Family Economy," p. 66.

[59] AN, Y15170, 22 June 1741. The woman, now a widow, is found running a café on the same spot ten years later in Y15180, 30 November 1751.

[60] Medick, "Plebeian Culture," pp. 93-94, notes that "The 'social exchange,' as it occurred in festivals, sports and celebrations, in the exchange of gifts, and also in the ordinary events of daily 'display,' could, in such circumstances, be more sensible, even in an 'economic' sense, than the hoarding of money earnings." Pierre Bourdieu, whom Medick cites as well, describes "the work of reproducing established relations—through feasts, ceremonies, exchange of gifts,

Drink, as we have seen, served as the medium of social exchange, around which friendships were made, renewed, and sometimes broken. Honor demanded that a drink accepted from a friend be reciprocated. Gambling simply functioned as another form of reciprocity. This kind of public consumption and exchange cemented the ties of friendship and neighborhood—in many ways as much a rational use of money as any explicitly economic behavior could be. The bonds of professional and communal solidarity were as important to the prosperity and were as certain in times of need as any investment could be and were indeed themselves a kind of investment.[61] The logic of such cultural reproduction clashed, however, with the immediate needs of the family and with the ethos of thrift and delayed gratification.

Men went to taverns regularly and gambled uninhibitedly; they also bore witness against neighbors like the one who "abandoned himself to his diversions." Even if personal rivalries might have inspired some such condemnations, men clearly objected to such excess. They showed no tolerance for men who jeopardized their professional honor, their solvency, or their family's livelihood through an irregular passion for gambling. But they were implicitly contrasting these abuses with an ideal of moderate behavior, an ideal that most men surely practiced successfully in their tavern comportment, where drinking and wagering for the price of drinks bound men together in public consumption. The most that could be hoped for was a delicate

visits or courtesies, and, above all, marriages—which is no less vital to the existence of the group than the reproduction of the economic bases of its existence," in *Outline of a Theory of Practice*, trans. Richard Nice (Cambridge, 1977), p. 171.

[61] Karp, "Beer Drinking," p. 89, says of beer drinking that, "like money, beer provides a measure of value in terms of which actors establish credit and bank labor." While Parisians did not rely on an exchange of labor, as did the Iteso, their economy did depend on a complex web of credit and the ability to get credit. See Kaplan, *Provisioning Paris*, pp. 147-152, for an illustration of this system.

balancing act between the two interests, and when a man failed to preserve the mean, he became a caricature of honorable behavior and offensive to all.[62]

The tension between competing evaluations of tavern sociability lies at the root of a complaint brought to a commissaire half a century before Brisset's case.[63] Two master founders drinking in a tavern had wagered for the price of a pitcher of wine. One lost three pitchers in quick order, but his wife in their shop across the street thought she had noticed some trickery and came over to warn him. "No need to teach an old monkey how to make love," she said of the winner. At this Revol, the winner, got mad and told the loser, Chibou, that he was a jean foutre to let himself be led by his wife. The winner insisted that the loser pay for the pitchers, which they then drank together, despite the objections of Chibou's wife who "knew Revol for a turbulent spirit who only sought to break the union between Chibou and his spouse." To make the woman angry, Revol insisted that they drink the last pitcher at a second tavern where they began to play boulles for the price of another pitcher. But when Revol lost he refused to pay and Chibou got mad and kicked him. Chibou then complained to the police, ostensibly because of Revol's treatment of his wife, but it is important to notice that Chibou was willing to keep him company despite his wife's misgivings. It seems more likely that Chibou was complaining because of Revol's bad faith. His complaint illustrates the tension between the "union of husband and wife" and the demands of fellowship and honor. Throughout the century, this tension revealed itself in and through the sociability of taverns.

[62] See Bertram Wyatt-Brown, *Southern Honor* (Oxford, 1984), p. 489, for a fine portrait, drawn from the society of the antebellum South, of the fear and contempt such behavior arouses in those who are closest to sharing the same traits.

[63] AN, Y14518, 15 October 1721.

FORMS OF FELLOWSHIP

Agulhon has called the cercle and the spontaneous association of men in taverns a "diffuse" sociability.[64] Certainly when compared with the elaborate organization and constitution of confraternities, the transient fellowship of tavern groups and the promiscuity of friends and strangers all together in a tavern room does seem diffuse and disorderly. But tavern sociability did not bring people together randomly or indiscriminately. There were patterns to the way men associated and rituals that allowed them to focus their socializing even in the midst of a public space. Indeed much of what men spent their time doing in taverns tended, whether deliberately or not, to define them as a group.

Alcohol provided the principal relational instrument, but other features of tavern comportment could intensify a group's isolation or its unity. The tables, at which practically all drinking was done, also drew a group together and distinguished it from others in a room. Two groups might share a table, but a number of fights that arose over such situations indicate how tense this arrangement could become. Upstairs rooms also afforded greater privacy and, as the examples of "sociétés" indicated, were popular among groups with a sense of particular identity. Private rooms allowed the elites to maintain a certain social distance, "to seclude oneself," as Restif put it, "in a room [apart]" in a cabaret to avoid rubbing shoulders with the populace.[65] The same friction between elites and populace in taverns presumably motivated an assault reported near the beginning of the century. Two domestics and a wig powderer had gone to a local cabaret to share a quart of wine and some bread, and the waiter had sent them to an upstairs room where they found "several empty tables and another with an abbé and an

[64] Agulhon, *Pénitents*, p. 240.
[65] Restif de la Bretonne, *Les Nuits de Paris*, 1:135.

258

officer in the army [who turned out to be a marquis]." The abbé, however, had objected to their presence, saying "Messieurs les bougres, you have only to get out," and when they objected that "they had paid to be there and ought to be free [to stay]," the marquis attacked and wounded them.[66]

Upstairs rooms in taverns more often gave privacy to men playing cards or dice than to disdainful elites. Gaming clearly functioned as one strategy to focus sociability, particularly when a group met regularly in such a room. Agulhon sees gaming as an embryonic form of more organized sociability, and certainly some examples of regular customers gambling in their neighborhood tavern indicate their self-conscious identity as well as their privileged position in the tavern.[67] A group of men playing cards in an upstairs room of a suburban cabaret were suddenly joined by a dozen workers (wood sawers) who had been taken to the tavern by their master "to refresh themselves" after having carried their tools to a new site. The workers were not from the vicinity of the tavern, whereas the cardplayers were. The workers seem to have come barging into the room, disturbing things, and perhaps disrupting the game of cards. At any rate, the cardplayers objected to their intrusion, pointing out that they had been there first, and a fight broke out.[68] One of them protested that he had never seen the workers there before; perhaps this was meant as a claim to the privileged use of the tavern. This was their neighborhood tavern, a place they could come when they wished to relax and where they evidently felt free to gamble.

The cardplayers certainly seem to have felt a right to keep the room to themselves and to exclude strangers. They were protesting in some degree against an invasion of privacy, a privacy all the more intense because of the gaming. A group of card-

[66] AN, Y14633, 30 November 1711.
[67] Agulhon, *Pénitents*, pp. 236-237; see also Castan and Castan, "Les Figures du jeu," pp. 235-236.
[68] AN, Y10993b, 2 November 1751.

players reacted similarly to a stranger, a soldier who probably was drunk, who had wandered into a cabaret in the northern part of the city. He had insulted the neighborhood—"There are a pack of scoundrels in this quarter"—and by implication insulted those who were in the neighborhood tavern. Then he went up to a table where some men from the neighborhood, "friends" of the wine merchant, were playing cards. "Are you playing cards in a cabaret at this hour?" he challenged them, to which the tavern owner interjected, "Yes, yes, they are playing and I wish it." The owner thus emphasized the cardplayers' position as regulars, enjoying his approval. He seems also to have angered the soldier, for the soldier became violent. The soldier hit one of the gamblers across the face and demanded that the man follow him outside. The man, a sergeant in the militia, immediately left to get a sword and returned to duel with, and kill, the soldier. The sergeant was later pardoned. The example suggests the atmosphere of the local tavern, where regulars came to associate quietly and in their own pastimes and ignored those they did not know.[69]

Other activities common to tavern recreation aimed also at focusing drinking groups. Dancing, singing, even talking could bring a group together and distinguish it from others in a room. Like gaming, singing reinforced the solidarity of the group performing. Singing, however, was more open to outside participation than either gambling or dancing and thus led occasionally to frictions. Two artisans arrested for causing a disturbance explained that they had been drinking together in a tavern when a party of men and women had come in and began, after a while, to sing. One of the two, an ironmonger's clerk, joined in, singing the bass part, but the group told him to stop and called him a fool. He objected but the others had thrown themselves on him and kicked him. After the two fled out a window (the tavern boy had closed the door), they were stopped

[69] AN, Y10228, 20 November 1759.

by the watch, which refused to hear their complaint.[70] The other party claimed that the two men started singing songs "that wound the modesty and reverence due to the women and girls who were there."[71] The story nicely demonstrates the tension that existed between a group's desire to maintain a degree of identity and privacy and the ability of others to intervene. The plaintiff in another case reported that, "being in a good humor," he had sung a song shortly after a person whom he knew slightly in another group in the tavern had finished a song. He had sung a song he had learned while provisioning the army in Flanders, "You have kissed my wife, I have kissed yours." Although the plaintiff had been "far from meaning anything malicious by this song," the other person had taken offense and had attacked him.[72] Again, the distinctions between drinking groups in small tavern rooms were easily crossed but could be hotly defended.

Dancing offered the popular classes another social recreation that commonly occurred in taverns, though it too was frowned upon and limited by the police.[73] Music and dancing enhanced the openness and accessibility of a tavern, emphasizing its public quality, as neighbors and customers appropriated its rooms for their recreation. Such dances were not generally organized by the tavern owner. Professional musicians made a living by going from cabaret to cabaret playing for dances. Their arrival in a tavern would inspire groups, of men and women or just of men, to begin dancing. Alternatively, if someone in a company of customers had an instrument, they might serenade themselves. A painter of the king's pottery told of going to a lunch with some friends at a cabaret, and after the meal of taking a

[70] AN, Y14511, 14 August 1711.

[71] AN, Y12337, 10 August 1711.

[72] AN, Y15348, 3 February 1751.

[73] A sentence de police, 1 April 1740, prohibited anyone from having "dancing assemblies or rooms on Sundays or holidays"; see Laingui and Lebigre, *Histoire du droit pénal*, 2:212. See also the ordonnance de police, 27 July 1777, in Isambert, *Recueil général*, 25:72.

flute and playing while they danced.[74] The owner did not generally invite the musicians in, nor does he seem to have had much say about what went on.

The sound of a violin emanating from the local tavern was a joyous tocsin. Music was an open invitation to all within reach of its sound. The police noted that "most young people and disturbers of the night believe themselves authorized by a supposed custom to enter, even by force, in all the places where there are violins."[75] This "supposed custom" was a claim to communal rights in any fête—music could not be monopolized. Thus two violin players appearing at a tavern in the city, in the fall of 1691, were enough to bring the neighbors flocking in, with wives and children. All in the tavern began to dance, somewhat to the consternation of the party that was paying the players, and a fight ensued.[76]

At the same time that the music was perceived as an open invitation, the fight suggests that dancing focused group identity and exclusivity. The group of six or seven artisans that was paying for the music displayed a proprietary attitude toward the dance and would not let everyone present join. They welcomed the women of the neighborhood, tolerated their husbands, but fought with two other men who had been drinking in the cabaret and who tried to join. It did not help matters that the two were noble. The noblemen had actually been invited to dance by one of the neighbors, who happened also to be the man's tailor and who had offered his wife to be the nobleman's dancing partner. But the artisans would have none of it. A dance, in this case, was circumscribed by the group, and one could not join without the invitation of that group. The neighbors were careful to note that two of the artisans were from the neighborhood,

[74] AN, Y14499, 5 September 1691.

[75] Arch.Préf.Pol., Fonds Lamoignon, 6 December 1737: the ordinance is referring to "assemblées et noces" at cabarets and traiteurs. The ordinance had to be repeated again in 1742; see Boislisle, *Lettres de M. de Marville*, p. 230.

[76] AN, Y11626, 15 October 1691.

in a partial justification of their intrusion. Nor was it a simple question of who paid the musicians. The artisans stopped the nobleman from trying to pay the players himself, saying "they were their violins and they would not let anyone dance but themselves."[77] The dance had become something private to the group of artisans, although they did not hinder the neighbors from joining.

Access to music, to a dance floor, to women, all became issues that identified a group and distinguished it from rivals.[78] The desire to control the music provoked a group of *auvergnats*, one of the most ethnically distinct groups in the city, to fight with a group of Parisians in a guinguette over the kind of instrument they would dance to. The auvergnats had been drinking in a room next to that in which the others had been dancing to a violin. The auvergnats joined the dancing but insisted on playing a bagpipe that one of them had brought. The others complained of being disturbed by the "auvergnats and by the sound of their bagpipe."[79] When a young man in another incident tried to organize a contradanse, instead of the minuet that most depositions speak of, he was opposed by the rest of the people in the cabaret.[80] Again the innovation was suggested by a provincial, a young man from the Franche Comté. Perhaps these fights exhibited tensions between native and newcomer; it would not be surprising if such tensions were commonly expressed through conflict over distinctive elements of popular culture.

The fact that most guinguettes offered music and dancing contributed to their appeal and to their distinct identity. People danced at taverns in town as well, but they seem increasingly to have visited guinguettes outside the city for this recreation.[81]

[77] AN, Y11626, 15 October 1691.
[78] See Muchembled, "Les Jeunes," p. 569, for a similar discussion.
[79] AN, Y11947, 31 May 1761.
[80] AN, Y14088, 11 October 1761.
[81] I have found several examples in the judicial archives of dances in an urban cabaret in 1691, but they become increasingly scarce after that.

Both inside and outside of town the dancing moved to the music of men calling themselves dancing masters, who claimed a monopoly over music in public places.[82] Since this monopoly was frequently contested in practice by foreigners or men identified simply as violin players, it was clearly not a rigorous organization. The presence of musicians in particular taverns was equally informal, although some guinguettes had dancing every Sunday.[83] Dancing was sufficiently important to the guinguette that some owners made special arrangements to have music available; one owner offered free room and board to four German musicians if they would play exclusively for her.[84] But most musicians seem to have visited a circuit of guinguettes on evenings when they thought there would be people to hire them. Some musicians spoke of playing every night at the same tavern, but they could take the initiative to move on to another if they thought the demand might be greater.[85] They

[82] A community of "maîtres à danser et joueurs d'instruments" had existed, under different names, since the fourteenth century. Their statutes claimed, in the seventeenth century, that "no one could . . . play their instruments in any weddings or assemblies" without belonging to the guild. By the eighteenth century, however, the head of the guild was described as a "dead title," and he felt compelled to ask for a renewal of the guild's privileges. These the king granted but suppressed them again in 1773; see Franklin, *Dictionnaire des arts*, s.v. "instruments (joueurs d')." A wedding party complained en masse of two "dancing masters" who had attacked members of their party who were playing violins for the wedding celebrations at a tavern. The dancing masters claimed that the violinists "did not have the qualification [qualité] to play for the public," even though they were not being paid (AN Y13187, 11 October 1701).

[83] AN, Y10987, 31 August 1741.

[84] The owner, a German, agreed to provide rooms in return for their willingness to play, to provide food when they did play, and to let them keep the "income from their playing" (AN, Y15180, 6 November 1751). Music for dancing was provided in one tavern by the waiter himself, who set out a money box with a sign reading, "Messieurs, after having danced well, put [something] in the box without being asked"; sentence de police, 1 April 1740, cited in Laingui and Lebigre, *Histoire du droit pénal*, 2:212.

[85] A maître de danse was "leading the dance daily" at a cabaret in the Porcherons (AN, Y9668, 9 December 1761). Two "violin players" spoke of "going from tavern to tavern at la Courtille [outside the barriers] to play violin to earn

presented themselves in a tavern, not always bothering to ask the owner's permission, and played for whoever would pay them.[86]

Dancing in the large rooms of a guinguette could not be controlled by one group as easily as in the more intimate setting of an urban cabaret. Witnesses spoke of whole rooms, *salons*, at guinguettes devoted to dancing. The musicians would still be paid for their performances by the tavern patrons, and are called "merchants of sound" in one poissard burlesque, but they played to larger assemblies in guinguettes, with the result that dancing became less the prerogative of the group that paid for the music and more available to everyone present. Men still fought over dancing, of course, when someone blocked the dance floor or joined a dance out of turn.[87] The fights at these dances arose over access to women more often than over access to music. "Where do you come from that you dance with this girl," a man's assailants had asked after he tried to invite a young woman from their group.[88] But another plaintiff expressed "shock" at such a refusal and demanded of a group to know why they had stopped a woman in their company from dancing with him.[89] Restif's rare visit to a guinguette was in the company of a young woman who danced for hire. He describes

---

their livelihood"; they had "looked into the tavern de La Raquette to ask if they could play" and been thrown out by one of the customers (Y14771, 3 May 1721).

[86] A violin player named Husson had "asked permission [of the wine merchant] to come and play violin at his tables to divert the people who came there" and it was granted, but the tavernkeeper soon relented and found that Husson refused to go and would come and play "despite the plaintiff" (AN, Y15180, 18 October 1751). Several examples show the wives of musicians along to "collect the money," again, independently of the tavernkeeper; see Y14088, 14 October 1761, and Y10987, 31 August 1741.

[87] Cailleau, *Le Waux hall populaire*, pp. 122-124, describes his porters waiting their turn to dance and being scandalized by the suggestion of the marchand de son that they try a new German dance. See also AN, Y12950, 18 July 1751; Y13387, 17 April 1761; and Y9668, 9 December 1761.

[88] AN, Y11651, 30 September 1721.

[89] AN, Y13376, 23 May 1751.

the cautious formality with which men asked his permission before inviting his companion to give them a dance, but a short burlesque written by Collé portrayed an artisan boldly seducing a young woman away from an abbé who was dining with her in a guinguette.[90] The openness of the dance floor and the greater access of men to women in other groups contributed greatly to the unique social dynamics of the guinguette. Unlike local cabarets in the city, where people assembled for sociability in self-consciously distinct drinking groups, the guinguette threw people together and provided entertainment and diversion indiscriminately to all. This greater openness and anonymity gave the guinguette a more commercial, more "modern" character than the neighborhood tavern.

Although tavern sociability was clearly more diffuse than the confraternity, drinking companions employed certain strategies to focus their interaction and to increase their sense of fellowship and unity. Such unity seems to have been a goal for every association, from the fleeting companionship at a tavern table, to the société of Brisset, to the confraternity of penitents.[91] In fact, the degree of continuity in form and function evident from the humblest tavern table to the most elaborate confraternity suggests that we might reconsider Agulhon's thesis regarding the genesis of popular chambrées in late eighteenth-century France. He suggests that the artisanal and then the popular chambre was adopted in imitation of the bourgeois cercle and, before that, of the confraternity. For Agulhon, the origins of organized popular sociability lie, on the one hand, in the existence of elite models and, on the other, in the inherent tendency of the popular classes to imitate their betters.[92] This model of cultural diffusion from upper to lower classes has

[90] Pitsch, *La Vie populaire*, pp. 14-15; Charles Collé, *Scènes détachées de la guinguette* (1753), in *Parades inédites de Collé* (Hamburg, 1864).

[91] Agulhon, *Pénitents*, p. 212.

[92] Ibid., pp. 233-239; see also Agulhon, *The Republic in the Village*, pp. 124-150.

been criticized recently, yet the evidence uncovered by Agulhon does seem to support such a shift.[93]

The sociability common to Parisian taverns, however, points to the existence of popular patterns and inclinations to focused association in the midst of seemingly diffuse and unorganized tavern life. Thus we might argue that the development of Brisset's "society" and perhaps of the chambrée in general was as much an intensification of a well-established propensity to give form to associations as it was an imitation of elite organizations. Agulhon seems to see the "diffuse" sociability of the tavern as some primordial incoherence, "open to all comers," and separated from organized sociability by a large gap. The idea and form of organization then would clearly come from above. Yet if we can see that organized associations existed in taverns, used common forms, and looked much like the informal patterns of tavern life, as they did in Paris, then we must revise our concept of a gap between the two and consider the possibility that a dynamic inherent in the popular classes pushed them to more elaborate, more private, and more regular associations. Perhaps the existence of a bourgeois model does help us understand why the Parisian "société" took the form that it did, yet its form was also firmly based on models of tavern sociability.

To the extent that attitudes can be discerned from behavior, men expressed a desire for fellowship through their congregating in taverns, their carousing, their gambling and consumption. This sociability is what Brisset and his friends were defending, belatedly, in their testimony. Their investment in sociability may have exceeded that of other men and manifested itself more formally, yet they shared the basic impulse to public

[93] See Ginzburg, *The Cheese and the Worms*, pp. xii-xxiv, for a discussion of the direction in which cultural forms migrated. He argues that the "trickle down" theory is too simplistic. See also Burke, "Popular Culture Between History and Ethnology," pp. 6-7, who revises the model of downward diffusion that he held in his earlier monograph on *Popular Culture*.

association and intercourse that motivated other tavern customers.

When taverns drew men away from work, when drinking or gambling took money away from the family, there were women and men who objected. However important time and money spent in taverns were to maintaining social networks, they were begrudged by wives and employers, by police and moralists. At the heart of this tension lies a disagreement over the role of the community, and the role of public drinking places in cementing communal ties. Many in this society condemned the worker's use of his leisure, and his prodigal use of income in sociability. Historians have been more aware of the condemnations than of the defense, for those who condemned such behavior wrote the laws and the records. They also enforced the laws and judged transgressors. It is likely that Brisset lost his case.

Six. The Police of Public Places

Throughout this study, the police's hostility to taverns has been contrasted with the evidence for the social conduct of tavern patrons. Although much of the evidence is drawn from police records, and at times refers to the flagrant violation of police regulations, it nevertheless portrays the basic dignity of popular culture. The dichotomy is worth pursuing for it raises basic questions about the reality of the tavern's social role. It also offers an interesting exercise in the interpretation of elite evidence about popular culture. For the accessibility of their records and the coherence of their vision make the police particularly attractive as witnesses and their hostility has contributed to the frequent dismissal of taverns as serious social institutions.

Edicts and ordinances warned of the criminals, vagabonds, prostitutes, debauchery, and general mayhem associated with cabarets. Police treatises condemned them as "caverns of debauchery" and "altars of pagan lust."[1] "The haunt of villains," one treatise called them, "the rendezvous of evil rogues, of fences, procuresses, vagabonds."[2] The police were wary of the public nature of the tavern, particularly its openness and accessibility. They often described the tavern as a no man's land, a "public place," into which all of the dangerous and criminal elements of the city were drawn by the tavern's inherent disorder, and often with the complicity of the tavern owner. No doubt there was some truth to these allegations; every city has its "underworld," and those who inhabited it were not likely to appear in the commissaires' records in the way that artisans and

[1] Fréminville, *Dictionnaire ou traité de la police*, s.v. "cabarets"; Delamare, *Traité de la police*, 1:719.
[2] Des Essarts, *Dictionnaire universel de police*, 1:422, cited in Kaplan, "Réflexions," p. 67.

workers did. But the police's blanket condemnation of cabarets, cafés, and "other suspicious places" arose from a more fundamental perception of the city and of its "public places." The police's concern grew in part out of their perception of a criminal class, ubiquitous and malevolent. This perception, linked with their profound ambivalence about "public places," led them to suspect and often to condemn cabarets. Yet the police's attitude actually attests to a complex mixture of insight and ideology, of observation and preoccupation. The cabaret was rarely, in fact, the den of vagabonds and thieves that the police suggested it was. Nor did police agents themselves find much to support their suspicions, as their reports make clear. We must look below the surface of the police's attitude, then, to find the reasons for their fears.

The police had the following cautionary tale, based on an incident in a village outside of Paris, printed for the edification of the Parisian population.

Three young men of Vernon sur Seine [were] drinking together in a tavern in Vernon and pushing their debauchery and drunkenness to an extreme . . . beyond the bounds of moderation and sobriety; the fumes and exhalations of new wine causing such trouble and disorder in the faculties of their brains, and extinguishing the little reason and judgment that could have remained to them, that they abandoned themselves to the envy of each other and to who would succeed best at uttering oaths and impious speech in terms and ways of speaking not yet in usage; agreed together that the one who managed to swear more boldly than the others, and who invented new expressions of impiety and of swearing, even curses, would be relieved and exempted from paying the tavern bill, having each put a *louis d'or* on the table by form of price and recompense to the most dissolute, and to the one who could first make the evil spirit come. . . . This behavior terrified the people in the tavern, who feared heavenly justice. One of the three finally announced he would win. . . . "I will commit the blackest act," and, taking a pan and some butter, fricasseed a crucifix that was in the tavern. To his surprise, thunder and lightning came flashing down the chimney, at which all three fled and have not been found since.[3]

The story manages to illustrate most of the deepest fears about the tavern. The combined perils of drink, gambling, blasphemy, and wicked companions that the police associated with taverns all culminated in the "blackest" sacrilege. Although the episode sounds faintly ludicrous to the modern ear, the police *sentence* reveals an obvious belief that divine retribution could be, and indeed had been, provoked by such behavior. An act of such evil was "capable of destroying the city," as the police notice put it; it represented a moral threat to the God-fearing people in the community. Not all taverns were so wicked, even in the police's eyes, but the threat was there nonetheless.

The moral contagion identified in taverns by the police posed a series of threats. The prominent jurist, Delamare, called taverns "places of assemblies, of debauchery," condemning them "because very often what goes on there degenerates into debauchery and drunkenness." His association of "assembly" and "debauchery" was made explicit elsewhere: "assemblies in places where wine is sold have ordinarily the aim of debauchery."[4] The fear of "illicit assemblies" was an ancient, but not always a clearly defined, one. A police sentence spoke of "cabarets, cafés . . . where one is in the custom of assembling" as places where "arguments arise."[5] Other eighteenth-century examples of assemblies in taverns referred to by the police ranged from an artists' gallery to periodic meetings of the Freemasons, both of which were strictly forbidden.[6] But a police treatise in the middle of the century warned of "clandestine assemblies, where the enemies of order seek to weaken in people's spirits

[3] AN, Y13187, 24 January 1701.

[4] Delamare, *Traité de la police*, 1:384.

[5] Arch.Préf.Pol., Fonds Lamoignon, sentence de police, 17 October 1698.

[6] Laingui & Lebigre, *Histoire du droit pénal*, 1:207-212; see also Arch.Préf. Pol., Fonds Lamoignon, sentence de police, 4 April 1727.

the principles of religion and of subordination to the Powers, established by God."[7]

Clearly one aspect of the preoccupation with assemblies involved the fear of political subversion. To justify this fear they could point to a handful of examples, such as an ink seller who was found in a tavern "holding discourse of the utmost insolence about the King of France." He was accused of saying that "King Louis XIV was an honest man but that Louis XV was a jean foutre." The man was arrested but was too drunk to be interrogated immediately. Upon sobering up, the ink seller claimed he could remember nothing of his comments but assured the police that "he knew him [Louis XV] to be a brave Prince and prayed God every day for the continuation of his health and that of his family." Furthermore, he had nothing to complain about the present government, and "when he heard someone speak of affairs of state he told them that our good King does not know everything." When asked if he did not talk sometimes in the cafés and cabarets of affairs of state, he assured them that he did not "get mixed up in things that did not concern him and that were above his level [portée], and that in any case the conversations that he might have with strangers never strayed from the respect that he had for the people who govern the state so wisely under the king's authority."[8] The man's answers were faultlessly respectful, but not unambiguous. Did he mean to absolve the king for the things he did not know about, while indicating that some affairs of state did not please him? What did he say, for instance, in conversations with people who were not strangers? There is the suggestion, at least, that politics was at times the subject of conversation among his friends.

A recent study has pursued the question of subversive talk [mauvais discours] against the king in some detail and argues that the state found little evidence of it until the 1750s. From

[7] Duchesne, Code de la police, 1:217.
[8] AN, Y14967, 6 December 1751.

then on, however, subversive talk becomes more common, and several examples of such behavior take place in taverns.[9] Yet cabarets were not debating societies or political clubs, unlike cafés later in the century, which had a generally richer, more literate clientele. The cabaret was seldom accused of political involvement. There were no *nouvellistes* to spread the latest news and little evidence of political discussions or discontent. The journeyman printer, Contat, describing a tavern gathering, insists that "one spoke not of theology or philosophy, still less of politics. Each spoke of his profession."[10] The police might accuse the cabaret of debauchery, but it was to the café as well as to the *promenades publiques* that the police spies went to eavesdrop on "public opinion about the king, and the ministers."[11] The distinction is revealing; the humbler clientele of the cabaret was considered "debauched" but not politically dangerous.

If the lower-class patrons of the cabaret did not generally indulge in political debates, they did occasionally discuss issues that were closer to their hearts. In the summer of 1691, silk workers met in cabarets to organize a strike. Certain ringleaders—or those whom the police characterized as ringleaders—were trying to hold the price of piece work up, from 3½ to 4 sous. They threatened to beat any worker who sold for less. Cabarets were the main meeting place of the movement, which was, of necessity, clandestine because such "cabales" were illegal. The ringleaders invited silk workers out to drink with them, and led them to guinguettes where other silk workers had gathered to enforce the will of the strikers.[12] Toward the middle of the following century, three journeymen curriers re-

[9] Dale Van Kley, *The Damiens Affair and the Unravelling of the Ancien Régime, 1750-1770* (Princeton, 1984), pp. 239-241; 253-254.

[10] Contat, *Anecdotes typographiques*, p. 40.

[11] BA, Arch. Bastille, Ms. 10156-10170, "Gazetons de la police secrète . . . 1724."

[12] AN, Y13037, 3 July 1691.

ported that five others took them to a tavern in the suburbs and tried to force them to become "*compagnons du devoir* [one of the major clandestine journeymen organizations, the *compagnonnages*], which leads to a continual debauch and forms a sort of brigandage [and] which the plaintiffs would not accept."[13] The police generally linked taverns to the few worker actions and strikes that they uncovered; in one case, they accused a tavern-keeper of being the leader of a plot.[14] These were the seditious assemblies that the police were forever expecting to find in cabarets. Where else could workers assemble, and under the guise of socializing as well?

More commonly the police were thinking of gambling when they talked of "illicit assemblies, and the gambling and debauchery for which they are most often an occasion."[15] Thus a royal ordinance condemned those cafés and cabarets that "suffered daily and publicly all sorts of prohibited gambling, by which means they gather a great number of idle vagabonds and vagrants."[16] The police blamed "suspicious people," who sought by gambling to "subsist at the expense of others," for these "ruinous assemblies."[17] They created thereby a "nearly universal disorder, as much by the thefts and domestic infidelities as by the scandal, riots and tumults that are the necessary results of these assemblies."[18] Gambling was certainly more prevalent than politics; indeed, as shown in Chapter Five, gambling was endemic to tavern sociability but perhaps not so disruptive as the police feared.

The police also accused taverns of encouraging public pros-

[13] BA, Arch.Bastille, Ms. 10060, 3 August 1761.

[14] Kaplan, "Réflexions," pp. 60-65, and for other examples of strikers meeting in taverns.

[15] Duchesne, *Code de la police*, 1:192.

[16] Arch.Préf.Police, Fonds Lamoignon, ordonnance du Roi, 18 February 1718.

[17] Duchesne, *Code de la police*, 1:192.

[18] Arch.Préf.Police, Fonds Lamoignon, ordonnance du Roi, 4 December 1717.

titution. As early as the fourteenth century the Provost of Paris had enjoined "all women of dissolute life to go live in the brothels and public places that are reserved for them."[19] The police continued in the eighteenth century to accuse cabarets of "attracting girls of evil life, public prostitutes, soldiers and vagrants with the purpose of favoring their debauchery."[20] Those wine merchants who abetted such debauchery then "shared at the end of the day the fruits that these girls gained from their infamous commerce."[21] As a result, the police were suspicious of women found in cabarets, especially at night, and arrested those who were with men they did not know.[22] At times the police's zeal went too far. A note from an irritated wine merchant to the lieutenant general of police asked if the police forbade even parties of "respectable" men and women from drinking at cabarets. A commissaire had closed his cabaret for serving a party that included women, although he insisted they had all been perfectly respectable.[23]

The police had many reasons, then, to be particularly concerned about taverns and to give them their special attention. Indeed, their responsibility for regulating taverns was a well-established one. A royal declaration of Francis I ordered the Provost of Paris to "appoint a lieutenant to visit the streets, cabarets, public places and there seize vagabonds, *gens-sans-aveu*, sturdy beggars, blasphemers." This precursor of the commissaire of the Châtelet would "visit daily the streets, crossroads, taverns, cabarets and other dissolute houses where vagabonds,

[19] Delamare, *Traité de la police*, 1:522, ordonnance du prévôt de Paris, 18 September 1367.

[20] AN, Y9499, 12 December 1732.

[21] AN, Y9538, 22 September 1757. Not all wine merchants were complacent. The owner of the Louis d'Argent, upon finding a woman in a "position of prostitution" with a male customer in one of the cabaret's rooms, ran in screaming at them and sent the servant to fetch the nightwatch (AN, Y14009, 3 February 1731). See also AN, Y15133, 20 August 1701.

[22] AN, Y11178, 28 March 1761.

[23] BA, Arch.Bastille, Ms. 11154, (1731).

[and others] . . . are accustomed to retire."[24] The edict of 1667 creating the Lieutenant General of Police in Paris spoke more generally of "visiting markets, hotels, inns, lodging houses, gaming houses, *tabacs* [taverns] and disreputable places."[25] By 1699 when the institution of the Lieutenant General of Police was extended to the rest of France, the edict explicitly ordered them to "visit the markets, hotels, inns, lodging houses, cabarets, cafés and other public places. . . ."[26] The police themselves spoke of "cabarets and other suspicious places," or "cabarets and other places subject to the police."[27] They noted that "police regulations compel wine merchants to open their doors and shops [to the police] as public places . . . whenever public order and tranquillity require it."[28] These, then, were the urban areas for which the police were particularly responsible.

The police's response to the tavern, embodied in the regulations they enacted to counter the threat presented by taverns, illustrates the nature of that perceived threat. To the fear of excessive publicness, the police reacted by restricting people's access to taverns. Edicts banished all local townspeople from a town's drinking places, and later settled for a strict closing hour. The police closed taverns during Mass on Sundays and feast days. In the fear that taverns sheltered a criminal or suspicious clientele, the police inspected all public drinking places to check for suspicious people. Their measures were designed to limit the tavern's openness and its use by "enemies of order."

For centuries there had been a general refusal to let any townsmen, particularly "those who are married and have a household, use the taverns in their own town."[29] Cabarets, ho-

---

[24] Isambert, *Recueil général*, 2:269, déclaration du Roi, 7 May 1526.

[25] Delamare, *Traité de la police*, 1:147, édit du Roi, March 1667.

[26] Ibid., 1:156. The phrase is "cabarets, cafés et autres lieux publics."

[27] See in BA, Arch.Bastille, Ms. 10129, any of several dozen procès-verbaux for 1751. A police sentence, BN, Ms. fr. 21710, 24 July 1720, added to that "the said limonadiers, coffee sellers, which are public."

[28] AN, Y9538, 21 January 1757.

[29] Delamare, *Traité de la police*, 3:719.

tels, and auberges were to be used only by travelers, on the theory that a person was less likely to misbehave while away from home.[30] Apparently travelers were deemed to have a legitimate need for a place to drink while away from home, a need the townsmen could not share. The ordinance was repeated in 1597 and again in 1635, but it was increasingly ignored. The jurist, Delamare, referred to it again at the beginning of the eighteenth century as a still-current law, but he admitted that the law was no longer enforced.[31] When the regulation was finally dropped from the books, the police of Paris had long since given up trying to enforce it. From at least the seventeenth century on their efforts were directed toward limiting the hours of the tavern's service rather than excluding its local clientele, and some evidence suggests that they were more tolerant of locals staying after hours than of strangers.[32]

As early as the fifteenth century the Parlement had admonished owners of cabarets and *tavernes* to stop serving during "late hours."[33] The police did not really approve of people out at night and had mandated a closing hour to maintain "public tranquillity." The police repeated this command at regular intervals through the sixteenth and seventeenth centuries, though which hours were "late" was not always made clear. Through much of the seventeenth century, cabarets had to close at seven

[30] Dion, *Histoire de la vigne*, pp. 487-488; he also claims that the law was applied more strictly to "gens de métier et gens de petit état."

[31] Delamare, *Traité de la police*, 1:137; 3:724.

[32] During a night visit to a cabaret on the rue St. Germain l'Auxerrois that was still open at eleven at night, the police discovered eighteen people at different tables (AN, Y9538, 27 December 1756). The tavernkeeper identified them all as "neighbors and locataires [living in the same building as the tavern]" but acknowledged three who were not, and these three were arrested. Similarly, a report in BA, Arch.Bastille, Ms. 10133, 19 July 1761, described going into a guinguette at one in the morning and finding, "among others, two individuals . . . [who were arrested] because of the lateness and the distance from their lodgings."

[33] Referred to in BN, Coll. Joly de Fleury, Ms. fr. na. 2414, p. 243, arrêt du Parlement, 10 February 1724.

during the winter months and at eight during the summer. By 1666 the closing hours had changed to six and nine, respectively. By 1700 the closing hours were eight in the winter and ten in the summer. They were moved back again some time before 1730 to nine and ten, at which hour they appear to have remained until 1777 when an ordinance listed them as ten in winter and eleven in summer.[34] Just as the police became increasingly lax in their enforcement of the ban on townsmen, so they gradually extended the closing hour by three hours over the course of a century.

The police's leniency probably took account of what was happening anyway. The police records show that closing hours were violated regularly.[35] The police patrols could find a dozen taverns open late on any night that they looked. Deponents' testimony before commissaires suggests that Parisians were accustomed to staying in the tavern past closing hour; they were certainly there past ten at night regularly. The rhetoric of police ordinances never stopped sounding determined to control the populace's use of taverns, but the commissaires were aware of popular pressure to make the tavern more accessible and responded by gradually easing their control.

One law the police did not make more lenient, however, was the closing of taverns and other shops during the hours of Sunday Mass. People were forbidden to go to public drinking places in those hours "because this frequenting of cabarets

[34] Delamare, *Traité de la police*, 3:719; AN, Y9498, 22 October 1700; BN, Ms. fr. 21709, fol. 76, sentence of 17 November 1730. See Marion, *Dictionnaire des institutions*, p. 63, for the ordinance of 27 July 1777. The hours were still eight and ten in Y9538, 27 October 1724, and still nine and ten in an ordonnance de police, 29 October 1760, Duchesne, *Code de la police*, 2:242. There seems to have been some confusion among the police at times as to what the closing hour was. An ordinance of 5 November 1677, Arch.Préf.Police, Fonds Lamoignon, gives four in the afternoon as closing hour in winter, whereas other sources give six. The dates for winter were given sometimes as "Toussaint à Pacques," and sometimes as 1 November to 1 April.

[35] See, for example, the registers of the audience de police, AN, Y9541b to Y9642.

hinders those who go from satisfying the duties of a parish-
ioner, which are to attend Mass and instructions."[36] Delamare
put the injunction in stronger terms: "Since the assemblies
which gather where wine is sold are ordinarily for the purpose
of debauchery, it is scandalous to allow them on these holy
days."[37] The police patrolled the city every Sunday morning for
violations, and inevitably there were cabarets and cafés found
open.

The police's principal means of restricting the cabaret's accessibility was by making frequent inspections of the city's
streets and public places at night and on Sundays. Their duty,
as they reported it, was to "make patrols and visits in streets and
cabarets and in suspicious houses in order to arrest suspicious
people, vagrants, vagabonds, and those suspected of theft."[38]
There seems to have been a *visite de nuit* at least once a week
through various sections of the city. A commissaire, with an inspector and several men from the nightwatch, would spend the
hours from ten to three at night checking the taverns in three
or four quarters. The inspector and the watch would go on foot,
out of uniform, and the commissaire would follow at some distance in a carriage, wearing his robes of office in case an arrest
had to be made.[39] The reports of these visits lie scattered
through the commissaires' archives and the registers of the police court, along with lists of fines for unswept doorways and
lists of "girls" taken to prison.

On a Wednesday evening in March 1771, a police inspector
and a commissaire patrolling the city's streets were looking for
"wine merchants, limonadiers, lodgers selling brandy and
other places where vagrants, vagabonds, night prowlers and

[36] BN, Coll. Joly de Fleury, Ms. fr. na. 2414, p. 247, letter of 5 November
1760.
[37] Delamare, *Traité de la police*, 1:384.
[38] François Ravaisson, *Archives de la Bastille* (Paris, 1866-1904), 17:398,
procès-verbal of 13 March 1749.
[39] LeMaire, "La Police de Paris en 1770," p. 77.

others suspected of threatening the safety of the city ordinarily retire and hang out."[40] A few weeks earlier a similar pair had gone "in search of thieves, night prowlers, vagabonds, and vagrants to verify the contraventions of wine merchants and café owners who give them refuge and give them drink after closing hours."[41] In fact there are thousands of reports like these two, identifying taverns in much the same terms.[42] The police accused cabarets of being a "retreat for all sorts of swindlers, vagabonds, men and women of evil life. . . ."[43] They accused wine merchants of "sheltering [*retirer*] disreputable people [gens-sans-aveu] and women of public prostitution."[44] Another cabaret owner was said to have "given refuge to public prostitutes, soldiers and gens-sans-aveu, and swindlers."[45] The expression "to shelter" or "to give refuge" appeared frequently in official records, usually in reference to various kinds of "suspicious people." The vocabulary of these reports implied that the cabaret provided protection from the law and from the police's scrutiny.

The tavern fit neatly into the police's vision of urban criminality and marginality. Crime, as the police saw it, was "most often committed by vagabonds and gens-sans-aveu."[46] Poverty in general was increasingly criminal and immoral in the eyes of the government and its agents, who instituted throughout the century a number of repressive measures to control the marginal elements in the population.[47] Criminals and beggars,

---

[40] AN, Y11697, 6 March 1771.

[41] AN, Y12989, 16 January 1771.

[42] See any of a number of inspectors' records in BA, Arch.Bastille, Ms. 10129-10139.

[43] AN, Y9499, 5 June 1733.

[44] BN, Ms. fr. 21710, Coll. Delamare, sentence de police, 9 January 1728; AN, Y9499, 21 June 1732; *Le Petit Robert*, s.v. "retirer."

[45] AN, Y9538, 20 October 1721.

[46] Duchesne, *Code de la police*, 1:208.

[47] Jacques Depauw, "Pauvres, pauvres mendiants, mendiants valides ou vagabonds? Les hésitations de la législation royale," *Revue d'histoire moderne et contemporaine* 21 (1974):408-416.

known generally as "suspicious people," were an important aspect of the police's perception of the taverns. By "suspicious people" the police meant a class of people who "subsist in Paris only through the aid of a criminal industry."[48] They existed outside of law-abiding, ordered society and were characterized by a malicious inclination toward crime. The police did not perceive criminals or suspicious people as either destitute or miserable. They were convinced, rather, that such people were able to make a living, and had chosen to do so simply by begging, stealing, or cheating. Their superiors instructed them to arrest all "able-bodied persons who beg only because of libertinism."[49] The vagabond, swindler, and "other evildoers [malvivants] look always to commit bad actions and to find by theft the wherewithal to subsist in the libertinism and debauchery in which they live."[50] The police were not alone in this belief, for Mercier maintained that "swindlers and brigands steal only in order to pass the rest of the night amidst women, wine and cards."[51] Thus the police and others depicted a coherent, identifiable group, distinct from ordered society, which was not only responsible for crime and disorder but actually preferred the life of crime. The police repeatedly pointed to cabarets and "suspicious places" as the refuge for such people.

On a more fundamental level, the police's rhetoric suggests that they perceived the tavern as an asylum and a haunt for people who would otherwise have had no access to the ordered and legitimate environs of a community. The police understood crime as something exogenous to the community, attributed to people from outside of the city living marginally in the urban community. These people, "for the most part transients . . .

---

[48] Arch.Préf.Police, Fonds Lamoignon, ordonnance du Roi, 4 December 1717.

[49] Delamare, *Traité de la police*, 1:227. At the same time commissaires were directed to help the "pauvres honteux" of their quartiers.

[50] Arch.Préf.Police, Fonds Lamoignon, ordonnance de police, 5 November 1677.

[51] Mercier, *Tableau de Paris*, 11:198.

bringing with them not only the obscurity of their birth but also the turpitude of their vices and their crimes . . . trouble the public order and tranquillity."[52] A treatise on the "antiquities of Paris" in 1724 agreed that "in Paris the thefts, the murders . . . are ordinarily committed by soldiers and men from the dregs of the populace [*lie du peuple*] who are not Parisians."[53]

Since the police did not consider the people who caused trouble to be indigenous to the city, they accounted for their presence by pointing to sanctuaries, places that gave them shelter when they would otherwise have nowhere to exist. An ordinance identified certain taverns "where very often during the night swindlers, vagabonds, libertines and thieves retire and seek refuge when they have committed some crime."[54] Such "people of evil life" were depicted as using taverns as a base from which they launched their particular mayhem into a quarter of the city. They would "take themselves every evening at the approach of night to whichever quarter seemed good, to the brandy sellers' shops as if to a meeting place." From here they would sally forth, "furious, at all hours of the night, committing great disorders."[55] Then, having "stolen hats, swords, and canes from bypassers they would seek refuge again in the cabarets."[56] As the police described it, the cabaret was a place where troublemakers regrouped, planned their assaults, and based their operations. "Most cabaretiers, limonadiers, [and so

[52] AN, Y9538, 21 January 1757.

[53] Sauval, *Histoire et recherches des antiquités de Paris*, 1724; quoted in Jean Chagniot, *Paris et l'armée au XVIIIe siècle* (Paris, 1985), p. 57.

[54] BN, Ms. fr. 21709, Coll. Delamare, fol. 71, ordonnance de police, 27 February 1725. The ordinance notes that "ordinary" taverns were thought too well patrolled to attract such riffraff, but at the same time the lieutenant general of police was sending patrols out to check any tavern that might harbor suspicious people.

[55] Arch.Préf.Police, Fonds Lamoignon, ordonnance de police, 5 November 1677.

[56] BN, Ms.fr. 21710, Coll. Delamare, sentence de police, 9 January 1728.

forth] . . . keep their houses open during the night, and receive people of every estate, and often give shelter to debauched
women, soldiers, beggars and sometimes to thieves, who by
these asylums find the means of continuing their disorders
without concern, and of escaping our searches for them."[57]
Thus, the police conceived of the tavern as such a shelter, and
consequently a threat to the rest of the city.

The evidence gained from the police's own pursuit of such
crime suggests a more complicated reality and indicates a need
for rethinking the tavern's role in the city. The poorest levels
of the city, those who survived by begging, seem to have been
guilty only of the crime of indigency. Although the police had
been directed to arrest those who "beg from pure idleness,"
most of those they found were begging out of dire necessity.[58]
Despite the theory that "marginals, criminals, and vagabonds
form a single family," very few vagabonds or beggars turned
out to have been "false" poor or to have been involved in
crime.[59] Most of the people who were involved in crime did
indeed come from the provinces, but so did roughly two-thirds
of the Parisian population in general.[60] Many thieves were
caught within weeks of their arrival in Paris; presumably they
were those among the recent immigrants who found the greatest difficulty in establishing themselves in Parisian life, for
clearly most newcomers did not turn to crime. Few if any of
these unfortunates appear to have belonged to bands of criminals or to have been professional crooks. The men and women
brought before the criminal courts for theft were poor, some-

[57] Duchesne, *Code de la police*, 2:242, ordonnance de police, 29 October
1760.
[58] Jean-Pierre Gutton, "Les Mendiants dans la société parisienne au début du
xviiie siècle," *Cahiers d'histoire* 13 (1968):134-140.
[59] Christian Romon, "Le Monde des pauvres à Paris au xviiie siècle," *Annales, économies, sociétés, civilizations* 37 (1982):729, passim.
[60] Petrovitch, "Recherches sur la criminalité à Paris," p. 238, find that pro-
vincials account for two-thirds among the Parisians in their sample; Farge, *Vol*,
p. 118, finds that they account for three-quarters among thieves.

times destitute. They could rarely name a domicile or a job, but they were hardly living the life of chosen idleness as it was portrayed by the police. Rather, their crimes were the desperate acts of starving people, forced to risk their lives to feed themselves.[61] Few would have had the money to frequent taverns. But in the same way that the police could find occasional vagabonds to fit their stereotype, they could be certain of the misbehavior of a few taverns. They had information from people like the young mason who had been arrested for theft and named half a dozen taverns where he was "known as a thief" and given help.[62] But this is certainly the exception. The behavior of a small minority, then, whether of poor, immigrants, or taverns, indicted the rest.

What the police found out about a few shady taverns simply confirmed their distrust of all taverns and provoked greater assiduity in their patrols. Yet the reports resulting from these patrols of taverns give some indication of the extent of the threat presented by suspicious people frequenting them. There were nearly always three or four cabarets and cafés found open after hours in an evening, though rarely the same ones. The offenders could be found all around the city rather than concentrating in any particular area, except for those in the place du Carousel, which were frequent contributors to the police records. Many of the taverns found open late had their doors closed and attempted to disguise their infraction, but the patrol could tell from the lights seen through windows and by the sound of people inside.[63] The commissaire would enter the cabaret and count the customers, for the size of the fine was related

---

[61] Farge, *Vol*, p. 212, describes a population out of work and driven to theft by poverty.

[62] BA, Arch.Bastille, Ms. 10727, fols. 255-259, March 1723.

[63] A patrol of 9 December 1732, for example, passing at midnight "in front of the shop of the widow Constant, heard people in the shop which obliged them to knock on the door." The servant and the widow refused to open the door and tried to smuggle several customers out through a hidden door, but the police caught them. See AN, Y9499, 12 December 1732.

to the number of people there. They found an average of four taverns breaking curfew per night in a series of patrols in 1751. The number found open on Sundays during Mass was generally a bit less. The average tavern breaking the curfew was serving eleven customers, while fewer could be found drinking during Mass. Twenty years later, police patrols found more taverns open, on average, both on Sundays and at night and the average number of customers inside had also increased.[64] The commissaire also determined if there were any "suspicious people" among the customers, for the main purpose of these patrols was to "examine the people who could be suspected of being vagrants, thieves, and vagabonds."[65] Suspicious people were arrested and identified in the report of the patrol. Commissaires described hunting through taverns and discovering men and women hiding behind staircases and in trunks. They were then questioned and arrested if they failed to satisfy the police of their honest reputation.

The reports of these patrols were sufficiently laconic that it is difficult to know really what the police were finding. One commissaire gave shape to his idea of "very suspicious persons" in the form of five men found drinking in a café. Three of them he recognized as "night prowlers [rôdeurs de nuit], vagabonds, drunkards [yvrognes], and brawlers and the other two for having been locked up in Bicêtre." All but one were natives of Paris, shoemakers and tanners, although one admitted to being "without work"; they were all sent to the Châtelet.[66] Yet over and over again the reports said simply "nothing to report," or "no suspicious people were found." In several hundred patrols taken from across the eighteenth century there were scarcely ten taverns in which suspicious people were arrested.[67] Even in

[64] See AN, Y9452a and Y9452b for 1751, and Y9474a and Y9474b for 1771.

[65] AN, Y15643, 28 March 1761.

[66] AN, Y12990, 12 November 1771.

[67] The sample was drawn from AN, Y9432; Y9538; Y9539; Y9627; Y9631;

these taverns the report would state that a certain number of customers were drinking after hours (usually under a dozen) of which only a few were "arrested as suspects." Nearly half of those arrested were women, although women accounted for less than 15 percent of the tavern customers in other judicial records. The majority of men arrested were soldiers, although two young workers drinking outside of the city were arrested "because of the late hour and the distance from their lodgings, which makes them suspect."[68] Of eight men found in a café at the market after midnight, one, a journeyman, was arrested because the inspector had just thrown him out of another café half an hour earlier. The others went free.[69] Yet a remark like the one made during a patrol by inspector Poussot, that in a house (not a tavern) they had visited "all those in the house were worth arresting [but] we were content to tell them that if we found them again we would send them to prison," makes one wonder just how thorough these patrols really were. The other inspector with Poussot reported this case in much the same way: "there were indeed suspicious people [in the house], but, nothing certain having been found against them, [they] were not arrested." When other commissaires were willing to arrest women simply for being out late, and men for "seeming suspicious," there would seem to be a certain amount of caprice at work.[70] To the extent, however, that the police were willing to

---

Y11744; Y12441 plus those mentioned in note 64. Some of these are registres d'audience de la police and some are extracts from these registers.

[68] BA, Arch.Bastille, Ms. 10133, 19 July 1761; the same formula appears occasionally; see, for example, Arch.Bastille, Ms. 10133, 27 March 1760, where the commissaire asked the suspects (four surgeons' helpers) why they were drinking "after hours and far from their lodgings" and locked them up "because some days ago some surgeons' helpers caused a very large riot in Paris."

[69] BA, Arch.Bastille, Ms. 10133, 9 February 1760.

[70] BA, Arch.Bastille, Ms. 10139, 21 November 1751, and Ms. 10129, 21 November 1751. Christian Romon, "Mendiants et policiers à Paris au XVIIIe siècle," *Histoire, économie, société* 2 (1982):271-283, provides evidence that the police did not actively pursue beggars until the second half of the eighteenth century, especially after 1767. Such diffidence surely explains the absence of sus-

identify people who seemed suspicious and warranted their jaundiced view of the tavern, the police were singularly unsuccessful in their search for "people of evil life" who supposedly haunted taverns.

They had more luck when they responded to citizens' complaints about disreputable taverns. The police encouraged this kind of information: they were told to establish a network of bons bourgeois who would keep them apprised of conditions in their quarter. Then the commissaire might find someone like the beer seller, Charbonnier, out in the faubourg St. Martin, who called his establishment the Café des Chiens. As the guard explained to the commissaire, "many bourgeois have complained at different times saying that all sorts of rascals [*polissons*], debauched women and gens-sans-aveu retire to this cabaret and debauch the youth and attack bypassers, and that this place is so detestable that bourgeois pretend that it is maintained by the guard . . . that the whole quarter has complained for a long time about this place."[71] On the other hand, a patrol arrested the "Lejeune woman," a beer seller, for "keeping an evil place" and for "causing scandal." The police then "interrogated the persons drinking in the shop, even obtaining information about them from the bourgeois of the neighborhood and, finding them *non suspects*," did not arrest them.[72] Isolated cases like these are difficult to interpret, and it is hard to know what impact they may have had on the police's perception of taverns. It is fair to say that the police had only a small minority of taverns to point to when they fulminated against the institution.

The frequent failure of the police patrol to discover criminals and suspicious people reveals a gap between their reiterated depiction of taverns and the generally innocuous nature of their reports. This gap suggests that police preoccupations with tav-

---

picious people in taverns to some extent, but I have not found a corresponding increase in arrests in taverns after 1767.

[71] AN, Y9474a, 12 April 1771.
[72] AN, Y14396, 2 August 1751.

erns originated in some different consideration, a less obvious but perhaps more fundamental basis for devoting special attention to taverns, which in turn sheds light on the tavern's function. Their perception of the tavern corresponded to a profound ambivalence toward public places and the role of the public drinking place in the society. To understand the reasons for this ambivalence and to discover what these perceptions can tell us about taverns, we must go beyond the police's conscious policies and statements. We must consider briefly their relationship to the urban community and the nature of their role in the city. In fact, the police were assigned to patrol taverns less because of the perceived danger of these institutions than because of the tavern's social role and place in urban space.

PUBLIC PLACES

The police identified taverns generically as open, accessible, unguarded—as "public places." The logic of their perceptions of the urban community as a whole led them to treat a public place as a dangerous, potentially debauched enclave in an otherwise peaceable community. Public places were categorically suspicious, less from any pattern of misbehavior than from their unique status in the urban community. For, unlike the houses and shops, taverns were the responsibility of no legitimate, sanctioned group in the city. Public drinking places were perceived as unsupervised, undisciplined, and essentially anarchic, in a society that based itself on order and hierarchy. The tavern's usual tranquillity, its normally peaceful and law-abiding clientele, had less to do with the police's responsibility for, and attitude toward, the tavern than did the tavern's place in the public space of the city. It is important to sketch, briefly, the outlines of this sense of public space and of the police's role.

The police's use of the phrase "public places" to identify the markets, streets, boarding houses, and taverns in their purview clearly evoked their accessibility and openness, yet there is reason to understand the phrase in another, related sense of serving the public and answering to public authorities.[73] A jurist near the end of the eighteenth century, for example, in an essay in the *Encyclopédie méthodique*, defined taverns as "public places" and "public houses" and spoke of them as "devoted to serving the public, their entire house, even their person are engaged in this service," as well as being "open to the first comer." For this reason, the essay went on to explain, the police had unimpeded access to taverns but not to other domiciles, which were "immune" and "privileged."[74] The author used the tavern to illustrate the realm of society that was directly the responsibility of the police, whom the author identified as "uniquely limited to the relations of things and persons with public order." Since "private actions do not regard them [the police], the respective interests of families, of individuals and of *corps* escape for this reason their considerations."[75] The tavern lay beyond this sphere of private actions and individuals. The implications of this status are revealing.

The *Encyclopédie méthodique* was not an unpolemical work, coming as it did just after the end of the old regime and embodying much of the Enlightenment's passion for liberty.[76] Its

[73] See Richard Sennet, *The Fall of Public Man* (New York, 1976), pp. 16-19, on the definitions of public in early modern Europe; see also S. I. Benn and G. F. Gaus, eds., *Public and Private in Social Life* (London, 1983), pp. 3-27.

[74] *Encyclopédie méthodique: jurisprudence*, 10:67-70. The two volumes in the *Méthodique* on "Police et municipalité" (that is, volumes 9 and 10 in the volumes on jurisprudence) were written by Jacques Peuchet, who is described by Darnton, *Business of the Enlightenment*, p. 435, as an "unemployed lawyer turned journalist and revolutionary bureaucrat." He later edited a *Collection des lois, ordonnances, et règlements de la police depuis XIIIe siècle jusqu'à 1818*, 8 vols. (Paris, 1818-1819).

[75] According to the *Encyclopédie méthodique: jurisprudence*, 10:837, "The police's laws are different from those of justice. The former have a bearing on public interactions [*rapports*] and the others on private interactions."

[76] The *Encyclopédie méthodique* was an enlarged and rearranged version of the *Encyclopédie*, organized by the original work's publisher, Pancoucke. See Darnton, *Business of the Enlightenment*, pp. 395-519. Darnton, pp. 447-454, argues

characterization of public and private spheres that delimited the police's function is not unproblematical either. The notion of public and private realms is strongly reminiscent of Seyssel or Bodin, both of whom spoke of such a distinction limiting in some way the king's power, whether constitutionally or voluntarily.[77] "All power to command is either public or private," according to Bodin. "The public power resides in the sovereign who makes the law, or in the person of the magistrates. . . . The private power to command is in the heads of the households, or in guilds and corporations generally."[78] The fact that the distinction could be articulated by both a constitutionalist and an absolutist did not, however, enable it to survive unchanged into the eighteenth century. The development of both absolutist and mercantilist thought in the seventeenth century led to the creation of a more active monarchy and, in particular, a more pervasive police. Particularly in the area of guilds and manufacturing, the absolute monarchy extended its control to most aspects of corporate life, and in general public authorities increasingly exerted power over private authorities.[79]

The treatises of jurists and the conduct of police commissaires reveal a vestige nonetheless of the earlier, sixteenth-century vision of society and its relation to the police. This is not to say that the police were constrained in any formal way.

that the *Méthodique* was less polemical, less challenging than the *Encyclopédie* and "appeared with the royal stamp of approval, virtually as an official publication."

[77] Nannerl O. Keohane, *Philosophy and the State in France* (Princeton, 1980), pp. 36-40, 69-73.

[78] Jean Bodin, *Six livres de la république*, 4th ed. (Paris, 1579), bk. I, ch. III, p. 19; quoted in Julian H. Franklin, *Jean Bodin and the Sixteenth-Century Revolution in the Methodology of Law and History* (New York, 1963), pp. 70-71.

[79] Marc Raeff, "The Well-Ordered Police State and the Development of Modernity in Seventeenth- and Eighteenth-Century Europe: An Attempt at a Comparative Approach," *American Historical Review* 80 (1975):1221-1243; William Farr Church, *Constitutional Thought in Sixteenth-Century France* (Cambridge, 1941), pp. 305-335; Herbert H. Rowan, *The King's State: Proprietary Dynasticism in Early Modern France* (New Brunswick, N.J., 1980), pp. 75-81; Keohane, *Philosophy and the State*, pp. 154-167.

Rather their behavior attests to degrees of responsibility, to variations in their concerns. A jurist like Delamare, who could claim that the police were responsible for "maintaining good order and discipline in all things," could still identify particularly public matters that he assigned to the police's function: "They [commissaires] are charged with the pursuit of all abuses . . . and crimes committed in public [*dans le public*]."[80]

Thus certain distinctions between public and private may still be detected. Some groups in society experienced a more direct and unrelenting supervision by the police than others. Equally, certain places occupied far more of the police's time than others. The rest did not escape police scrutiny, yet certain groups and places, by virtue of their own inherent order, took initial responsibility for policing themselves. The family was one such group; a father exercised a kind of police over his own, though his jurisdiction was not well defined.[81] Parents retained their authority over their children until they reached the age of twenty-five, and sometimes even later.[82] The father's traditional rights over his family were then reinforced by the police, who would implement a father's wishes to have a family member put in jail for "libertinage."[83] Although it was often seen as a notorious intrusion into domestic life, the *lettre de cachet* was also a service the police offered to parents and spouses to buttress the family's own policing. Thus a person's

[80] Delamare, *Traité de la police*, 1:220.
[81] According to Honoré Antoine Frégier, *Histoire de l'administration de la police de Paris* (Paris, 1850), 2:363, "The respect for paternal authority . . . established in the family a sort of domestic tribunal authorized to judge the acts of children or members of the family."
[82] Jean-Louis Flandrin, *Famille, parenté, maison, sexualité dans l'ancienne société* (Paris, 1976), p. 129. See also Mousnier, *Institutions*, pp. 84-91.
[83] See Mousnier, *Institutions*, pp. 89-90, and Farge, *Vivre*, p. 235. Farge claims that the lettre de cachet was an "intrusion of the police apparatus in family life," but in many cases the police's powers were being used by parents to maintain family discipline. When the police began to review carefully the granting of lettres de cachet (after 1769), their interests and perceptions arguably became more intrusive in the process.

morality was first and foremost the responsibility of his parents. The police did their best to support the authority of the father and of the family, not just of the upper-class families but of the laboring-class families as well. By extension, the police regarded the family's domicile as internally ordered and noted that "each citizen is obliged to watch out for the protection and safety of his house."[84] The police even recognized some limits on their rights to enter domiciles, having been told they could not "go to the houses of individuals without written summons, or judicial ordinance, except in the case of *flagrant délit*."[85]

The guild was another inherently ordered group, "a privileged group . . . [that] enjoyed a more advantageous position than that in common law, which is isolation and the absence of all private [*particulière*] protection."[86] Guild members did live within the immunity of private law, a private sphere in which they organized themselves, and the police's treatment of guilds recognized this status. The police placed themselves squarely at the pinnacle of the guild hierarchy, demanding a review of all account books, all new masters, the guild statutes, and all corporate decisions. Yet much of the internal affairs of the guild was left largely in the guild's own hands. "The syndics, guards, and jurez of the communities are charged to see that order is kept." This regulation meant that the guild was responsible for "internal discipline" and was expected to police itself. "The rights of guilds, or rather of masters, consist of . . . [the power] to exercise a sort of police over their members."[87] The

---

[84] Duchesne, *Code de la police*, 1:182.

[85] Arrêt, 9 July 1712, and arrêt, 7 February 1701, cited in the *Encyclopédie méthodique: jurisprudence*, 10:68; 9:566. Marc Chassaigne, *La Lieutenance générale de police de Paris* (Paris, 1906), pp. 188-189, agrees that "numerous arrêts prohibited them . . . from going into [se transporter dans] the houses of domiciled individuals [particuliers domiciliés]."

[86] François Olivier-Martin, *L'Organisation corporative de la France d'ancien régime* (Paris, 1938), p. 230.

[87] "The syndics . . . make their visits alone to the merchants or masters of their guild . . . this internal discipline . . . is always initiated [excitée] by their

jurés and syndics, as "semipublic persons," continued to conduct the visits of their own members, usually on their own, although they were expected to call in a commissaire for any serious infraction or when a nonmember was being visited.[88] Thus the guild juré or syndic joined the police of the early modern state in ordering society, and the police recognized and worked with the guild's policing authorities.[89] However much the police may have felt the need to dominate the guild, they acknowledged its inherent order, its internal policing.

In contrast, certain places and kinds of people could be distinguished from the rest of society by a lack of order, a lack of internal policing. Men who worked outside of any guild, or did not work at all, and women who gave up their family for prostitution all felt the cold suspicion and unsympathetic scrutiny of the police.[90] The police found no intermediaries, no internal "police" upon which to rely when dealing with these kinds of people, unlike their experience with the guilds. Such

---

[the corps'] officers." Delamare, *Traité de la police*, 1:226; *Encyclopédie méthodique: jurisprudence*, 9:361; François Olivier-Martin, *Histoire du droit français des origines à la révolution* (Paris, 1951), pp. 620-621.

[88] Olivier-Martin, *L'Organisation corporative*, p. 217. According to Kaplan, "Réflexions," p. 27, "Intensely jealous of the autonomy, communities (guilds) solicited the intervention of the police only in particular cases where they could not do without them. For its part the police preferred equally to remain outside of the ordinary run of affairs." Duchesne, *Code de la police*, 1:460, also points out that the syndics "make their visits alone to the merchants or masters of their corps, but in visits to others [nonmembers] who encroach on their profession [that is, their monopoly] they ought to be assisted by a commissaire."

[89] Williams, *The Police of Paris*, p. 118, points out that "the police managed to convert each set of corporate officers into auxiliary agents." Kaplan, "Réflexions," p. 26, also claims that "in a strictly administrative sense, the corporation was an active branch of the police." Perhaps it would be as accurate to say that the traditional "police" of the guild relied increasingly on the greater power and authority of the state's police. Raeff, "The Well-Ordered Police State," pp. 1227-1229, recognizes the tension between the state's desire to "foster" and to control corporate bodies.

[90] Sewell, *Work and Revolution*, pp. 20-21, 24. See Jill Harsin, *Policing Prostitution in Nineteenth-Century Paris* (Princeton, 1985), p. 212, for a similar discussion.

people lacked privilege and thus a civic or public identity, yet, at the same time, this status thrust them into the public realm more nakedly than the person who belonged to some corporate group. Without any "private protection," the unprivileged person was also a peculiarly public person, exposed to an increasingly rigorous treatment by public authorities. The public woman, the *fille publique*, had long been a matter of police concern. Belonging to no family, accessible to all, the prostitute was of course an anomaly, though one that bothered the police less, apparently, before the sixteenth century than by the eighteenth. Prostitutes were routinely incarcerated, although some, living in specific brothels (and therefore policed), were tolerated. It was the poorest (and thus the most accessible, most public) women who bore the brunt of police repression. Equally the poorest men, the vagabond and beggar, were subjected to summary justice and repression.[91] Many men belonged to no guild in the eighteenth century, although the state had made the attempt to create guilds for everyone and force everyone to belong to one.[92] The police themselves exercised the immediate supervision of such men. Their reports on the laborers in the market, for example, can be found between the lists of men and women imprisoned for crime and debauchery (also public people), most described as loyal subjects but some as brutal or drunkards.[93] The mass of day laborers, all

[91] Jacques Rossiaud, "Prostitution, Youth, and Society in Towns of Southeastern France in the Fifteenth Century," in Orest Ranum and Robert Forster, eds., *Deviants and the Abandoned in France*, trans. Elborg Forster (Baltimore, 1978), pp. 17-31. See Nicole Castan, "Summary Justice," in Ranum and Forster, eds., *Deviants and the Abandoned*, pp. 111-116.

[92] Olivier-Martin, *L'Organisation corporative*, p. 217.

[93] Olivier-Martin, *Histoire du droit français*, p. 621, notes that "they [the 10,000 artisans and sellers in Paris who were still not organized en jurande] are under the direct surveillance of the police authorities." The police gave special attention, for instance, to "professions nonerigées en communauté." See AN Y9508 for a register of those revendeuses, logeurs de nuit, crieurs de vieux chapeaux, and other groups who were registered by the police. See BA, Arch. Bas-

with little or no corporate identity or "police," many with no fixed abode, drew particular police attention. Even journeymen, only marginally attached to the formal guild by the eighteenth century, and insufficiently subordinate to their employers in the eyes of both guild masters and police, worried the police. For all these men, the police instituted a system of passbooks, identifying employment record and some employer who was responsible for the worker. Workers without an employer, someone to police them, for more than two weeks were liable to prison.[94]

Along with the control of unprivileged, public people went the control of public places. The public places repeated over and over in ordinances and judgments—the streets, markets, cabarets, lodging houses, and so forth—were the object of police scrutiny in a way that domiciles or workshops were not. To be sure, the police could go anywhere they wanted and might check domiciles, with a warrant, or workshops, at least some of the time—but not on a regular basis, not with the frequency of their supervision of streets and markets, taverns or lodging houses. The street and market had long been the police's particular responsibility and the majority of the police court's time was spent on matters relating to the street.[95] Streets not swept, garbage in the street, anything blocking or jeopardizing the street all produced a constant source of police infractions. Markets drew the police's attention both for being the meeting place of so many different people in the city and for their role in provisioning the city.[96] The street and market existed outside of, or rather between, the more private realms of home and guild.

tille, Ms. 10141, for the list of forts de la halle; and the related discussion of this in Kaplan, *Provisioning Paris*, pp. 556-557.

[94] Day laborers, manoeuvriers, were checked by the police for certificats from their employers "where they are actually employed, or else have them imprisoned," according to Delamare, *Traité de la police*, 1:227. See Kaplan, "Réflexions," pp. 56-57.

[95] LeMaire, "La Police de Paris en 1770," pp. 15-16.

[96] Kaplan, *Provisioning Paris*, p. 28.

Here the intersections of individual producers and consumers emerged onto a public level.

Lodging houses, on the other hand, were public in a different way. Despite being enclosed spaces, owned by individuals, they were accessible to all and indeed were used in most cases by the unordered people who drew the police's particular attention. The police required every lodging-house manager to keep a log of his boarders to help them provide order to these people.[97] Taverns, finally, like streets and markets, provided the point of intersection for men in urban society. At the same time, taverns were enclosed spaces like the lodging house, open to all, and because they did not order their space, they were accused of catering particularly to unordered people and were scrutinized, like lodging houses, for their clientele. They were reprimanded for having customers meet in upstairs, private rooms—a common enough practice as we have seen—because the privacy allowed might obscure the very unprivileged, public people whom the police wished to find. Taverns and lodging houses supposedly attracted these people because they were public places, open and accessible. And by attracting such people, many of them a danger to society, they were considered public, unordered, and dangerous places.[98] The logic was impeccably circular and not always accurate. At its basis, however, lay the recognition that the public place too was inherently unpoliced and unordered. This lack of internal order meant that the state's police had direct responsibility, but it also meant, as far as they were concerned, that the public place was inherently dangerous, disordered, and associated with people who were equally so.

The association of public people and places, of suspicious

[97] LeMaire, "La Police de Paris en 1770," pp. 78-79.

[98] Farge, *Vol*, p. 165, cites a nineteenth-century author, H. Monin, *L'Etat de Paris en 1789*, who made the equation explicit in a chapter entitled "Logement garnis–Cabarets–Débauche": "the lodging house is suspect in the eyes of the authorities and the police because the lack of money and stability are also."

people and public drinking places, was an essential part of the police's perception of the city. The street, the tavern, the lodging house, all of the "public places" and "suspect places" were particularly accessible to those "suspicious people" who "have neither profession nor craft, nor certain domicile nor wealth with which to live."[99] To be sure, there were taverns that aided prostitutes in their trade, drew a particularly shiftless clientele, or flouted the closing hours. The police were forever on the alert for such infractions, but their distrust of taverns was due to more than the isolated cabaret of ill-repute or to the general exuberance of many drinking places. The police's conception of the urban community divided the inhabitants of the city into ordered and unordered individuals, internally policed or publicly policed groups, and divided the space of the city similarly. The police's duty lay in the public realm, where the state ordered individual interests for the common good and defended public welfare against an "infinity of enemies." Those who inhabited the public domain because they lacked the identity of the guild, or trade, or family, were undisciplined and suspicious, readily perceived as a threat and automatically associated with public places.

If the tavern was filled with vagabonds and suspicious people, the police did not find many of them, although they were looking carefully. Their hostility arose as much from their basic conception of the city, and because they had recognized that disorder was the very essence of the tavern. Thus they assigned the tavern to the public domain, along with other places in the city that existed outside of the order of work and family. Their association of taverns with suspicious people was due more to their identification of the tavern as a public, unordered, and permissive place than to any discovery of criminal bands working out of cabarets. They realized that the public drinking place was outside of the organization of private life and space,

99 Duchesne, *Code de la police*, p. 208.

each with its own inherent order. To the tavern's clientele, as we shall see, the license of the public drinking place meant that one could "do what one wanted" there, that it was an arena free from the hierarchy of profession and family. In this way the tavern provided a socially useful role of neutral space. To the police, however, charged with maintaining order, patrolling taverns "to reestablish good order," as one commissaire said, disorder was associated with scandal, debauchery, and crime.[100] To be sure, they occasionally found debauchery, along with much that was peaceful and respectable. But the police's perception of the tavern, the category of urban space into which they put the public drinking place, was what kept the police at the ceaseless patrols.

PEOPLE

Popular perceptions of taverns were surprisingly similar to those of the police, although the fact that much of the evidence for the popular viewpoint comes through the police records may account for some of the similarity. The populace also expressed an awareness of the tavern as a public place and recognized its inherent lack of order. Both the testimony and the behavior of the laboring classes reveal a concern about access to taverns and about comportment appropriate to such places.

Unlike the police, who were concerned with the disorderly, even criminal, aspects of the tavern, the people of Paris saw it as an integral part of everyday life. All but the richest and poorest Parisians went to taverns regularly, to dine, to relax, and to drink. Far from being a den of thieves, as the police would suggest, the tavern was popularly perceived as a generally respectable gathering place, a legitimate part of the community. Through their actions, their behavior, and the testimony in

[100] AN, Y12660, 20 January 1761. An inspector also spoke of making his patrols of taverns to "maintain good order," in BA, Arch.Bastille, Ms. 10129, 27 March 1751.

their complaints to the police, Parisians—at least male Parisians—expressed an attitude toward the tavern as a communal space, in which all had rights of access and freedom of action. Public space implied an openness, a freedom of access. But the right of access and the freedom of action inside had limits that varied according to one's viewpoint. The police and the church, for example, held the tavern owner responsible both legally and morally for access to the tavern and to the wine supply.[101] The owner was at fault if the tavern was open too late or during Sunday Mass. In theory the police court levied a fine for the infractions discovered by the visites de nuit against both the wine merchant and the customers found breaking the curfew, but in practice only the wine merchant paid.[102] The owner was expected to deny alcohol to customers who were drinking too much or who appeared suspicious. Owners found themselves in a remarkably difficult position, however, because their customers disputed their authority at every turn. The question of access to taverns was a constant source of conflict, as customers refused to leave at closing time and revelers attempted to gain entrance far into the night. A café owner, chided by a woman for serving after hours, mockingly replied that "his house was public."[103] Legally the tavern's public character did not affect the closing hour, but the reply raises the question of just how accessible the public drinking place was. If it was public, who could enter and when? More importantly, who had control over its access?

The owner of a tavern represented a clear limit to the freedom of a public place. Just as the police held him legally responsible for access to his establishment, and fined him if it was open late, there were others who held the owner responsible for limiting access to the tavern. Complaints to the police from irate neighbors accused owners of "giving drink to people of all

[101] "Cas de conscience sur l'yvrognerie."
[102] Duchesne, Code de la police, 1:56.
[103] AN, Y15940, 4 January 1741.

kinds after closing hours" and having "sheltered vagrants both night and day."[104] Although these complaints generally went on to mention the disturbances made by customers—such as singing, playing trumpets and drums—the implication was that the owner was responsible for having served these people in the first place. The sentiment that the owner was responsible is evident in the heated words recorded in several complaints. A wine merchant was charged with having "sheltered thieves day and night and giving them drink" by a woman who had tried to take her brother from a cabaret. The woman was the wife of a beer merchant across the street from the wine merchant. The wine merchant replied that "he was not like [the beer seller] who shelters all sorts of people."[105] Another woman trying to persuade her husband to leave a cabaret turned on the owner and accused her of "always serving people who pass the nights drinking."[106]

It is worth noting, first of all, the similarity here with the perceptions of the police; the phrases are identical to police accusations. Does this indicate a borrowing of the police's perceptions of the tavern as well? Or were they simply used to cast aspersion in terms that everyone, especially the magistrate, could understand? The charges, at any rate, censured the owner for the type of people who used his establishment and for his consent in accommodating them. The implication was that he did control the space and the access to it. It is important, however, that two of the accusers were women who were angry, in each case because their husbands spent too much time in the cabaret. In other words, they projected their anger at being unable to control access to the cabaret (their husband's access, that is) onto the owner for being unwilling to do so. Thus the owner was accused of "indiscreet complacency toward those who come to

---

[104] AN, Y9538, 8 July 1721; 20 October 1721; BN, Ms. fr. 21710, Coll. Delamare, sentence de police, 9 January 1728.

[105] AN, Y14056, 10 December 1720.

[106] AN, Y10987, 5 December 1741.

drink there."[107] The freedom of access threatened the roles of women as wives; they expanded the personal threat into what was recognizably a threat to the community. Most people did not share these women's perceptions. Complaints brought before the commissaire reveal substantial opposition to the owner's right to control the social life of the tavern. To the extent that behavior indicates attitudes, the populace perceived the tavern as theirs, accessible and public, and resisted the owners' attempts to control it. Nearly one-third of the violence in taverns that came before the various judicial officers consisted of conflict between a tavernkeeper and his customers. The majority of these cases involved the owners complaining of violence by customers but over one-third found customers bringing action against the owner. The plaintiffs in such cases were quite similar to plaintiffs in the other cases of tavern violence, with nearly one-half (47 percent) belonging to levels of society that included employers and the leisured class. The culprits in complaints by owners resembled too the accused in other cases of tavern violence, so that workers and employees were far more common among culprits than among plaintiffs. If some of the customers involved in these cases, either as plaintiffs or culprits, were rowdies trying to cause trouble, many were neighbors expressing their anger at being excluded from a public place.

Disputes over closing hours figured as a frequent source of friction between customers and owners. There are numerous cases of revelers appearing before the door of a cabaret long after closing hours, demanding to be let in. The nightwatch would find people outside of a cabaret "who wished to force the owner to give them drink, rioting at the door and trying to break it."[108] Even more common were instances of patrons refusing to leave when the owner wished to close. In some cases

[107] Ibid.
[108] AN, Y12952, 30 December 1751.

the patrons became violent, refusing to go until they had been served more wine and threatening to stay all night. Their position was not unreasonable. Owners were sufficiently lax about closing hours that it often seemed to be a matter of personal discretion. Not all tavernkeepers tried to exclude customers, as the weekly list of infractions demonstrates. When neighbors appeared at closing time in the tavern on the rue de Clery, the owner simply gave them a bottle and asked them to leave when it was done. He went to bed.[109] The printer, Contat, describes the negotiations with a tavernkeeper over extending the time of their banquet. The printers managed to stay into the early morning hours.[110] Understandably, owners would be more complacent about neighbors and regular customers than strangers.

Yet customers were not willing to let the owners exercise their prerogative to choose. They complained when they had been refused wine "even though there were still people in other rooms who had been served."[111] A master joiner who had been told that it was the closing hour "observed that the wine merchant ought not to refuse him wine since he had just served others who were at several tables."[112] When one beer seller tried to close, three customers had gone upstairs to where friends of the owner were still drinking and, in a quixotic attempt to apply the closing hour uniformly, insisted on repeatedly blowing out their candles. The three were finally thrown out and spent the next two hours throwing stones at the door and cutting it with their knives.[113] The objections were bitter, perhaps, because the owner had been so patently arbitrary, but all were essentially disputing his right to control the cabaret, to

[109] AN, Y14066, 10 May 1741.
[110] Contat, *Anecdotes typographiques*, pp. 40-41.
[111] AN, Y11238, 23 July 1751.
[112] AN, Y11947, 10 March 1761. See also Y10732, 23 October 1701, and Y9663, 24 May 1761.
[113] AN, Y14761, 5 October 1711.

make it less public. Owners explained and defended their attempts to control in terms of police ordinances, "wishing to conform to the regulations of the police which he has always observed very religiously since he was established."[114] If much of this was for the benefit of the magistrate taking the deposition, it was, nonetheless, a function of the owner's lack of authority. Patrons were not impressed with police regulations. Nor were they impressed with the claims of ownership advanced by the tavernkeeper, although the response of one customer to an owner, "If you were outside *chez toi* you would see how I would take care of you," was essentially a recognition of that ownership.[115] But a wine merchant who had tried to silence several customers "scandalizing all the neighbors with shameful songs," was challenged, and when he informed them that he was the "master of the house," they "mocked him" and attacked him.[116]

Owners seem to have been generally incapable of excluding people for other than official reasons. A brandy seller had refused entrance to his house to a person whose attentions to the seller's wife were becoming the subject of neighborhood gossip. Yet the person had "used the pretext of coming to drink morning and evening in order to insult and threaten him."[117] It took the seller three weeks to complain to the police. Even then the complaint was in terms of violence done him rather than trespassing. A merchant apparently could not exclude anyone who presented himself as a customer. A café owner complained of a person insulting his wife and the customers in the café for six months, but seems not to have been able to stop him.[118] Again, he complained not of being unable to exclude the person

[114] AN, Y12950, 23 July 1751.

[115] AN, Y12951, 6 September 1751.

[116] As the watch led the three troublemakers away, a witness heard one say to the wine merchant, "you are nothing but a bankrupt and a scoundrel . . . and I will burn down your cabaret," (AN, Y12925, 1 November 1741).

[117] AN, Y13926, 21 June 1741.

[118] AN, Y14761, 10 April 1711.

but of being insulted. Some owners did try to assert themselves. A beer seller, in the course of a fight with some of her customers, told them not to come back because "they did her more harm than profit." The seller herself did not admit to having said this, nor did it stop the customers from coming back and insulting her.[119] But other owners found it difficult to eject even those who made a habit of picking fights with other customers.[120] Owners found it very hard to remove anyone and could call on the nightwatch only for real violence or when the hour had become excessively late. Even then the watch might not come or, in one instance, left the customers there to stay as late as they wanted, for "they were honnêtes gens."[121] Turning regular customers away was particularly difficult, and we find one owner resignedly opening his door in the middle of the night to "some bourgeois of the quarter who lived in the neighborhood."[122]

The problem was partly one of force. An owner's lack of authority was exacerbated by a lack of physical power to enforce it. Some cabaret owners who were big enough to do so undoubtedly policed their cabarets themselves and, since they did not go to the commissaire, they left no record. There were customers, however, who complained at such treatment, objecting at the same time to the owner's attempt to control the space of his cabaret.[123] In such cases the customers expressed a perception of the cabaret as public and accessible in opposition to the owner's authority.

More than ownership or brute force, the merchant's strongest leverage was probably the wine supply. If the owner had lit-

---

[119] AN, Y10987, 5 December 1741.
[120] AN, Y14761, 10 April 1711.
[121] AN, Y10732, 18 December 1701.
[122] AN, Y14611, 9 January 1691.
[123] AN, Y14056, 8 March 1720. A woman having an argument with another customer complained that the wine merchant "auroit prit la partie" of the other customer—had interfered, that is, in a private matter—and had tried to throw her out (AN, Y14518, 21 August 1721).

tle control over access to the cabaret, he had far greater control over the alcohol. He could decide, for example, which customers would get credit. His refusal could make it effectively impossible for some men to drink regularly at his tavern, and there are bitter fights that arose out of customers' inability to get credit.[124] Or he might simply refuse to serve customers in the first place. His attempts to control alcohol were an important aspect of controlling behavior, for drinking was a central function of the cabaret. Thus one wine merchant tried to control access by withholding wine, refusing to serve two men because one of them had been laughing and yelling at a procession of monks from the Abbey of St. Germain des Prés that was passing by the door. The rowdy customer warned her that "if she refused him beer, he would buy it elsewhere and drink it *chez elle* and stay until midnight."[125] Thus, while admitting his inability to force her to serve him, he emphasized his ability to remain in the tavern. When she steadfastly refused, however, he became furious and started breaking things. Another fight reveals a different approach. Having been insulted by a customer, the wine merchant "asked him not to come back or he would give him vinegar (because every time he came he never failed to start a fight)."[126] Threatening him with bad wine was probably the merchant's strongest defense. Other disputes over bad wine show that merchants used it as a conscious weapon. When a merchant grocer complained to the tavernkeeper that

[124] Saint-Germain, *La Reynie*, pp. 294-295, describes such a fight. Many of the complaints brought against customers who refused to pay for wine they had drunk may have originated in a struggle over credit.

[125] AN, Y10143, 5 April 1751. Interestingly, one of the two customers was the playwright Toussaint Gaspard Taconnet. He identified himself as a "machiniste à la Comédie Française," but refused to testify or to sign the police report. Later on in the day, Taconnet's mother went to the cabaret and threatened the beer seller. In another case, a customer who was refused wine because of his inebriation brought food back to the cabaret and insisted that owner had to serve him wine with his meal; see AN, Y10141, 27 April 1751.

[126] AN, Y14499, 26 October 1691.

the wine was bad, he responded that it "was too good for people like him," which "scandalized the plaintiff's companions" and they left.[127]

There was not much else they could have done other than leave. Still the frequency with which people tried to force the tavernkeeper to provide wine indicates an expectation of being served. As one plaintiff pointed out, "a cabaret servant ought to do what one tells him."[128] When merchants refused to serve drink, they provoked frustrated assaults and rage. Their control of the wine supply was far more certain than their control over access, but they found themselves then with furious customers in their establishments. Other than blackmailing the merchant with violence or the threat of it, the customer had little means of forcing the merchant to serve him. But such blackmail could be effective, either by intimidating the owner directly or by threatening damage to the owner's reputation. When two customers began to fight in a new tavern, the owner's wife asked them to leave, "begging them not to quarrel chez elle." One of them turned on her and, yelling "atrocious and scandalous words and other shocking speech which he repeated, caused a quantity of people to assemble with great scandal, [since] the plaintiff is not yet known on the quay."[129] For the same reason a wine merchant's widow, insulted in her tavern, brought a complaint because "it was in her interest that her reputation not be tarnished among the people with whom she has long been well established."[130] Like all those engaged in business, and perhaps more than most, tavernkeepers depended on the goodwill of their customers and neighbors and on their reputation among them.[131] The extravagance of customers' as-

[127] AN, Y12308, 14 June 1701. See Y15180, 30 November 1751, for the same insult.
[128] AN, Y11218, 28 September 1731.
[129] AN, Y10739, 24 October 1711.
[130] AN, Y15238, 25 September 1731.
[131] Neighbors with windows overlooking the courtyard of a tavern could hold

saults against tavernkeepers makes sense when their actions are seen as attacking that reputation by deliberately creating a public scandal.

Customers were even less willing to have the owner control their recreation. They resisted when owners tried to stop them from playing cards or, in one case, attempted to deny entrance to the women in a party.[132] The owner did not interfere generally in the fights that took place in his tavern. Troublemakers were usually ejected by other customers. If they were objecting to an illegal activity, owners could threaten to bring in the police, but there was little they could do if the customers were simply raucous. Similarly, a joiner who had argued with a tavern waiter because, according to the waiter, he had been refused wine, admitted only that he had argued "because the waiter had stopped him from singing."[133] The waiter's interference with the defendant's singing would appear to have been more objectionable than his interference with the supply of alcohol. But owners did not often interfere. Their authority, contested even with regard to wine and access, clearly did not go beyond that. As customers fought with owners over the control of taverns they expressed, if only implicitly, the assertion of their right to appropriate the public place. The attempts by the owner to police the tavern violated their sense of its legitimate role.

Another perception of the tavern's unordered quality was stated in an extreme form by a drunken clockmaker who had urinated on the floor of a tavern. Two witnesses had done nothing about it, fearing a disturbance, but the plaintiff told the clockmaker that "it was not proper to perform such indecencies

---

the tavernkeeper hostage by occasionally pouring things out of their window on customers below; see, for example, AN, Y13018, 9 June 1751.

[132] AN, Y15133, 20 August 1701.

[133] When a sergeant of the guard appeared in response to the tavernkeeper's call for help, the joiner turned on him: "j——f——, have you [tu] come to take the cabaretier's side?" The sergeant replied that he was there "to stop disorders" (see AN, Y15946, 11 February 1751). For a similar case, see AN, Y14527, 27 August 1731.

in the company of honest people." The clockmaker replied that "at the cabaret and at the brothel one could do what one wished and that one could piss and shit there when one wanted." The plaintiff objected still and a fight broke out.[134]

The exchange is revealing, if not terribly edifying. To the clockmaker's way of thinking, the cabaret and the brothel were unlike other places, and one could do what one wanted there. Here in a drunken overstatement is most clearly articulated the perception of the cabaret as an unordered, even anarchic, space, with the freedom of action that lack of order entailed. There was also a sense of disorder and disrepute; the comparison with the brothel was not flattering, nor were the actions that the clockmaker advocated. Yet he was clearly championing a degree of license and of freedom in the cabaret. Other testimony expressed similar sentiments, such as the man who insisted on his right to sing in a tavern, despite the objections of other customers. He maintained that he was in a "free place because he was in a cabaret," although his opponents proceeded to assault him anyway.[135]

The clockmaker's statement did not go unchallenged either, but it is worth noting that the plaintiff and the defendant in this case were not arguing about the same thing. The defendant's argument addressed the function of certain places: the cabaret was a free place where there was no limiting code of conduct. The plaintiff's objections, however, were couched in social terms. One did not commit such indecencies "in the company of honest people." To the freedom of the cabaret, he opposed the restrictions of one's honor. If there was no standard of behavior associated with a cabaret, there was one demanded by the

---

[134] AN, Y14957, 31 August 1741. Bakhtin, *Rabelais*, pp. 146-155, points to a general link between excremental language and the "festive marketplace" where he sees popular culture having its freest expression.

[135] AN, Y14511, 14 August 1711; Yves Castan, *Honnêteté*, p. 565, notes several dozen cases in his study that refer to the "liberty to conduct oneself at the tavern as in one's home."

presence of "honest people." Thus freedom of action, even in a cabaret, was not accepted by everyone, although the greatest limitations were those imposed by the presence of others. At first glance the police appear to have shared few of the popular perceptions of the tavern. There was relatively little sign of the police's hostility and suspicion of taverns among the populace, at least among men, little of the police's association of taverns with debauchery. Popular perceptions emphasized instead the openness of the tavern, its accessibility and lack of constraints, its public and licensed character. Yet the police perceived the cabaret in much the same way. They too referred to its openness and license, its unrestrained and public nature. The difference lay rather in the police's attitude toward what they perceived. The police translated the lack of control, of inherent order, in cabarets into debauchery. Disorder meant degeneration to the police and threatened the tranquillity of the society. To the populace, however, disorder meant leisure and fête; it meant an opportunity to step out of constraints of daily life and ordered society, a kind of "carnival license" in their daily lives.[136]

Yet the notion of carnival can identify only some of the activity in taverns. To be sure, there were elements in tavern culture of antistructure and liminality, as these concepts have been developed by Victor Turner.[137] Antistructure is understood by Turner and others as a temporary supplanting, and reaffirmation, of structured social life. Liminality is the state of being "betwixt and between," outside of normal order and hierarchy. In particular, the liminality of various rites is seen as a way of creating an egalitarian solidarity, or "communitas." Clearly the tavern shared some of these characteristics.[138] The emphasis in

---

[136] Davis, "Reasons of Misrule," p. 117 and passim.

[137] Victor Turner, *The Ritual Process: Structure and Anti-Structure* (Chicago, 1969), pp. 94-108.

[138] Taylor, *Drinking, Homicide, and Rebellion*, pp. 66-67, portrays the tavern in colonial Mexico in terms similar to these.

tavern comportment on the communal and bond-reestablishing nature of wine, and on fellowship in general, shares elements of communitas, and the elite perception of marginality and of danger in taverns underscores their liminality.

Yet the clockmaker's fight over acceptable comportment in the tavern indicates that there were limits to the license countenanced even by fellow tavern customers. Indeed the evidence presented in previous chapters makes clear that popular culture in taverns respected very definite rules and structures: of fighting, of drinking, and of associating. Men in taverns lost neither their awareness of honor and reputation, or of social differences, or of distinctions between friend and foe. They asserted limits to what one could do before "honorable men" and created a distinct social order through their networks of drinking companionship. Popular culture meant more than an inversion of social norms and hierarchies. Although it might stand society on its head to make a point, popular culture in its quieter, everyday moments was engaged in articulating people's social bonds, their productive relations, and their values.

The customers' opposition to the ordering of taverns by the police and the owner involved something more than the establishment of a liminal arena, or a festive occasion. They sought not disorder, but their own ordering, and refused to surrender to the ordering of others. Men appropriated the tavern as a place for popular culture in all its forms, some riotous and unstructured, others intensely formal. They resisted the increasing commercialization and elite control of their cultural expressions and spaces, striving to maintain the tavern as a place where they could express the meaning of their culture in their own way.

Conclusion

Taverns were many things to many people, but dismissing them as marginal to Parisian society is not an adequate assessment of the role they played. They might have been suspicious in the eyes of the police and debauched in the eyes of moralists, and some taverns unquestionably lived up to these indictments. The fact remains that thousands of Parisians, many insisting on their *honnêteté*, can be found in the judicial archives describing their use of taverns in terms that suggest neither criminality nor debauchery. Clearly the moralists had missed something, and historians have been largely guilty of following their lead. Hence, this analysis has aimed principally at correcting a caricature by offering another dimension to the picture. The communal, sociable uses of taverns must be understood in order to comprehend both their social function and the important role of taverns in popular culture.

It is perhaps perverse to have started with the disruptive, contentious aspects of tavern sociability to understand its role, but the fights in taverns and the complaints that resulted clearly demonstrate the respectable self-image of many customers and the seriousness with which they competed for honor. Their umbrage also expresses the importance of an audience, of being "in public" in a tavern, as contestants played to their friends and mobilized supporters. Although some of the customers met in these archives were as dangerous as the police feared, most look more like the common men and women of the laboring classes. The innocuous clientele cannot refute the existence of the "suspicious" ones, of course. The tavern customers and their comportment, as presented in this study, provide a significant but still only partial picture of urban society or of public drinking. They have been given center stage, nonetheless, for several reasons. In large part the documentary evidence has determined what can be known about the populace: the men who fought to defend their honor have left evidence through their judicial contests and the rest have left little.

Furthermore, the laboring classes in this study warrant further consideration for their prominence in urban society and for the role they would later assume in national affairs. The laboring classes have achieved fame as the "revolutionary crowd," but their prerevolutionary lives and culture remain in relative obscurity. They have received little attention from historians until recently for they were neither elevated enough to engage in politics under normal circumstances nor poor enough to be included in the studies that have been made of the criminals and abandoned elements of the society. Their appearance in taverns, however, placed them on a more public stage, where their fights and rivalries gained them a small place in the historical records and allow us to glimpse the routines of their daily lives.

By finding these people in taverns, we see them at their leisure. They are not protesting the price of bread or the inadequacy of wages. Of course, they protested when the time came, but seeing them at their leisure provides a different perspective on their lives. The laboring classes lived uncomfortable, exhausting lives and were poorly paid for their work, yet they managed to enjoy their leisure. The sociable uses of leisure in taverns—whether drinking, gaming, dancing, or congregating—are largely obscured by the tradition of elite censure of popular culture. Yet we must recognize that these activities were very much a part of daily leisure, rather than an excuse for excesses and debauchery (although a more extravagant form of entertainment was emerging in the guinguette). Excess, too, had its role in this culture, in fêtes and carousing, but the routine gatherings that occupied most customers aimed at a different goal.

These men, and some women, made a point of congregating at taverns, of drinking together and buying each other drinks, of gambling and paying the bill with the losses. They consumed, publicly and without restraint. Their consumption is almost incongruous in the face of wage and price records that point to their limited means. It was this incongruity that disturbed the elites in part, and to some extent it disturbs us, because we expect a certain relationship between income and consumption, a relationship shaped by modern attitudes. The popular classes of the old regime calculated costs and benefits with a different rule. Public consumption celebrated their public identities, cemented their networks of mutual aid and obligation, and created their social capital. They articulated this sociability through public drinking and used taverns to create their communities and their culture.

Appendix

This study is based on a sample of the voluminous archives of the Châtelet, and particularly of the commissaires of the Paris police. From each year ending in 1, from 1691 to 1771, I examined the records of at least twelve commissaires (one-quarter of the total number of any year but a much higher fraction of those whose records survive). The fact that some commissaires' records were nearly devoid of police or criminal cases compelled me to include additional commissaires in the survey in the interest of achieving a rough parity of cases for each year. As a result, 1691 and 1711 include twelve commissaires, 1701 contains thirteen, 1771 has fourteen, 1721 and 1761 have fifteen, 1741 has sixteen, and 1731 has eighteen. In the interest of achieving a more comprehensive survey of one year, I looked at twenty-five commissaires for 1751, over one-half of the commissaires in Paris and over three-quarters of those whose records survive. For earlier years, fewer documents survive—only twenty commissaires' minutes for 1691 and scarcely more for 1701. Thus, I have consulted roughly one-half of the available commissaire documents in most years.

Despite the differences in numbers of records consulted each year, the numbers of people and cases included in each year, except for 1751, were similar. Other researchers have remarked upon the unequal distribution of caseloads among commissaires, even within the same quarter, and have hypothesized a division of labor based upon seniority or zeal. Whatever the reasons, some commissaires' records included very few cases of police or criminal matters, whereas others were full. On average, a commissaire's records would contain eight cases on taverns, but if those with two cases or less are ignored, the average was fifteen tavern cases per liasse.

My choice of individual commissaires was essentially a random selection but guided by a desire for geographical coverage. Thus, I consulted four to six commissaires' records for each of the twenty quartiers, plus a few more in some of the quarters in which there were three commissaires stationed rather than two. The survey achieved a fairly comprehensive overview of the city as a whole.

I supplemented this basic source with the records of the guard, the inspectors, and the different criminal and police courts. These records are all quite scarce before the middle of the century, so they contributed relatively little to the survey.

Bibliography

UNPUBLISHED PRIMARY SOURCES

Archives de la Ville de Paris et de la Seine
Series D_4B^6: 1-27, 1695; 1-35, 1695; 1-82, 1739; 2-98, 1740; 2-101, 1740; 2-107, 1740; 2-117, 1740; 3-144, 1741; 3-147, 1741; 3-163, 1741; 3-173, 1742; 5-222, 1743; 7-330, 1747; 7-354, 1748; 7-359, 1748; 10-460, 1751; 10-466, 1751; 10-488, 1752; 14-642, 1754; 14-662, 1755; 14-695, 1755; 15-715, 1755; 19-912, 1758; 20-971, 1759; 21-1020, 1759; 21-1065, 1760; 23-1169, 1762; 23-1198, 1762; 29-1561, 1766; 33-1777, 1768.

Series D_5B^6: 248 (1707-1716), 525 (1749-1753), 657 (1740-1752), 694 (1749-1758), 754 (1717-1718), 965 (1722-1725), 1240 (1769-1778), 1430 (1750-1759), 1643 (1755), 2521 (1768-1769), 2704 (1721-1723), 2783 (1764-1765), 2854 (1712-1716), 3103 (1727-1728), 3343 (1769), 3734 (1770), 3847 (1772-1778), 3881 (1723-1725), 4097 (1760-1763), 4143 (1750-1751), 4453 (1752), 4933 (1763-1770), 5022 (1722), 5775 (1726), 6210 (1764).

Archives Nationales
Minutier Central: III-901 (1741); VII-279 (1751); XXI-387 (1751); XXVII-180 (1731); XXVIII-23 (1694); XXVIII-176 (1721); XXVIII-176 (1721); XXVIII-219 (1730); XXVIII-221 (1731); XXVIII-222 (1731); XXVIII-320 (1751); XXVIII-323 (1751); XXVIII-323 (1751); XXXVIII-387 (1751); XXXVIII-387 (1751); XLVI-329 (1751); XLVII-137 (1751); LXI-385 (1731); LXVI-489 (1751); LXI-451 (1751); LXVI-489 (1751); LXXXII-311 (1751); XCIII-22 (1751); CII-290 (1730).

Series Y: Mss. 9432, 9434, 9452, 9474, 9498-9499 (minutes . . . de la chambre de police); 9508 (professions non érigées en communauté); 9535 (informations . . . en la chambre de police); 9538-9539 (roles . . . de police); 9625-9626 (registres . . . chambre de police); 9657, 9663, 9668, 9776, 9782, 9787 (chambre criminelle . . . petite criminel); 10029, 10040, 10082-10086, 10088, 10095, 10139-10148, 10226-10228, 10230, 10233, 10264, 10318 (chambre criminelle . . . grande criminel); 10623 (rapports du guet); 10726, 10732, 10739, 10765, 10837, 10851, 10982, 10987, 10993b, 11035, 11150, 11178, 11218, 11228, 11238, 11247, 11344, 11558, 11626, 11641, 11650-11651, 11661, 11697, 11744, 11788, 11798, 11933, 11947, 11959, 12000, 12025, 12100, 12107, 12115, 12123, 12154, 12177, 12307-12308, 12337, 12356-12357, 12416, 12441, 12538, 12548, 12567, 12621, 12660-12661, 12924-12925, 12949-12952, 12989-12990, 13016, 13037, 13092, 13166, 13187, 13197, 13228, 13239, 13271, 13334, 13376, 13387, 13399, 13468, 13493, 13513, 13548, 13742, 13782, 13880, 13886, 13888, 13901, 13908, 13911, 13926, 13942, 14009, 14056, 14066, 14088, 14174, 14195, 14263,

14284, 14334, 14396, 14489, 14511, 14518, 14527, 14537, 14611, 14633, 14643, 14661, 14671, 14681, 14761, 14771, 14877, 14894, 14915-14916, 14944, 14957, 14967, 14984, 14990, 15047, 15062, 15133, 15170, 15180, 15190, 15219, 15228, 15238, 15279, 15348, 15366, 15449, 15643, 15748, 15798, 15904, 15931, 15940, 15946 (archives des commissaires au Châtelet).
Series Z^{1G}: Mss. 343^A, (1771); 343^B (1771); 343^B, (1771); 350, (1773) (rôles de tailles).

Archives de la Préfecture de Police
Fonds Lamoignon (41 volumes of collected edicts, sentences, and decrees from the eleventh to the eighteenth century).

Bibliothèque de l'Arsenal
Archives de la Bastille *(Mss. 10001-12725)*: Mss. 10028, 10060, 10094, 10129, 10133, 10137, 10139-10140, 10143, 10169, 10727, 11154, 11562, 11727, 11736, 11743.

Bibliothèque Historique de la Ville de Paris
Pièces diverses concernant les marchands de vin. Paris, 1626-1762.

Bibliothèque Nationale
Fonds français Ms. 21710 (from the Delamare collection).
Nouvelles acquisitions françaises, Mss. 1273-1280, 2414 (from the Joly de Fleury collection).

PRINTED PRIMARY SOURCES

Brac, François. *Le Commerce des vins, réformé, rectifié et épuré ou nouvelle méthode pour tirer un parti sur, prompt et avantageux des récoltes en vins.* Amsterdam, 1769.
Cailleau, André Charles. *Le Waux hall populaire.* Paris, 1769. In *Three Centuries of French Drama.* Louisville, Ky., 1969. Microfiche edition.
Collé, Charles. *Scènes détachées de la guinguette.* Paris, 1754. In *Parades inédites de Collé.* Amsterdam, 1864.
Contat, Nicolas. *Anecdotes typographiques où l'on voit la description des coutumes, moeurs et usages singuliers des compagnons imprimeurs.* Edited by Giles Barber. Oxford, 1980.
Dancourt, Florent Carton. *Le Moulin de Javelle.* Vol. 2. In *Les Oeuvres de M. D'Ancourt.* 7 vols. Paris, 1711.
Delamare, Nicolas. *Traité de la police.* 4 vols. Paris, 1705-1738.
Des Essarts, Nicolas Toussaint Lemoyne. *Dictionnaire universel de police.* 8 vols. Paris, 1786-1790.
Diderot, Denis, et al. *Encyclopédie, ou dictionnaire raisonné des sciences, des arts et des métiers.* 35 vols. Paris, 1751-1780.

Duchesne. *Code de la police ou analyse des règlements de police*. 4th ed. rev. and enl. Paris, 1767.

Dumont, Ch. H. Fr. *Nouveau style criminel*. Paris, 1778.

Encyclopédie méthodique: commerce. 3 vols. Paris, 1783. Vols. 78-80 of the *Encyclopédie méthodique*. 185 vols. Paris, 1782-1832.

Encyclopédie méthodique: jurisprudence. 10 vols. Paris, 1782-1791. Vols. 133-142 of the *Encyclopédie méthodique*. 185 vols. Paris, 1782-1832.

Expilly, Jean-Joseph. *Dictionnaire géographique, historique et politique des gaules et de la France*. 6 vols. Amsterdam, 1762-1770.

Farin de Hautemar. *Impromptu des harangères, opéra-comique*. Paris, 1754. In *Three Centuries of French Drama*. Louisville, Ky., 1969. Microfiche edition.

Fougeret de Monbron, Louis-Charles. *Le Cosmopolite ou le citoyen du monde; suivi de la capitale des gaules ou la nouvelle Babylonne*. Paris, 1750-1759. Reprint, Bordeaux, 1970.

Fréminville, Edme de La Poix de. *Dictionnaire ou traité de la police générale des villes, bourgs, paroisses et seigneuries de la campagne*. Paris, 1758.

Furetière, Antoine. *Dictionnaire universel*. La Haye, 1727.

Genlis, Félicité Ducrest de Saint-Aubin, Madame de. *Mémoires inédits sur le XVIIIe siècle et la révolution française*. Paris, 1825.

Isambert, François, et al. *Recueil général des anciennes lois françaises depuis l'an 420 jusqu'à la révolution de 1789*. 29 vols. Paris, 1821-1833.

Lavoisier, Antoine. *Résultats extraits d'un ouvrage intitulé De la richesse territoriale du royaume de France*. Vol. 6 in *Oeuvres de Lavoisier*. 6 vols. Paris, 1893.

LeMaire, Jean Charles. "La Police de Paris en 1770." Edited by Augustin Gazier. *Société de l'histoire de Paris et de l'Ile de France* 5 (1878):1-131.

LeSage, Alain René. *Les Désespérées*. Paris, 1703. In *Three Centuries of French Drama*. Louisville, Ky., 1969. Microfiche edition.

Marville, F. de. *Lettres de M. de Marville, lieutenant général de police, au ministre Maurepas*. 3 vols. Edited by Arthur-Michel de Boislisle. Paris, 1896-1905.

Ménétra, Jacques-Louis. *Journal de ma vie: Jacques-Louis Ménétra, compagnon vitrier*. Edited by Daniel Roche. Paris, 1982.

Mercier, Louis-Sébastien. *Tableau de Paris*. 12 vols. Amsterdam, 1782-1788.

Montaigne, Michel de. *The Complete Essays*. Translated by Donald M. Frame. Stanford, 1958.

Muyart de Vouglans, Pierre-François. *Les Loix criminelles de France dans leur ordre naturelle*. New ed., enl. 2 vols. Paris, 1780.

Nemeitz, J. C. *Les Séjours de Paris: instructions fidèles pour les voyageurs de condition*. Leiden, 1727. Reedited by Alfred Franklin as *La Vie de Paris sous la régence*. Paris, 1897.

Peuchet, Jacques. *Collection des lois, ordonnances, et règlements de la police depuis le XIIIe siècle jusqu'à l'année 1818*. 8 vols. Paris, 1818-1819.

Restif de la Bretonne, Nicolas-Edme. *Les Nuits de Paris*. In *Les Oeuvres de Restif de la Bretonne*. 9 vols. Paris, 1930-1932.

Tableau général des maîtres distillateurs, limonadiers et vinaigriers de Paris pour l'année 1789. Paris, 1790.

BIBLIOGRAPHY

Taconnet, Toussaint Gaspard. *L'Impromptu de la foire.* In *Théâtres français.* Paris, 1732-1791.

————. *La Mariée de la Courtille.* In *Ballets, pantomimes, tableaux, etc.* 5 vols. Paris, n.d.

————. *Les Ecosseuses de la halle.* Vol. 1. In *Taconnet Théâtre.* 10 vols. Paris, 1759.

Vadé, Jean-Joseph. *La Pipe cassée.* In *Oeuvres de Vadé.* Paris, n.d.

Voltaire. *Letters on England.* Translated by Leonard Tancock. Harmondsworth, 1980.

Young, Arthur. *Travels in France during the Years 1787-1789.* Edited by Jeffry Kaplow. Garden City, N.Y., 1969.

SECONDARY SOURCES

Agulhon, Maurice. *Pénitents et francs-maçons de l'ancienne Provence.* Paris, 1968.

————. *The Republic in the Village.* Translated by Janet Lloyd. Cambridge, 1982.

Andrews, Richard Mowery. "Social Structures, Political Elites and Ideology in Revolutionary Paris, 1792-94: A Critical Evaluation of Albert Soboul's *Les Sans culottes en l'an II.*" *Journal of Social History* 19 (1985):71-112.

Ariès, Philippe. *Centuries of Childhood: A Social History of the Family.* Translated by Robert Baldick. New York, 1962.

Austin, Gregory. *Alcohol in Western Society.* Santa Barbara, 1985.

Babeau, Albert. *Les Artisans et les domestiques d'autrefois.* Paris, 1886.

Bakhtin, Mikhail. *Rabelais and His World.* Translated by Helene Iswolsky. Cambridge, Mass., 1968.

Barrows, Susanna. "After the Commune: Alcoholism, Temperance, and Literature in the Early Third Republic." In *Consciousness and Class Experience in Nineteenth-Century Europe,* edited by John M. Merriman, pp. 205-218. New York, 1979.

————. *Distorting Mirrors.* New Haven, 1981.

Barthes, Roland. *Mythologies.* Translated by Annette Lavers. New York, 1972.

Baulant, Micheline. "Les Salaires des ouvriers du bâtiment à Paris de 1400 à 1726." *Annales, économies, sociétés, civilizations* 26 (1971):463-468.

Beik, William. "Searching for Popular Culture in Early Modern France." *Journal of Modern History* 49 (1977):266-281.

Benn, S. I., and G. F. Gaus, eds. *Public and Private in Social Life.* London, 1983.

Bergeron, Louis. "Paris dans l'organization des échanges intérieurs français à la fin du XVIIIe siècle." In *Aires et structures du commerce français au XVIIIe siècle, Colloque national de l'association française des historiens économistes, 4-6 October 1973,* edited by Pierre Léon, pp. 237-263. Lyon, 1975.

Bott, Elizabeth. *Family and Social Networks.* New York, 1971.

Bourdieu, Pierre. *Outline of a Theory of Practice.* Translated by Richard Nice. Cambridge, 1977.

Braudel, Fernand. *Capitalism and Material Life.* Translated by Miriam Kochan. New York, 1973.

————. *The Wheels of Commerce.* Translated by Siân Reynolds. New York, 1982.

Burke, Peter. *Popular Culture in Early Modern Europe.* New York, 1978.

————. "Popular Culture between History and Ethnology." *Ethnologia Europaea* 14 (1984):5-13.

Cahen, Léon. "Communication sur les marchands de vin et débitants de boissons à Paris au milieu du XVIIIe siècle." *Bulletin de la société d'histoire moderne* (March 1910):109-111.

————. "La Population parisienne au milieu du XVIIIe siècle." *Revue de Paris* 5 (1919):146-170.

Cameron, Iain. *Crime and Repression in the Auvergne and the Guyenne, 1720-1790.* Cambridge, 1981.

Castan, Nicole. *Justice et répression en Languedoc à l'époque des lumières.* Paris, 1980.

————. *Les Criminels de Languedoc (1750-1790).* Toulouse, 1980.

Castan, Yves. *Honnêteté et relations sociales en Languedoc, 1715-1780.* Paris, 1974.

Castan, Yves, and Nicole Castan. "Les Figures du jeu dans la société languedocienne au XVIIIe siècle." In *Les Jeux à la renaissance: actes du XXIIIe colloque international d'études humanistes,* edited by Philippe Ariès and Jean-Claude Margolin, pp. 235-242. Paris, 1982.

Chagniot, Jean. *Paris et l'armée au XVIIIe siècle.* Paris, 1985.

Chartier, Roger. "Culture as Appropriation: Popular Cultural Uses in Early Modern France." In *Understanding Popular Culture,* edited by Steven L. Kaplan, pp. 229-253. Berlin, N.Y., 1984.

Chassaigne, Marc. *La Lieutenance génerale de police de Paris.* Paris, 1906.

Chevalier, Louis. *Laboring Classes and Dangerous Classes in Paris during the First Half of the Nineteenth Century.* Translated by Frank Jellinek. Princeton, 1973.

Church, William Farr. *Constitutional Thought in Sixteenth-Century France.* Cambridge, 1941.

Clark, Peter. *The English Alehouse: A Social History, 1200-1830.* London, 1983.

Clark, Stuart. "French Historians and Early Modern Popular Culture." *Past and Present* 100 (1983):62-99.

Clinard, Marshall. "The Public Drinking House and Society." In *Society, Culture and Drinking Patterns,* edited by David Joshua Pittman and Charles R. Snyder, pp. 270-292. Carbondale, Ill., 1962.

Cobb, Richard. *The Police and the People: French Popular Protest, 1789-1820.* London, 1970.

————. *Death in Paris: The Records of the Basse Géôle de la Seine, 1795-1801.* Oxford, 1978.

Coffey, T. G. "Beer Street, Gin Lane: Some Views of Eighteenth-Century Drinking." *Quarterly Journal of Studies on Alcohol* 27 (1966):669-692.

Cohn, Samuel Kline. *The Laboring Classes of Renaissance Florence.* New York, 1980.

Cole, Charles W. *Colbert and a Century of French Mercantilism.* 2 vols. Hamden, Conn., 1964.

Colombey, Emile. *Ruelles, salons, et cabarets.* Paris, 1858.

Coornaert, Emile. *Les Corporations en France avant 1789.* Paris, 1941.

Coste, Jean-Paul. *La Ville d'Aix en 1695; structure urbaine et société.* 2 vols. Aix-en-Provence, 1970.

Darnton, Robert. *The Business of the Enlightenment.* Cambridge, Mass., 1980.

————. "The High Enlightenment and the Low Life of Literature." In *The Literary Underground of the Old Regime,* pp. 1-40. Cambridge, Mass., 1982.

————. *The Great Cat Massacre and Other Episodes in French Cultural History.* New York, 1983.

Daumard, Adeline. "Une Référence pour l'étude des sociétés urbaines en France aux XVIIIe et XIXe siècles: projet de code socio-professionel." *Revue d'histoire moderne et contemporaine* 10 (1963):185-210.

Daumard, Adeline, and François Furet. *Structures et relations sociales à Paris.* Paris, 1961.

Davis, Natalie Zemon. *Society and Culture in Early Modern France.* Stanford, 1975.

Delamain, R. *Histoire du cognac.* Paris, 1935.

Desmaze, Charles. *Le Châtelet de Paris, son organization, ses privilèges.* Paris, 1863.

Deyon, Pierre. *Le Temps des prisons. Essai sur l'histoire de la délinquance et les origines du système pénitentiaire.* Lille, 1975.

Dion, Roger. *Histoire de la vigne et du vin en France des origines au XIXe siècle.* Paris, 1959. Reprint, 1977.

Durand, Georges. *Vin, vigne et vignerons en Lyonnais et Beaujolais (XVIe-XVIIIe siècles).* Paris, 1979.

Enjalbert, Henri. "Comment naissent les grands crus." *Annales, économies, sociétés, civilizations* 8 (1953):315-328, 457-474.

Farge, Arlette. *Délinquance et criminalité: le vol d'aliments à Paris au XVIIIe siècle.* Paris, 1974.

————. *Vivre dans la rue à Paris au XVIIIe siècle.* Paris, 1979.

Farge, Arlette, and André Zysberg. "Les Théâtres de la violence à Paris au XVIIIe siècle." *Annales, économies, sociétés, civilizations* 34 (1979):984-1015.

Farge, Arlette, and Michel Foucault. *Le Désordre des familles.* Paris, 1982.

Fillaut, Thierry. *L'Alcoolisme dans l'ouest de la France pendant la seconde moitié du XIXe siècle.* Paris, 1983.

Flandrin, Jean-Louis. *Familles, parenté, maison, sexualité dans l'ancienne société.* Paris, 1976.

——. "La Diversité des goûts et des pratiques alimentaires en Europe du xve au xviiie siècle." *Revue d'histoire moderne et contemporaine* 30 (1983):66-83.

Forster, Robert, and Elborg Forster. *European Society in the Eighteenth Century.* New York, 1969.

Fosca, François. *Histoire des cafés de Paris.* Paris, 1934.

Foucault, Michel. *Madness and Civilization: A History of Insanity in the Age of Reason.* Translated by Richard Howard. New York, 1965.

Franklin, Alfred. *Dictionnaire historique des arts, métiers et professions exercés dans Paris depuis le XIIIe siècle.* Paris, 1906.

Franklin, Julian H. *Jean Bodin and the Sixteenth-Century Revolution in the Methodology of Law and History.* New York, 1963.

Frégier, Honoré Antoine. *Histoire de l'administration de la police de Paris depuis Philippe-Auguste jusqu'aux états généraux de 1789.* 2 vols. Paris, 1850.

Furet, François. "Structures sociales parisiennes au xviiie siècle: l'apport d'une série fiscale." *Annales, économies, sociétés, civilizations* 16 (1961):939-958.

Garden, Maurice. *Lyon et les lyonnais au XVIIIe siècle.* Paris, 1970.

Garrioch, David, and Michael Sonenscher. "*Compagnonnages*, Confraternities, and Associations of Journeymen in Eighteenth-Century Paris." *European History Quarterly* 16 (1986):25-45.

Geertz, Hildred. "An Anthropology of Religion and Magic." *Journal of Interdisciplinary History* 6 (1975):71-89.

George, M. Dorothy. *London Life in the Eighteenth Century.* London, 1951.

Ginzburg, Carlo. *The Cheese and the Worms.* Translated by John and Anne Tedeschi. New York, 1982.

Gutton, Jean-Pierre. "Les Mendiants dans la société parisienne au début du xviiie siècle." *Cahiers d'histoire* 13 (1968):131-141.

Hampson, Norman. *Will and Circumstance: Montesquieu, Rousseau and the French Revolution.* Norman, Okla., 1983.

Hanagan, Michael P. *The Logic of Solidarity: Artisans and Industrial Workers in Three French Towns, 1871-1914.* Urbana, Ill., 1980.

Hanlon, Gregory. "Les Rituels de l'aggression en Aquitaine au xviie siècle," *Annales, économies, sociétés, civilization* 40 (1985):244-268.

Harsin, Jill. *Policing Prostitution in Nineteenth-Century Paris.* Princeton, 1985.

Hufton, Olwen H. *The Poor of Eighteenth-Century France, 1750-1789.* Oxford, 1974.

Isherwood, Robert M. "Entertainment in the Parisian Fairs in the Eighteenth Century." *Journal of Modern History* 53 (1981):24-48.

——. *Farce and Fantasy: Popular Entertainment in Eighteenth-Century Paris.* New York, 1986.

Jellinek, Frank. "Cultural Differences in the Meaning of Alcoholism." In *Society, Culture and Drinking Patterns*, edited by David Joshua Pittman and Charles R. Snyder, pp. 382-388. Carbondale, Ill., 1962.

Jones, Gareth Stedman. *Languages of Class: Studies in English Working Class History, 1832-1982.* Cambridge, 1983.

Kaplan, Steven L. *Bread, Politics and Political Economy in the Reign of Louis XV.* 2 vols. The Hague, 1976.

———. "Réflexions sur la police du monde du travail, 1700-1815," *Revue historique* 261 (1979):17-77.

———. "Note sur les commissaires de police de Paris au XVIIIe siècle." *Revue d'histoire moderne et contemporaine* 28 (1981):669-686.

———. "The Luxury Guilds of Eighteenth-Century Paris." *Francia* 9 (1982):257-298.

———, ed. *Understanding Popular Culture.* Berlin, N.Y., 1984.

———. *Provisioning Paris: Merchants and Millers in the Grain and Flour Trade during the Eighteenth Century.* Ithaca, 1984.

———. "The Character and Implications of Strife among the Masters inside the Guilds of Eighteenth-Century Paris." *Journal of Social History* 19 (1986):631-647.

Kaplow, Jeffry. *The Names of Kings: The Parisian Laboring Poor in the Eighteenth Century.* New York, 1972.

Karp, Ivan. "Beer Drinking and Social Experience in an African Society." In *Explorations in African Systems of Thought,* edited by Ivan Karp and Charles S. Beard, pp. 6-119. Bloomington, Ind., 1980.

Keohane, Nannerl O. *Philosophy and the State in France.* Princeton, 1980.

Labrousse, Claude-Ernest. *Esquisse du mouvement des prix et des revenues en France au XVIIIe siècle.* 2 vols. Paris, 1933.

Lachiver, Marcel. "Fraude du vin et fraudeurs en l'Ile de France, XVIIIe siècle." *Revue d'histoire moderne et contemporaine* 21 (1974):419-444.

———. *Vin, vigne et vignerons en région parisienne du XVIIe au XIXe siècle.* Pontoise, 1982.

———. "L'Approvisionnement de Paris en vin." *Mémoires de la fédération des sociétés historiques et archéologiques de Paris et de l'Ile de France* 35 (1984): 277-287.

Lacroix, P. *Dix-huitième siècle. Institutions, usages et coutumes.* Paris, 1875.

Lafarge, Catherine. "Paris and Myth: One Vision of Horror." *Studies in Eighteenth-Century Culture* 5 (1976):281-291.

La Fizilière, Albert de. *Vins à la mode et cabarets au XVIIIe siècle.* Paris, 1886.

Laingui, André, and Arlette Lebigre. *Histoire du droit pénal.* 2 vols. Paris, 1979.

Laslett, Peter. *The World We Have Lost.* New York, 1968.

Lavisse, Ernest. *Louis XIV.* 2 vols. 1911. Reprint, Paris, 1978.

Leclant, J. "Le Café et les cafés à Paris, 1644-1693." *Annales, économies, sociétés, civilizations* 6 (1951):1-14.

Lottes, Günther. "Popular Culture and the Early Modern State in Sixteenth-Century Germany." In *Understanding Popular Culture,* edited by Steven L. Kaplan, pp. 147-175. Berlin, N.Y., 1984.

Lottin, Alain. "Vie et mort de couple; difficultés conjugales et divorce." *Dix-septième siècle* 102-103 (1974):59-78.

———. *Chavatte, ouvrier lillois, un contemporaine de Louis XIV.* Paris, 1979.

MacAndrews, Craig, and Robert Edgerton. *Drunken Comportment: A Social Explanation.* Chicago, 1969.

Mandrou, Robert. *Introduction à la France moderne (1500-1640): essai de psychologie historique.* Paris, 1961. Reprint, 1974.

———. *De la culture populaire aux XVIIe et XVIIIe siècles: la bibliothèque bleue de Troyes.* Paris, 1964.

Marion, Marcel. *Dictionnaire des institutions de la France aux XVIIe et XVIIIe siècles.* Paris, 1923. Reprint, 1976.

Marrus, Michael. "Social Drinking in the *Belle Epoque.*" *Journal of Social History* 7 (1974):115-141.

———, ed. *The Emergence of Leisure.* New York, 1974.

Maza, Sarah C. *Servants and Their Masters in Eighteenth-Century France: The Uses of Loyalty.* Princeton, 1983.

Medick, Hans. "Plebeian Culture in the Transition to Capitalism." In *Culture, Ideology and Politics. Essays in Honor of Eric Hobsbawm,* edited by R. Samuel and Gareth Stedman Jones, pp. 84-112. London, 1983.

———. "The Proto-industrial Family Economy." In *Industrialization before Industrialization,* edited by Peter Kriedte et al., translated by Beate Schempp, pp. 38-73. Cambridge, 1981.

Mehl, Jean-Michel. "Les Jeux de dés au xve siècle d'après les lettres de rémission." In *Les Jeux à la renaissance: actes du XXIIIe colloque internationale d'études humanistes,* edited by Philippe Ariès and Jean-Claude Margolin, pp. 625-634. Paris, 1982.

Michel, Francisque, and Edouard Fournier. *Histoire des hôtelleries, cabarets, hôtels, garnies, restaurants et cafés.* 2 vols. Paris, 1859.

Midelfort, H. C. Erik. "Madness and Civilization in Early Modern Europe: A Reappraisal of Michel Foucault." In *After the Reformation. Essays in Honor of J. H. Hexter,* edited by Barbara C. Malament, pp. 247-267. Philadelphia, 1980.

Mols, Roger. "Population in Europe, 1500-1700." In *The Fontana Economic History of Europe: The Sixteenth and Seventeenth Centuries,* edited by Carlo Cipolla, pp. 15-82. London, 1974.

Moore, Alexander Parks. *The Genre Poissard and the French Stage of the Eighteenth Century.* New York, 1935.

Mousnier, Roland. *The Institutions of France under the Absolute Monarchy, 1598-1789.* Translated by Brian Pearce. Chicago, 1979.

———. *La Stratification sociale à Paris aux XVIIe et XVIIIe siècles.* Paris, 1975.

Muchembled, Robert. *Culture populaire et culture des élites dans la France moderne.* Paris, 1978.

———. "Les Jeunes, les jeux, la violence en Artois." In *Les Jeux à la renaissance: actes du XXIIIe colloque internationale d'études humanistes,* edited by Philippe Ariès and Jean-Claude Margolin, pp. 565-579. Paris, 1982.

Olivier-Martin, François. *L'Organization corporative de la France d'ancien régime*. Paris, 1938.

―――. *Histoire du droit français des origines à la révolution*. Paris, 1951.

Ourliac, Paul, and J. de Malafosse. *Histoire du droit privé*. Paris, 1968.

Peristiany, J. G., ed. *Honour and Shame. The Values of Mediterranean Society*. Chicago, 1966.

Perrot, Jean-Claude. *Genèse d'une ville moderne: Caen au XVIIIe siècle*. 2 vols. Paris, 1975.

Petrovich, Porphyre. "Recherches sur la criminalité à Paris dans la seconde moitié du XVIIIe siècle." In *Crimes et criminalité en France sous l'ancien régime, XVIIe et XVIIIe siècles*, edited by André Abbiateci et al., pp. 190-268. Paris, 1971.

Peveri, Patrice. "Les Pickpockets à Paris au XVIIIe siècle." *Revue d'histoire moderne et contemporaine* 29 (1982):3-35.

Pillorget, René, and Jean de Viguerie. "Les Quartiers de Paris aux XVIIe et XVIIIe siècles." *Revue d'histoire moderne et contemporaine* 17 (1970):253-277.

Pitsch, Marguerite. *La Vie populaire à Paris au XVIIIe siècle*. 2 vols. Paris, 1949.

Prestwich, P. E. "French Workers and the Temperance Movement." *International Review of Social History* 28 (1980):36-52.

Raeff, Marc. "The Well-Ordered Police State and the Development of Modernity in Seventeenth- and Eighteenth-Century Europe: An Attempt at a Comparative Approach." *American Historical Review* 80 (1975):1221-1243.

Ranum, Orest. *Paris in the Age of Absolutism*. New York, 1968.

Reinhardt, Steven G. "Crime and Royal Justice in Ancien Régime France: Modes of Analysis." *Journal of Interdisciplinary History* 13 (1983):437-460.

―――. "The Selective Prosecution of Crime in Ancien Régime France: Theft in the Sénéchaussée of Sarlat." *European History Quarterly* 16 (1986):3-24.

Roberts, James S. *Drink, Temperance and the Working Class in Nineteenth-Century Germany*. Boston, 1984.

Roche, Daniel. *Le Peuple de Paris: essai sur la culture populaire au XVIIIe siècle*. Paris, 1981.

―――. "Le Temps de l'eau rare." *Annales, économies, sociétés, civilizations* 39 (1984):388-399.

Romon, Christian. "Le Monde des pauvres à Paris au XVIIIe siècle." *Annales, économies, sociétés, civilizations* 37 (1982):729-763.

―――. "Mendiants et policiers à Paris au XVIIIe siècle." *Histoire, économie, société* 2 (1982):259-295.

―――. "L'Affaire des 'enlèvements d'enfants' dans les archives du Châtelet (1749-1750)." *Revue historique* 270 (1983):55-95.

Rorabaugh, W. J. *The Alcoholic Republic, An American Tradition*. Oxford, 1979.

Rose, R. B. *The Making of the Sans-culottes: Democratic Ideas and Institutions in Paris, 1789-1792*. Manchester, 1983.

Rossiaud, Jacques. "Prostitution, Youth, and Society in the Towns of Southeastern France in the Fifteenth Century." Translated by Elborg Forster. In *Deviants and the Abandoned in France*, edited by Orest Ranum and Robert Forster, pp. 1-46. Baltimore, 1978.

Roubin, Lucienne. "Male and Female Space Within the Provençal Community." Translated by Patricia M. Ranum. In *Rural Society in France*, edited by Orest Ranum and Robert Forster, pp. 152-180. Baltimore, 1977.

Rowen, Herbert H. *The King's State: Proprietary Dynasticism in Early Modern France*. New Brunswick, N.J., 1980.

Rudé, George. "Prices, Wages and Popular Movements in Paris during the French Revolution." In *Paris and London in the Eighteenth Century*, pp. 163-197. New York, 1973.

———. *The Crowd in the French Revolution*. Oxford, 1959. Reprint, 1967.

Ruff, Julius. *Crime, Justice and Public Order in Old Regime France. The Sénéchaussées of Libourne and Bazas, 1696-1789*. London, 1984.

Sahlins, Marshall. *Stone Age Economics*. New York, 1972.

Saint-Germain, Jacques. *La Reynie et la police au grand siècle*. Paris, 1962.

———. *La Vie quotidienne en France à la fin du grand siècle*. Paris, 1965.

Sewell, William H. *Work and Revolution in France*. Cambridge, 1980.

Slavin, Morris. *The French Revolution in Miniature*. Princeton, 1984.

Soman, Alfred. "Deviance and Criminal Justice in Western Europe, 1300-1800: An Essay in Structure," *Criminal Justice History* 1 (1980):3-28.

Sonenscher, Michael. "Work and Wages in Paris in the Eighteenth Century." In *Manufacture in Town and Country before the Factory*, edited by Maxine Berg, Pat Hudson, and Michael Sonenscher, pp. 147-172. Cambridge, 1983.

———. "Les Sans-culottes de l'an II: repenser le langage du travail dans la France révolutionnaire." *Annales, économies, sociétés, civilizations* 40 (1985):1087-1108.

Swartz, Marc J., ed. *Local-Level Politics*. Chicago, 1968.

Swartz, Marc J., Victor W. Turner, and Arthur Tuden, eds. *Political Anthropology*. Chicago, 1966.

Taylor, William B. *Drinking, Homicide and Rebellion in Colonial Mexican Villages*. Stanford, 1979.

Thomas, Keith. "Work and Leisure." *Past and Present* 29 (1964):50-66.

Thompson, E. P. "Time, Work Discipline and Industrial Capitalism." *Past and Present* 38 (1967):56-97.

Turner, Victor. *The Ritual Process: Structure and Anti-Structure*. Chicago, 1969.

Van Kley, Dale. *The Damiens Affair and the Unravelling of the Ancien Régime, 1750-1770*. Princeton, 1984.

Weissman, Ronald. *Ritual Brotherhood in Renaissance Florence*. New York, 1982.

Williams, Alan. *The Police of Paris*. Baton Rouge, La., 1979.

Wills, Antoinette. *Crime and Punishment in Revolutionary Paris*. Westport, Conn., 1981.

Wissant, George de. *Le Paris d'autrefois: cafés et cabarets*. Paris, 1928.

Wyatt-Brown, Bertram. *Southern Honor*. Oxford, 1984.

Yeo, Eileen, and Stephen Yeo. "Ways of Seeing: Control and Leisure versus Class Struggle." In *Popular Culture and Class Conflict, 1590-1914: Explorations in the History of Labor and Leisure*, edited by Eileen Yeo and Stephen Yeo, pp. 128-154. Brighton, 1981.

Index

Library of Congress Cataloging-in-Publication Data

Brennan, Thomas Edward.
Public drinking and popular culture in eighteenth-century Paris.

Bibliography: p.
Includes index.
1. Drinking of alcoholic beverages—France—Paris—History—18th century.
2. Drinking customs—France—Paris—History—18th century. 3. Labor and
laboring classes—France—Paris—History—18th century. 4. Hotels, taverns,
etc.—France—Paris—History—18th century. 5. Paris (France)—Social
conditions. I. Title.

HV5470.P37B74   1988   394.1'3'0944361   87-29122
ISBN 0-691-05519-X